T.S. ELIOT:

The Critic as Philosopher

T.S. ELIOT:

The Critic
as *Philosopher*

By Lewis Freed

Purdue University Press
West Lafayette, Indiana
1979

Library of Congress Catalog Card Number 77-85598
International Standard Book Number 0-911198-54-7
Printed in the United States of America

For
Mark and David —
and Charlie

The arts
without intellectual context
are vanity

ELIOT
Notes towards the Definition of Culture

Contents

Preface

This is my second attempt to write about Eliot and F. H. Bradley, the first being *T. S. Eliot: Aesthetics and History* (1962). I had not, at the time of writing that work, read Eliot's Harvard dissertation on Bradley, which was published for the first time in 1964. And without the dissertation there is much that is impossible to show—though with the dissertation it is only a little less impossible.

Still, the thesis of *Aesthetics and History*—that Eliot's literary theory is based on Bradley's philosophy—is, I think, sound, though inadequately presented. Of positive errors there is perhaps only one worth mentioning. I wrote (p. 124): "There can be little doubt that the point of view implicit in Eliot's criticism of Leibniz and Bradley is that of scholasticism. We must assume that Eliot at one time was engaged in what Bradley calls 'a sincere metaphysical endeavor,' and that the endeavor ended in theoretical scepticism, which Bradley defines as 'the mere denial of any known satisfactory doctrine, together with the personal despair of any future attainment.'"

That statement is, I now believe, in error. Eliot's metaphysical endeavor did not end in theoretical scepticism, nor is the point of view implicit in his criticism of Leibniz and Bradley that of scholasticism. If we go by the evidence of *Knowledge and Experience* and the critical prose, Eliot was not an adherent of the scholastic philosophy; rather, the philosophy in his critical prose, late and early, is the version of Bradley sketched in *Knowledge and Experience*.

The use that Eliot makes of his philosophy is not confined to his critical prose; he uses it in writing about education, culture, politics, and religion. And I have given some indication of this, that is, of the philosophic ingredient in his discussion of these subjects. The philosophy also gets into the poetry, and I have given some indication of this, too—though we must not, according to Eliot, confuse the ideas that can be elicited from a poem with the philosophic beliefs of the author. But I am not concerned in this work with Eliot's politics or religion or with his poetry, but only with his idea of poetry—for example, with his view of the status of ideas in poetry. His position on this question is, like his other critical positions, an aspect of a definite literary theory, or, to give it a more formal designation, of a philosophic aesthetics.

Though the present work argues in effect the same thesis as the earlier one, it is from first to last a new study, made possible by the publication of *Knowledge and Experience*.

In chapter 3 I have undertaken a brief review of the work done on Eliot and Bradley—brief in the sense that it is selective rather than exhaustive. Though I quote there from Anne C. Bolgan's doctoral dissertation (1960), I make no reference to "The Philosophy of F. H. Bradley and the Mind and Art of T. S. Eliot: An Introduction" (1971) or to *What the Thunder Really Said: A Retrospective Essay on the Making of "The Waste Land"* (1973). The essay and the book somehow escaped me, and it was only after my work was completed that I learned of these writings; it was Shyamal Bagchee, editor of the *T. S. Eliot Review*, who drew my attention to Bolgan's book, and I subsequently discovered her essay. Bolgan initiated the process that led to the publication of *Knowledge and Experience*, and she was responsible for the editing of it.

In appendix II of her book she gives an account of "the genesis and the development of the Bradleian vein in Eliot studies." I find that in this account, as well as in her essay, she is doing in her way the same sort of thing that I have tried to do in mine. Her primary concern is, however, with the poetry, and mine is with the criticism; and the poetry and the criticism, it seems to me, present somewhat different problems. In any case, we are of one mind about the criticism, and about the general importance of Eliot's philosophy for the understanding of his literary work.

I had hoped to have this work ready by 1976, and by way of celebrating the Bicentennial I have turned British spelling into its American form.

I wish to thank H. B. Knoll, Loy E. Davis, and William J. Stuckey for reading the first draft of this work. I also wish to thank Cheryl L. Knott, Viola J. Flint, and Elizabeth P. Smith for typing the manuscript of the final draft.

Introduction

The question of Eliot's relation to Bradley is both important and difficult, and the difficulty has served to obscure its importance. Though I have tried to show why this is so in the text, it is well perhaps to say something here about the question and about my approach to it.

Eliot, as critic, is still regarded as a mere *littérateur*,[1] and his relation to Bradley is treated as just another fact to be filed under "sources and influences," useful perhaps as a footnote. Yet Eliot's critical prose is largely unintelligible apart from his philosophy, and in order to direct attention to this fact I have tried to show that commentators who ignore or discount the philosophy cannot as a rule find a meaning for Eliot's language.[2] My argument thus has a negative as well as a positive side; and I have seen nothing since setting down the negative side that has not shown the need for it. It is a familiar situation: a man who feels he has something to say which no one cares to listen to tends to raise his voice. That is the whole explanation of my criticism of Eliot's commentators.

To sketch in the background, prior to 1964 the common assumption about Eliot's critical writing was that it is innocent of any definite theory or philosophy, or, as John Crowe Ransom expressed it in *The New Criticism*, is marked by "theoretical innocence," and again, in the second of the essays entitled "The Concrete Universal," "philosophy as a part of the critical discipline" is not "according to Eliot." At the time Ransom made those statements, he did not know of Eliot's two *Monist* essays. Even so, his own theory of logical structure and irrelevant texture is a version of philosophic aesthetics; and though in the essay mentioned above he came to think of it as Kantian, in his earlier speculations he was influenced by the neo-Hegelians. Thus in *The World's Body*, criticizing I. A. Richards's "pseudo-statements," he says that poets make assertions: "their images are perceptions, and perceptions are assertions"; and it is from the "neo-Hegelians," he goes on to say, that he received this "understanding of what is implied in a perception." But, if so, the image qualifies, and is qualified by, the logical object, so that the green of the sea is not the same as the green of the trees. That is according to Eliot, who got it from Bradley and Bosanquet. Though Ransom abandoned this doctrine for what he calls a Kantian version, it is both strange and ironic that he should have overlooked the philosophic character of Eliot's critical writing.

And it is still overlooked, despite the work done on Eliot and Bradley. Thus, according to Kristian Smidt, though Bradley was an influence on Eliot, the critical writing lacks a theoretical basis, consisting, as he puts it, of scattered pronouncements from which something like a body of opinion may be compounded. Similarly, according to Hugh Kenner, though Bradley's mind lies behind certain statements of Eliot's, the critical work is not a theory of poetry but a collection of incidental remarks and *ad hoc* writings, and in Kenner's view none the worse for that.

When in 1964 *Knowledge and Experience* was published, it received very few reviews—if some of them can be called reviews. For instance, "a dreary thesis" is the whole comment of the reviewer in *American Literature*—though Josiah Royce, it may be noted, spoke of the dissertation as the work of an expert. To give one more instance, the reviewer in the *Times Literary Supplement*, though he used more words than the reviewer in *American Literature*, had little more to say, his justification being that Eliot said that he can present the book "only as a curiosity of biographical interest."

And that is how it continues to be regarded. Thus in *Selected Prose of T. S. Eliot*, edited with an introduction by Frank Kermode (1975), there is no mention of *Knowledge and Experi-*

ence in the introduction or the index. As for Bradley, he is mentioned once in the introduction, in conjunction with Babbitt. But Babbitt, in spite of all the talk about his influence on Eliot, has, so far as I can see, little or no relevance to Eliot as *literary* critic.[3]

Eliot and his commentators have been talking at cross-purposes, and it has seemed to me necessary to draw attention to this fact in order to show the need for a reexamination of the critical prose. After all, if, as Kermode says, Eliot has "profoundly changed" our thinking about poetry and criticism, it is worthwhile trying to understand what brought about the change.

The trouble is that, when we go to *Knowledge and Experience* for light on the literary work, we find, if we are plain readers, that the dissertation reads like "Greek"—or, as the Greeks say, "Chinese." Eliot himself is reported to have said that his dissertation was accepted at Harvard because it was unreadable.[4] It is, Richard Wollheim says, "a painfully obscure work." And speaking of his own study of Bradley, Wollheim says: "Certain parts of his thought I have omitted . . . because I can see no way of making them intelligible to the general reader: and others, because I continue to find them incomprehensible. It would be no service to Bradley to pretend he is an easy philosopher."[5] Yet, as Bolgan says, "Bradley is the way to understand Eliot," and there is no "easier way."[6]

There is really no way that is satisfactory. And what I have tried to do is to show the use that Eliot makes of his philosophy, without attempting to expound the philosophy. In other words, I deal with the philosophy only from the outside and only to the extent that is necessary for my purpose, which is twofold: first, to show that the critical prose—reviews, prefaces, essays, lectures—is informed by a definite theory or philosophy, and, second, to show how Eliot transcribes his philosophy without exposing it, and in this sense my work is a study of the style of the critical prose.

This is, then, in the sense explained, a literary and not a philosophic study. All the same, it depends throughout on Eliot's Bradleyan philosophy, and this requires a word of explanation.

The dissertation is a defense of Bradley's main positions as given in *Appearance and Reality*; and though Eliot has certain criticisms to make of Bradley, his argument, Eliot insists, is in keeping with Bradley's metaphysics. His procedure in defending Bradley is to criticize theories of knowledge that are based on assumptions other than Bradley's, and in doing so he sketches only so much of his own position as is required for his argument, and the argument itself is highly condensed. The consequence is that much is left unelaborated and unexplained. Further, it is not his intention, as Eliot says in his opening remarks, to cover the whole field of epistemology, and there are many questions he does not discuss or even hint at. For example, he does not discuss the theory of judgment and inference, a theory that is essential to the understanding of his aesthetic doctrine. Not everything, then, that gets into the critical prose is dealt with in the dissertation, so that we must eke out the account given there by going to other writers of the New Idealism. Though Bradley is Eliot's man, he is not always the best expositor of Eliot; on some points Joachim is more helpful, or Bosanquet, or Nettleship, or A. E. Taylor—and I have found that Brand Blanshard throws a retrospective light on certain aspects of Eliot's philosophizing.

Eliot's philosophy, then, has first to be put together before its relation to the critical work can be studied (and this, if one likes to say so, is like dealing with a relation between unknown terms). Nor is Eliot, to mention another complication, always the best guide in this matter. Thus he says in praise of Bradley that he is "wholly and solely a philosopher" remote from "the dignified vacuity of Bosanquet."[7] That is unjust to Bosanquet, and it can also be misleading.

Bosanquet is, of course, a different philosophic personality from Bradley; but, though he began by criticizing Bradley's logical writing, it is hardly too much to say that, allowing for differences of emphasis, he and Bradley are saying, each in his own way, very much the same thing.[8] Moreover, Bradley deals with logic as a special science, whereas for Bosanquet, as for Joachim, logic is philosophy, though not the whole of it;[9] and this seems to be Eliot's view. In aesthetic doctrine there is little to choose between Bosanquet and Bradley, once Bradley accepted Bosanquet's criticism of his treatment of the imagination.[10] Indeed, the most explicit statement of Eliot's aesthetic doctrine is to be found in Bosanquet's "On the Nature of Aesthetic Emotion" and *Three*

Lectures on Aesthetic, though Eliot handles the subject in his own way.

If I have said nothing about Royce, it is because his is a different form of idealism from that of Bradley, Bosanquet, and Joachim. Royce's main interest was in the moral and religious aspect of philosophy, and he is, accordingly, of little help in dealing with Eliot's logical view of aesthetics. Royce, like many other idealists of his time, was unhappy about Bradley's view of the self or personality;[11] and it is assumed that, since Eliot was a critic of Bradley's Absolute, he adopted some Christianized view of the Absolute. There is no evidence of this in his early reviews of books dealing with philosophy and religion, where, when he is not noncommittal, he seems to adhere to Bradley's position.[12] It is in any case a question that concerns the poetry rather than the criticism. I have assumed, for the purposes of this work, that for Eliot, as for Bradley, religion has two contexts; and though Eliot superposes one on the other, they are for him distinct.

There are various forms of idealism, and Eliot's is, as he says, substantially in agreement with Bradley's version. In the dissertation his position is that "no view is original or ultimate"; that knowledge is "essentially relative"; and that knowledge is "invariably a matter of degree," the division of experience into real and ideal being a "clumsy substitute" for degrees of truth and reality. If this is a sceptical conclusion, it is the outcome of a metaphysical inquiry, in which the theoretical criterion is supreme, so that to call it scepticism is to turn in a circle. For Eliot, as for Bradley, the solution of the problem of knowledge (so far as there is a problem of knowledge) is found in the doctrine of degrees of truth and reality.[13] This doctrine offers an intellectual standard for a scale of values, and seeks to justify the meaning, and the place in the world, of art, knowledge, morality, and religion. It is the doctrine that underlies my first chapter.

1

A Problem of Order

That Eliot is a difficult writer hardly needs to be said; but the difficulty has not been connected with his philosophy, and in this respect there is a problem that still remains to be defined. It is not that, when we take Eliot's philosophy into account, we shall find an easier Eliot; on the contrary, we shall find that Eliot is a far more difficult writer than we have thought, but at the same time a more intelligible one—more intelligible, certainly, than the unphilosophic Eliot of the commentators.

The problem is large and complex. Moreover, it is one thing for the poetry and another for the prose. Here we are concerned only with the prose, and in the prose only with the part that is theory.

The trouble is, to begin with, that Eliot, it is believed, has no theory—or if he has, it is only in the popular and not the specific sense of the word. Thus, for instance, the late Richard P. Blackmur, in "In the Hope of Straightening Things Out," says that Eliot "begs off both the talent and the bent for abstract thought"; that his criticism "has lacked a general character, and has lacked even the intention of sustained generalization"; that "it is the order of his personality that gives force to his thought about literature, and it is not a logical, nor a theoretic, nor in any way a systematic order."[1] That is a rather complete statement of the generally accepted view. And so long as that view obtains, I see little hope of "straightening things out."

Indeed Blackmur, an excellent critic, brings to his work on Eliot assumptions that are a considerable obstacle to this hope. Thus in "T. S. Eliot: From 'Ash Wednesday' to 'Murder in the Cathedral'" he says:

> He has an air of authority in his prose, an air of having said or implied to the point of proof everything that could be said; when as a matter of fact he has merely said what he felt and demonstrated his own conviction. Conviction in the end is opinion and personality, which however greatly valuable cannot satisfy those who wrongly expect more. Those who parrot Mr. Eliot think they share his conviction but do not understand or possess his personality. Those who have, dissatisfied, turned against him have merely for the most part expected too much. The rest of us, if we regard his prose argument as we do his poetry—as a personal edifice—will be content with what he is.[2]

Blackmur is defending Eliot against himself—Eliot the exponent of "this Impersonal theory of poetry." What is theory for Eliot is for Blackmur "opinion and personality." Blackmur even speaks of Eliot's "rich personal insistence on impersonality." Everything, including theory, is to be explained in terms of personality.

It is not clear whether Blackmur means that it is wrong to expect more from Eliot or wrong to expect more from any critical prose. In any event, in the field of literature, unlike that of science, few expect more than "opinion and personality." Indeed, if, as Blackmur says, conviction in the end is "opinion and personality," what more is to be expected? Or what could be more valuable? Theory, in this view, would be irrelevant—and it is in fact widely distrusted. Yet not everything connected with literature is "opinion and personality." There is, for one thing, literature itself. If there is such a thing as literature—as a distinct department of thought—it must, like other such departments, presuppose conditions that are independent of "opinion and personality." That, at any rate, is Eliot's position, as he indicates, for example, in "The Perfect Critic," where he refers the reader to the opening phrases of the *Posterior Analytics*. Just as in the study of geometry, say, it is assumed that the meanings of the terms triangle, square, and circle are understood and that the objects defined by these terms *are* or exist, in literary study it is assumed that there is such a thing as literature and that this term is understood. As Eliot puts it: "*If* there is 'literature,' *if* there is 'poetry'. . . . But I have assumed for this essay that these things exist and that these terms are understood."[3]

In "Arnold and Pater," quoting Pater's remark that "we shall hardly have time to make theories about the things we see and touch," Eliot says:

> Yet we have to be "curiously testing new opinions"; so it must be—if opinions have anything to do with theories, and unless wholly capricious and unreasoning they must have—that the opinions we test can only be those provided for our enjoyment by an inferior sort of drudges who are incapable of enjoying our own free life, because all their time is spent (and "*we* hardly have time") in making theories. And this again is only a development of the intellectual Epicureanism of Arnold.[4]

That is a different attitude toward theory from the one represented by Blackmur, or, according to Eliot, by Arnold and Pater.

It is not easy to set out Eliot's criticism of Arnold—though, as we shall see, it centers on Arnold's confusion of disciplines. Eliot sees Arnold as a forerunner of humanism as well as the father of Pater's view of life; and the criticism that he makes of Arnold is in principle the same that he makes of humanism in "The Humanism of Irving Babbitt," "Second Thoughts about Humanism," and "Experiment in Criticism." For Eliot, Arnold is a type of modern literary humanist: a moralist whose morals are based on literary taste and culture. (According to Arnold, the best stay of morals is the Bible, and the Bible is poetry or literature.)

Though Arnold, Eliot says, was a champion of "ideas," he could not take philosophy seriously. Again, the effect of Arnold's religious campaign is "to divorce Religion from thought"[5]—that is, from theology, which is the intellectual or theoretical aspect of religion. Further, though Arnold placed an exaggerated emphasis on morals, "systems of thought and belief," Arnold held, falsify morals.[6] For Eliot, Arnold's moralism is "irrational moral prejudice,"[7] for it is divorced from thought in any of its systematic forms: philosophical, theological, or scientific. Similarly, of humanism Eliot says: "Where do all these morals come from? . . . I can understand, though I do not approve, the naturalistic system of morals founded upon biology and analytical psychology . . . ; but I cannot understand a system of morals which seems to be founded on nothing but itself."[8]

The resemblance between Arnold and humanism is that "literature, or Culture, tended with Arnold to usurp the place of Religion." The difference is that humanism repudiates religion, and the aim of Arnold's religious writings is "to affirm that the emotions of Christianity can and must be preserved without the belief." From this proposition Arnold drew the conclusion that "Religion is Morals," and Pater that "Religion is Art."[9]

From one point of view, "Arnold's theory of Art and his theory of Religion are quite harmonious."[10] Arnold, that is, confuses poetry and morals and morals and religion.

Further, Arnold was "so conscious of what, for him, poetry was *for* [the moral and educational value of poetry], that he could not altogether see it for what it is."[11] Similarly, though Pater's "peculiar appropriation of religion into culture was from another side: that of emotion," he was, like Arnold, "primarily a moralist," and, like Arnold, "he was incapable of seeing any work of art simply as it is."[12]

Finally, according to Arnold, "Poetry is the reality, philosophy the illusion."[13] And poetry—or literature, or literary culture—supersedes philosophy as well as religion.

That is the substance of Eliot's criticism of Arnold. And the common view is, I believe, that this criticism, as well as that of humanism, is to be explained by reference to Eliot's religious attitude. Thus, for instance, René Wellek writes: "Arnold's 'culture' and classicism are behind Eliot's [theory of classicism], though Eliot rejected Arnold's views on religion."[14] But Eliot is also a critic of Arnold's views on art, on morals, and on philosophy. I am not, of course, saying that Eliot's religious attitude does not enter into it. But the motive is one thing, and the criticism another; and indeed there is a philosophic motive as well as a religious one, and that is what concerns us here.

For Eliot, it is true, "culture, after all, is not enough," but, on the other hand, "nothing is enough without culture." For Eliot, however, culture is not, as it is for Arnold, a substitute for philosophy, any more than it is a substitute for religion. Arnold, Eliot says, represents "a point of view which is particular though it cannot be wholly defined." Similarly, "humanism, because it is general culture," rests on "unformulable axioms." Culture or humanism is "critical rather than constructive"; it operates "by taste, by sensibility," and its business is to *"persuade."* But culture does not "refute anything" or "overthrow . . . *arguments*"; its function is not to provide "philosophical theories," nor is it concerned with "philosophical foundations." In short, humanists who take culture as a positive philosophy are "confusing two points of view."[15]

Eliot shows as much concern for the integrity of philosophy as he does for that of poetry or religion. Thus, remarking that with academic men of letters literature tends to be "a means of approach to something else," "an amateur substitute for that other thing," he says: "Nevertheless, there is a philosophical training, and it is not the literary training; there are rules of the philosophical game about the use and the definition of terms, and they are not the literary rules. One may consider the study of philosophy vain, but then one should not philosophize." His objection to culture or humanism is that it is not "humanistic enough": it plays "the games of philosophy and theology without knowing the rules."[16]

It is no accident that in "Francis Herbert Bradley" Eliot quotes a passage from *Ethical Studies* in which Bradley says:

> But here once more "culture" has come to our aid, and has shown us how here, as everywhere, the study of polite literature . . . makes needless also all further education; and we felt already as if the clouds that metaphysics had wrapped about the matter were dissolving in the light of a fresh and sweet intelligence.[17]

Eliot introduces this passage with the remark that "the greatest weakness of Arnold's culture was his weakness in philosophical training."[18] Arnold, he says elsewhere, "lacked the mental discipline, the passion for exactness in the use of words and for consistency and continuity of reasoning, which distinguishes the philosopher."[19] "Nothing in his prose work, therefore, will stand very close analysis, and we may well feel that the positive content of many words is very small."[20]

Let us begin with Arnold's confusion of morals and religion. Thus Bradley:

> Are we to say then that morality is religion? Most certainly not. . . . Nor does it help to say that religion is "morality touched by emotion"; for loose phrases of this sort may suggest to the reader what he knows already without their help, but, properly speaking, they *say* nothing. *All* morality is, in one sense or another, "touched by emotion." Most emotions, high and low, can go with and "touch" morality; and the moment we leave our phrasemaking, and begin to reflect, we see all that is meant is that morality "touched" by *religious* emotion is religious; and so, as answer to the question What is religion? all that we have said is, "It is religion when with morality you have—religion." I do not think we learn a very great deal from this.[21]

Arnold, Eliot says, had little gift for "definition," and he sometimes "confuses words and meanings."[22]

As for Pater, Eliot says:

> Pater undoubtedly had from childhood a religious bent, naturally to all that was liturgical and ceremonious. Certainly this is a real and important part of religion; and Pater cannot thereby be accused of insincerity and "aestheticism." . . . His High Churchmanship is undoubtedly very different from that of Newman, Pusey and the Tractarians, who, passionate about dogmatic essentials, were singularly indifferent to the sensuous expression of orthodoxy. It was also dissimilar to that of the priest working in a slum parish. He was "naturally Christian"—but within very narrow limitations: the rest of him was just the cultivated Oxford don and disciple of Arnold, for whom religion was a matter of feeling, and metaphysics not much more.[23]

With Bradley, though morality and religion are not the same thing, they are both practical. Morality survives within religion, so that all moral duties are also religious duties: "religious-moral acts." Religion also implies a "theoretic" element: orthodoxy, or having right opinions. This element is not, however, an end in itself, but is subordinate to the practice of religion, and if taken apart from that is not religion. It is the same with the element of churchgoing, ceremony, meditation, and prayer: so far as these subserve practice, they may be "a production of feeling *at least in part*" religious; but by themselves they are "the isolating a sphere of religion which, so isolated, loses the character of religion" and "degenerates into what may be well enough as aesthetic or contemplative, but, for all that, is . . . irreligious."[24]

Eliot, in the passage quoted above, analyzes religion into the same three elements: the "theoretic" element is exemplified by the Tractarians, and the practical element by the priest working in a slum parish; what is left to Pater is the feeling produced by liturgy and ceremony. But Pater was "naturally Christian," so that he cannot be accused of "aestheticism." It is, with the exception of this subtlety, a Bradleyan analysis.

Eliot, explaining why all of Bradley's writings are in some sense "essays," says:

> It is that he perceived the contiguity and continuity of the various provinces of thought. "Reflection on morality," he says, "leads us beyond it. It leads us, in short, to see the necessity of a religious point of view." Morality and religion are not the same thing, but they cannot beyond a certain point be treated separately. A system of ethics, if thorough, is explicitly or implicitly a system of theology; and to attempt to erect a complete theory of ethics without a religion is none the less to adopt some particular attitude towards religion. In this book, as in his others, Bradley is thoroughly empirical, much more empirical than the philosophies that he opposed. He wished only to determine how much of morality could be founded securely without entering into the religious questions at all.[25]

We must note, to begin with, that Bradley was not a theologian, and the statement about a system of ethics being a system of theology is not Bradley's but Eliot's. Further, we must distinguish between Eliot's philosophic and his religious position. He holds, as does Bradley, that morality and religion are not the same thing. Accordingly, in criticizing Arnold's confusion of morals and religion he is following Bradley, and his position is so far a philosophic one.

What Bradley says about religion in *Ethical Studies* is said from the point of view of philosophy. It is an analysis of the

"religious consciousness," as distinct from the "moral consciousness," and it has nothing to say about the "origin" or the "ultimate
truth" of religion. Here, as elsewhere, Bradley's remarks about
religion belong to the philosophy of religion, which is neither
religion nor theology. As Bradley says: "That a man should treat
of God and religion in order merely to understand them, and
apart from the influence of some other consideration and in-
ducement, is to many of us in part unintelligible, and in part also
shocking."[26] The motive is that of all speculative philosophy,
knowing or understanding for its own sake.

Now, though Eliot was a religious person, and for him religion involves theology, he holds the same view of philosophy that
Bradley does: for him, as for Bradley, philosophy is distinct from
religion and theology.

Eliot has, in one way or another, a good deal to say about
"the use and the definition of terms" as they concern the various
provinces of thought. Thus in "The Perfect Critic," speaking of
"verbalism," or the tendency of words to lose their "definite
meanings" and become "indefinite emotions," he says that this
tendency is especially marked in the professional philosophers of
the nineteenth century, and "their corruption has extended very
far." Its most prodigious exponent, he adds, is Hegel.[27] This sin-
gling out of Hegel is, like much else in Eliot's critical prose,
disconcerting; for Bradley, according to textbooks, is a British
Hegelian. Eliot recurs to the same point in "Francis Herbert
Bradley," where he says that "it is easy to underestimate Hegel,
but it is easy to overestimate Bradley's debt to Hegel; in a philosophy like Bradley's the points at which he *stops* are always important points." Further, remarking that "words have a way of
changing their meaning—as sometimes with Hegel," he says:
"But Bradley, like Aristotle, is distinguished by his scrupulous
respect for words, that their meaning should be neither vague nor
exaggerated; and the tendency of his labors is to bring British
philosophy closer to the Greek tradition."[28]

With Hegel, philosophy was the completion of religion; but,
according to Bradley, "metaphysics has no special connection
with genuine religion, and neither of these two appearances can
be regarded as the completion of the other." Metaphysics, Bradley says, "takes its stand on this side of human nature," and there

is no claim on its part "to supersede other functions of the human mind."[29] Thus, by way of contrast, Eliot says of Bergson: "Has not his exciting promise of immortality a somewhat meretricious captivation?" "But the question is, for philosophy, says Bradley somewhere dryly, not whether the soul is immortal, but whether, and in what sense, it may be said to exist here and now."[30] Similarly: "Aristotle was not embarrassed by a belief in personal immortality, and his philosophy confines itself with fair success to an examination of the actual, the present life." And explaining "the entelechy of Aristotle," he says: "Soul is to body as cutting is to axe: realizing itself in its actions. . . . For Aristotle reality is here and now; and the true nature of mind is found in the activity which it exercises."[31]

There is, as it happens, a certain ambiguity in Aristotle's usage, for he speaks, though only on two occasions, of "first philosophy" as "theology." In other contexts, however, "theology" is but one species of theoretical thought: it deals with pure form (God), whereas what Eliot in the passage quoted above calls Aristotle's philosophy deals with embodied form, the form of living things (plant, animal, man).[32]

As for Eliot's usage, he says of Arnold that "in philosophy and theology he was an undergraduate; in religion a Philistine."[33] Theology is coupled with philosophy because both are speculative studies, whereas religion, though it implies a "theoretic" element, is essentially practical. Again: "Possibly theology is what Bradley said philosophy was: 'the finding of bad reasons for what we believe upon instinct'; I think it may be the finding of good reasons for what we believe upon instinct."[34] Philosophy and theology are alike in being theoretical, but they deal with different objects. Thus in his essay on Leibniz Eliot carefully distinguishes between the philosophic and the theological aspects of Leibniz's thought. For instance: "Theology and physics join forces (so to speak) to rob metaphysics of its due." He notes, too, that "his metaphysics and his scientific achievements—logical and mathematical—are two different values."[35]

For Eliot, then, metaphysics is neither theology nor science (in the restricted English sense of the word). There is, however, a certain difference between Eliot and Bradley in regard to the relation of metaphysics to the special sciences, especially psychology, and perhaps logic. I shall try first to indicate Bradley's position and then the aspect in which Eliot differs from Bradley, confining myself to a bare sketch of the question.

With Bradley, reality is a whole with distinctions but no divisions.[36] And it is in virtue of this view that, as Eliot says, Bradley "perceived the contiguity and continuity of the various provinces of thought." Again, in *Ethical Studies* Bradley "wished only to determine how much of morality could be securely founded without entering into the religious questions at all." Bradley, indeed, deals with ethics without entering into the metaphysical questions, at least explicitly. Thus he says at the outset of *Ethical Studies:* "Beyond us lie the fields of metaphysic, which the reader must remember we are, so far as possible, not to enter but merely to indicate."[37] There is the same restriction in his book on logic and in his essays on psychology. And yet in these writings his metaphysics, though not expounded, is everywhere assumed. In short, Bradley deals with ethics, logic, and psychology as special sciences; and though he treats these subjects in the light of his metaphysics, he insists that as special sciences they are independent of metaphysics. That is, I believe, a fair description of Bradley's position, and it is a position that to certain of Bradley's disciples seemed open to question.[38]

Here, in "A Defense of Phenomenalism in Psychology," is Bradley:

> A limited science is . . . made what it is . . . by studying whatever it studies with a limited end and in a limited way. If you ask for instance unconditionally what are matter and force, that is a question for metaphysics. It becomes a question for physics if you ask what they are for a certain limited purpose and in a certain limited sense. And exactly the same thing in principle holds with the science of mind. If you ask about the soul unconditionally, what is the truth about its nature, the inquiry is metaphysical. But if, on the other hand, you confine yourself to a limited kind of question about the soul, that limitation keeps you within empirical psychology and is the boundary of your science. And this in principle seems as clear as it is evident and visible in practice.[39]

Bradley is here stating a general doctrine about the differ-

ence between metaphysics and the special sciences, and defending the status of psychology as a separate science. Now while
Eliot holds the general doctrine, he differs with Bradley on the
question of psychology.

But let us first hear Bradley again. In "Association and
Thought," after offering a psychological definition of the soul, he
says:

> The above definition is of course open to metaphysical objections,
> as are the conceptions which *must* be used in all empirical science.
> The objections are therefore irrelevant.

Similarly:

> A definition in psychology is for me a working definition. It is not
> expected to have more truth than is required for practice in its
> science; and if when pressed beyond it contradicts itself, that is
> quite immaterial.[40]

Eliot is critical of this position. "Whether psychology is independent of metaphysics, will be one of the questions involved."
Further, he finds in Bradley's treatment of psychology as a separate science "a confusion of the psychological point of view with
the metaphysical"; and again he says of a statement of Bradley's
that "this explanation I protest against as metaphysics and not as
psychology." But Eliot goes further. Psychology, he holds, is not
a scientific discipline at all—psychology, that is, as distinguished
from psychophysics and the study of behavior. These last are, to
be sure, important fields of study, but they are "knowledge either
of physiology, biology, or of the external world." Psychology
proper—what Eliot calls "rational psychology"—"will be not a
scientific but a philosophical discipline."[41]

We need not pursue this matter here. I introduce it at this
point only to show that in metaphysics Eliot insists on being
rigorously metaphysical. The main point is that Eliot holds the
same view of metaphysics that Bradley does, and he holds, too,
the same general doctrine of the special sciences (or disciplines or
departments of thought). These last, which are limited in the
kind of questions they ask (they are *special* sciences), deal with
truths that are relative and provisional, whereas metaphysics is

concerned with questions of ultimate truth and reality. That is the difference, in Eliot's terms, between "theory" and "practice and natural science" or "theory of practice."[42]

The nineteenth century, Eliot says in "The Perfect Critic," was responsible for "vast ignorance" as well as for "vast accumulations of knowledge—or at least of information." "When there are so many fields of knowledge in which the same words are used with different meanings . . . it becomes increasingly difficult for anyone to know whether he knows what he is talking about or not."[43] Similarly, in "Lancelot Andrewes" he speaks of "the vague jargon of our time, when we have a vocabulary for everything and exact ideas about nothing—when a word half-understood, torn from its place in some alien or half-formed science, as of psychology, conceals from both writer and reader the meaninglessness of a statement."[44]

With Bradley, every empirical science is "half-formed." Though its ideas are useful for practice in its science, if pressed beyond, they contradict themselves; or, as Eliot expresses it, "if you do not stop arbitrarily . . . ; and whether or no psychology has the right to stop."[45] Ideas on this level cannot be thought out—that is, cannot be defended against philosophical (metaphysical) criticism, which pushes, so far as it can, every question to the end.

Bradley's philosophy, Eliot says, is "a *pure* philosophy: it borrows none of the persuasiveness of science, and none of the persuasiveness of literature" (utility and appeal to emotion). It is "a *purer* philosophy" than that of either Bergson or Bertrand Russell. Bergson "makes use of science—biology and psychology—and this use sometimes conceals the incoherence of a multitude of points of view, not all philosophic." With Russell, the trouble is rather that "he has never been really convinced that philosophy was possible at all: he was educated as a mathematician, and the mathematician in him is impatient of the philosopher."[46]

Every science represents a particular point of view, but the point here is that science and philosophy represent different points of view. And the strange thing is, from a modern point of view, that science is not "theory" but "theory of practice." This distinction is in principle that of Aristotle, who classifies knowledge or science as theoretical, practical, and productive. And Bradley: "The distinction between theory and practice can never, I presume, lose its theoretical importance." Bradley's whole position, it may be said, depends on this distinction. To deny it, he holds, is to deny the independence of the intellect and thereby the possibility of philosophy or metaphysics.[47]

With Bradley, as with Aristotle, theory means *theoria*, the inquiry into what is or exists, and exists in some sense independently of the inquirer; and practice means the "alteration of existence." Philosophy is "mere theory," and the aim is knowing or understanding for its own sake. In practice and science, on the other hand, thought is subordinated to some end other than that of knowing, or contemplation; here thought stops at some point determined by practical interest, and the inquiry is, accordingly, limited and provisional. Thus the aim cf empirical science is prediction and control, and whatever ideas serve this end are the best ideas; if they are inconsistent with other ideas, or even with themselves, that is nothing against them. And exactly the same thing is true of morality and religion. In these spheres, as in empirical science, ideas are working ideas, ideas that find their justification not in theory but in practice. Since "theory" and "theory of practice" are different values, philosophy does not contradict morality or religion, any more than it contradicts physics or biology; it looks at these fields from an independent point of view.[48]

Bradley's *Ethical Studies* and *Principles of Logic* are about philosophical sciences: bodies of theory, or branches of philosophy. And what is true of the whole is true of the parts: they are "pure" disciplines. Thus, according to Bradley, the direct and primary purpose of logic is to set out "a general theory of reasoning, which is true in general and in the abstract"; and "any usefulness in practice falls . . . outside of the main end and purpose of a true logic." Similarly, ethics, when it goes beyond general theory, ceases to be a (philosophical) science, ceases to be ethics. For it is a mistake to think that "logic has to tell us how we are to reason from special premises" and that "ethics must inform us how we are to act in particular cases." In other words, there neither is nor can there be an "art of reasoning" or an "art of morality."[49] It is the same with aesthetics. Thus Eliot: "And while theories of poetry may be tested by their power of refining sensibility by increasing our understanding, we must not ask that they serve even that purpose of adding to our enjoyment: any more than we ask of ethical theory that it shall have a direct application to and influence upon human behavior."[50]

Though the purpose of aesthetic theory is not to teach us how to be literary critics, criticism implies some assumption about what poetry is and is not. Hence "to ask 'what is poetry?' is to posit the critical function" and "you cannot deplore criticism unless you deprecate philosophy."[51]

Eliot, as we have seen, associates Bradley not so much with Hegel or with the philosophy of the nineteenth century as with Aristotle and the Greek tradition. And I must say a word here about Aristotle.

In "Lancelot Andrewes," Eliot remarks that reading Andrewes on the Incarnation is "like listening to a great Hellenist expounding a text of the *Posterior Analytics*."[52] The allusion is, surely, to Harold Joachim, Bradley's disciple and Eliot's tutor at Merton College, Oxford, of whom Eliot says in the preface to *Knowledge and Experience*: "To Harold Joachim I owe a great deal: the discipline of a close study of the Greek text of the *Posterior Analytics*, and, through his criticism of my weekly papers, an understanding of what I wanted to say and how to say it." In "The Perfect Critic" (where Aristotle is praised above Coleridge), Eliot says: "Aristotle is a person who has suffered from the adherence of persons who must be regarded less as his disciples than as his sectaries. One must be firmly distrustful of accepting Aristotle in a canonical spirit; this is to lose the whole living force of him."[53]

Eliot's Aristotle is Aristotle read in the light of Bradley and after the fashion of Joachim. Eliot, as we shall see in a later chapter, also reads Leibniz in the light of Bradley, and in his essay on Leibniz (where he has almost as much to say about Aristotle as about Leibniz) he explains this procedure. In studying a philosophy, he says there, we must first isolate the work and attempt to comprehend it in its own terms; but the true value of a philosophy can never be extracted solely in that way; we must go on to "effect a radical restatement, find in it motives and problems which are ours." And in the dissertation, "the novelties in philosophy are only in the elaboration, and never in fundamentals."[54]

That explains in part Eliot's generalizing style: statements which (to use Frege's distinction) make sense while omitting the meaning or reference, the consequence being that each reader is left to supply, intuitively, his own reference, though these references are apt to be incompatible with one another as well as with Eliot's meaning.

In "The Perfect Critic," Eliot says of the *Poetics* that it is analysis carried to "the point of principle and definition," whereas "a precept, such as Horace, or Boileau gives us, is merely unfinished analysis. It appears as a law, a rule, because it does not appear in its most general form; it is empirical."[55]

That is, it may be said, an account of two levels of generalization according to Aristotle's theory of induction. As Eliot notes in his essay on Leibniz: "In *An. post* . . . we are told how the knowledge of the universals arises through experience of particulars. 'First principles' are arrived at by induction."[56] Experience, according to Aristotle, is developed from sense perception and memory, and from experience—that is, from the universal—"originate the skill of the craftsman and the knowledge of the man of science."[57] Knowledge is always of universals; but the knowledge of the craftsman, being nearer to sense, is obscure and limited by irrelevant details, whereas the man of science exhibits the universal disentangled from its irrelevant context: he exhibits it in its most general form.[58]

The precepts of Horace and Boileau are unfinished analysis, and the empirical sciences are half-formed, though their laws are on a higher level than the rules of Horace and Boileau. As Eliot says, there are "degrees of intelligence," and "we may doubt whether the level of intelligence among men of letters is as high as among men of science."[59]

Aristotle is not, however, the ordinary man of science. "Aristotle had what is called the scientific mind—a mind which, as it is rarely found among scientists except in fragments, might better be called the intelligent mind." The mind of "the ordinary scientific specialist" is "limited in its interest," is "good only for certain classes of objects"; but Aristotle was a man of "universal intelligence," and "universal intelligence means that he could apply his intelligence to anything."

It is, Aristotle says in the *Metaphysics*, "the function of the philosopher to be able to investigate all things."[60] This brings us back to philosophy and the special sciences. By a "science" is meant here not only or necessarily what Aristotle calls a demonstrative science or what in English is called a science, but any distinct discipline or department of thought. And the point to be indicated is that Bradley's conception of what a science is and of the relation of philosophy to the special sciences is in principle that of Aristotle, but Aristotle reproduced in a different philosphic context.

Eliot remarks that "Arnold, as Master of Arts, should have had some scruple about the use of words"; "we notice that he employs *truth* and *thing* as interchangeable."[61] The allusion is to Aristotle, who in the *Metaphysics* writes that "falsity and truth are not in things . . . but in thought";[62] or to Bradley, who also treats of "the distinction between things and my thoughts about them."[63] Again, metaphysicians, Arnold says, "were altogether above entertaining such a tyro's question as what *being* really was."[64] Aristotle, in the *Metaphysics*, says: "There is a science which investigates being as being and the attributes which belong to this in virtue of its own nature. Now this is not the same as any of the so-called special sciences; for none of these others treats universally of being as being. They cut off a part of being and investigate the attribute of this part; this is what the mathematical sciences for instance do."[65]

Students of special studies—this is the sense of Aristotle's doctrine—take their subject for granted; and that is perfectly proper, for the conditions or presuppositions of their subject are no concern of theirs. These conditions require for their investigation an external point of view, an investigation that is the complement of the special study.[66] Thus it belongs to philosophy to discuss the basic truths—the laws of thought, which are also the laws of being—from which every special inquiry starts and in virtue of which "all the sciences have communion with one another."[67] It also belongs to philosophy to discuss the assumptions that are peculiar to the particular disciplines, including such questions as what is the nature of the objects of which a discipline treats and whether and in what sense these objects may be said to exist.

Bradley's treatise on history is titled *The Presuppositions of Critical History*. It is one thing, Bradley says there, for history "to be aware of its aims and the character of its work," and another thing "to attempt to comprehend the conditions of its being, and the justification of its empire." Though this is now what history mostly needs, it "cannot, except by its actions, justify itself. Confined as it is to one limited sphere, to reflect on the grounds of its existence is for it to pass beyond that sphere; and the principles which regulate its practice are thus, because it cannot account for them, its presuppositions."[68]

That is a restatement of Aristotle's view of the relation of philosophy to the special sciences. Plato apparently held the same view, for he tells us that, though Theaetetus is an excellent mathematician, he is a poor philosopher: he can do mathematics, but he cannot account for the principles presupposed by his mathematics.

According to Aristotle, each special science investigates some sphere of being or department of the real, or some determinate class of things. A science is thus constituted by selection and abstraction: it isolates by definition some aspect of things and inquires into the properties of the abstracted aspect. Thus arithmetic marks off the numerable or countable side of things, and geometry the side that is extended and shaped; and these aspects (number and spatial magnitude) are, as defined, assumed to be or exist. This assumption of the being of the subject of a science Aristotle calls the hypothesis of a science, and the hypothesis is included in "the premises of the science."[69] Though the objects as abstracted and posited are fictions, this procedure is both legitimate and necessary, for "each question will be best investigated in this way—by setting up by an act of separation what is not separate, as the arithmetician and the geometer do."[70]

All this is restated by Bradley. For instance, the "world of mathematics . . . rest[s] upon certain conditions";[71] arithmetic "seems to assume a real system in which the relations of every possible unit and integer *are*."[72] Again, between psychology and logic there is a "difference of interest and of object": each has a "restricted end"; and if either "is to exist, [it] must abstract."[73] Similarly, the side of art, as well as that of science, is constituted "by an abstraction."[74] In sum, every distinct sphere and region "is set apart by an act of abstraction, and in that abstraction alone it essentially consists."[75]

Though without abstraction there could be no knowledge, the worlds thus constituted hold good "only for certain purposes and only under certain conditions"; and though we ignore these conditions, the conditions are not "absolutely true and real," and the constructed worlds have only "a relative truth and reality."[76]

Eliot, speaking of Arnold's "conjuring trick" of making poetry a substitute for philosophy and religion, says that the "most generalized form" of his own view is simply this: "nothing in this world or the next is a substitute for anything else"; it is not "the same desires that are satisfied," nor do we "have in effect the same thing under a different name."[77]

There are, Bradley says, "certain modes of experience which satisfy"—intellectual, practical, and aesthetic—and the whole question turns on the difference between these modes of experience. The aim of philosophy is truth, and truth is that which satisfies the intellect, according to the intellect's own standards (theoretical consistency). Accordingly, if there is to be philosophy, its proper business is "to satisfy the intellect." By "practice" is meant morality and religion; and the purpose of religion, and on a lower level of morality, is to satisfy the desire for goodness. With Bradley, as with Aristotle, the good is not *ipso facto* true. In any case, though religion has its ideas, the function of these ideas is something more and other than the satisfaction of the intellect. Then there is the "aesthetic attitude," and "this aspect of the world satisfies us in a way unattainable by theory or practice, and it plainly cannot be reduced and resolved into either." These are all "special aspects," and "not any one is resolvable into the others."[78]

A science, Eliot says, "is such because it is able to deal with objects of one type"; each science marks off a "field of reality," which is "assumed and selected"; and such spheres imply "selection and exclusion," which is a function of "a particular point of view."[79]

This brings us to what Eliot in "The Function of Criticism"

calls "a problem of order."[80] The underlying idea is that of the coherence theory, which, as we shall have occasion to see, applies to every sphere of experience. For our present purpose it is enough to note that the idea of order is not that of a sum or a collection of independent elements. It is, rather, that of "organic wholes" (though, as we shall see later, such wholes are *"more than organic"*);[81] or it is what Bradley calls the "idea of system,"[82] or, as Eliot puts it, "systems in relation to which, and only in relation to which," the elements have their significance. Again, what the critic needs is "a very highly developed sense of fact," for there are "many spheres of fact to be mastered." The essay concludes on the following note: "But if any one complains that I have not defined truth, or fact, or reality, I can only say apologetically that it was no part of my purpose to do so, but only to find a scheme into which, whatever they are, they will fit, if they exist."[83]

In the dissertation, "facts are not merely found in the world and laid together like bricks, but every fact has in a sense its place prepared for it before it arrives, and without the implication of a system to which it belongs the fact is not a fact at all."[84]

Eliot recurs to this point in his note on the *Posterior Analytics*, where, after remarking that first principles are arrived at by induction, he goes on to say that "what is not made clear is the status of the particulars after scientific knowledge is established." What Aristotle does not make clear is that facts are not independent of the science that deals with them (all facts are context-bound). And the "problem of order" is the problem of the various "spheres of fact."[85]

Eliot, in his "definition of Fact," instances two spheres: "a sphere of historical Reality" and "a sphere of aesthetic values," in which judgment is made upon the ground of "internal evidence."[86] In "The Function of Criticism," "it is difficult," he says, "to confirm the 'interpretation' by external evidence," though "to any one who is skilled in fact on this level there will be evidence enough." The other sphere belongs to scholarship, which gratifies "a taste for history, let us say, or antiquities, or biography—under the illusion that it is assisting another."[87]

For Bradley, Eliot says in "Francis Herbert Bradley," "no one 'fact' of experience in isolation is real or is evidence of anything."[88] There are no independent facts. As Eliot says, "the real is the organized,"[89] and organization means the idea of system. Thus criticism is "an organization of . . . experiences,"[90] or it is the communication of "a co-ordinate system of impressions."[91] In such a system, "the new impressions modify the impressions received from the objects already known. An impression needs to be constantly refreshed by new impressions in order that it may persist at all; it needs to take its place in a system of impressions. And this system tends to become articulate in a generalized statement of literary beauty."[92]

Speaking of *The Sacred Wood*, Eliot says that the problem there is "the problem of the integrity of poetry, with the repeated assertion that when we are considering poetry we must consider it primarily as poetry and not another thing," though this is "an artificial simplification, and to be taken with caution."[93]

Though art is but one abstracted aspect of things, we must treat it as relatively independent. Thus, for instance, Bradley: "The various sides of our nature appear to be connected, and more or less this connection everywhere shows itself. But the complete truth as to this connection seems not to be within our grasp. And hence the main aspects of our being must be allowed, each for itself, to have a relative independence."[94]

The reason, to restate it, is this. Though the various aspects are connected, the way in which they are connected is inexplicable. To understand that, we should have to explain the relation of the unity to the diversity, and the unity in its detail is unknowable.[95] Hence, as Eliot says: "Certainly poetry is not the inculcation of morals, or the direction of politics; and no more is it religion or an equivalent of religion, except by some monstrous abuse of words"; "on the other hand, poetry as certainly has something to do with morals, and with religion, and even with politics perhaps, though we cannot say what."[96]

There is unity, then, as well as diversity—though the unity is a matter of faith, in the sense of a principle whose details are unverifiable.[97] And there is, further, a distinction of degrees. Thus Eliot writes that "out of absolute idealism we retain what I consider its most important doctrines, Degrees of Truth and Reality and the Internality of Relations."[98] And in "A Dialogue on Dramatic Poetry": "For man lives in various degrees. We need (as

I believe, but you need not believe this for the purpose of my argument) religious faith. And we also need amusement. . . . Literature can be no substitute for religion, not merely because we need religion, but because we need literature as well as religion."[99] We also need philosophy, for "life includes both philosophy and art."[100] Though these are all essential, they do not stand on the same level. In some respects religion stands higher than art and philosophy, and in other respects art and philosophy stand higher than religion.

With Eliot, religion has two contexts, philosophic and theological; and when he speaks of religion in his critical prose (and in certain other texts), he does so, as a rule, from the point of view of his philosophy, and from this point of view religion is one aspect of the "problem of order."

Consider, for example, the following statement from "Arnold and Pater": "The dissolution of thought in that age, the isolation of art, philosophy, religion, ethics and literature, is interrupted by various chimerical attempts to effect imperfect syntheses. Religion became morals, religion became art, religion became science or philosophy; various blundering attempts were made at alliances between various branches of thought. Each half-prophet believed that he had the whole truth. The alliances were as detrimental all round as the separations."[101]

And Bradley: "Is then religion a mere mode of theoretic creation and contemplation, like art and science? Is it a lower form or stage of philosophy, or another sort of art, or some kind of compound mixture? It is none of these, and between it and them there is a vital difference."[102]

With Bradley, it was noted above, reality is a whole with distinctions but no divisions ("though we may not divide, yet we have to distinguish"). For Eliot's version we must turn to *Notes towards the Definition of Culture*, where he writes:

> The reader may have difficulty in reconciling these assertions with the point of view set forth in my first chapter, according to which there is always, even in the most conscious and highly developed societies that we know, an aspect of identity between the religion and the culture. I wish to maintain *both* these points of view. We do not leave the earlier stage of development behind us: it is that upon which we build. The identity of religion and culture remains on the

unconscious level, upon which we have superimposed a conscious structure wherein religion and culture are contrasted and can be opposed. The *meaning* of the terms "religion" and "culture" is of course altered between these two levels. . . . Hence, for the purposes of this essay, I am obliged to maintain two contradictory propositions: that religion and culture are aspects of one unity, and that they are two different and contrasted things.[103]

First a word about the "unconscious level." It is not what is called the unconscious but immediate experience or feeling. Thus Bradley, after explaining the notion of the unconscious as used in German philosophy (a notion made popular by von Hartmann), says: "Against any interpretation here of immediate experience in the above sense I would desire specially to warn the reader." Eliot, taking up the same point, says that experience "both begins and ends in something which is not conscious," and "this 'not conscious' is not what we call 'unconscious.'"[104]

What comes first is immediate experience or feeling: "an experienced non-relational unity of many in one." This immediate unity "is not a stage which shows itself at the beginning and then disappears, but it remains at bottom throughout as fundamental. And further, remaining, it contains in itself every development which in a sense transcends it."[105] Out of this unity are developed "the intellectual, the practical, and the aesthetic aspect of things"; "each must thus be regarded as a one-sided and special growth from feeling. And feeling still remains in the background as the unity of these differences, a unity that cannot find its complete expression in any or all of them."[106]

Eliot writes: "In order to apprehend the theory of religion and culture which I have endeavored to set forth in this chapter, we have to try to avoid the two alternative errors: that of regarding religion and culture as two separate things between which there is a *relation*, and that of *identifying* religion and culture." And Bradley: "Everything therefore, no matter how objective and relational, is experienced only in feeling, and . . . still depends upon feeling. On the other side the objective and the relational transcend the state of mere feeling and in a sense are opposed to it. But we must beware here of an error. We cannot speak of a relation, between immediate experience and that which transcends it, except by a license. It is a mode of expression found convenient in our reflective thinking, but it is in the end not defensible."[107]

Similarly, in the dissertation Eliot writes: "And now we are in a better position to inquire into the situation (in order not to say relation) of feeling, thought and object in experience." And in *Notes:* "No culture can appear or develop except in relation to a religion. But the use of the term *relation* here may easily lead us into error. The facile assumption of a relationship between culture and religion is perhaps the most fundamental weakness of Arnold's *Culture and Anarchy*."[108]

No culture can appear or develop except in relation to a religion, and Eliot might have added that no religion can appear or develop except in relation to a culture; for "art and science and religion are distinguishable elements or aspects of this one whole process," and "neither art nor science nor religion can exist as a thing by itself, and the two former will necessarily imply the latter."[109]

Though no one aspect by itself and taken apart from the others is truly real or significant, each is relatively independent. Moreover, there is no one aspect to which the others are subordinated. Nor can any one aspect serve as the explanation of the others or of the whole. Further, there is no direct way from one to the others. Thus a belief that supports religious practice need not be true for philosophy. Similarly, no inferences about morality or religion can be drawn from art. Again, though morality has something to say about whether and how far a man should pursue art and knowledge, it has nothing to say about how these pursuits are to be carried on. And though religion may determine that a novelist practices his art in a spirit that is irreligious, it has nothing to say about how a novel is to be written (any more than it has to say about how "to ride a horse or to play on a piano"). In short, morality and religion are external to the specific principles of artistic and intellectual activity.[110]

That is, I believe, as far as Eliot, as philosopher, carries the "problem of order"; and the reason is that the problem is not altogether explicable. But for Bradley and Eliot philosophy is not called upon to explain everything—and neither is religion. Eliot, like Bradley, defends only what he takes to be a sound general view of reality. And, so far as I can see, he nowhere does violence to his philosophy.

There are, to be sure, complications arising from his religious position. For instance, in "Religion and Literature" he is concerned with the application of religion to the criticism of literature. This essay, it should be noted, is dated 1935; the essay on culture is dated 1948, and the theory of religion and culture that is set forth there certainly seems to have a philosophic basis.

The purpose of "Religion and Literature" is to support the proposition that "literary criticism should be completed by criticism from a definite ethical and theological standpoint." That is a type of extraliterary criticism. But "whether it is literature or not can be determined only by literary standards." And this question—"what is poetry?"—belongs to philosophy. As Eliot says of the problem of the integrity of poetry and his assertion that poetry is primarily poetry and not another thing, "I do not, on the whole, repudiate it."[111]

In "Religion and Literature" he supports his proposition with philosophic argument. If, as Bradley says, one believes in "the unity of our nature," there can be "no one-sided satisfaction," for the various aspects "imply one another" and "must condition one the others." And Eliot: "If there could be a complete separation, perhaps it might not matter: but the separation is not, and never can be, complete." Hence "what we read does not concern merely something called our *literary taste*," but affects "the whole of what we are." Again, in "our individual literary education" we meet "very different views of life," and these, "cohabiting in our minds, affect each other," and we give "each a place in some arrangement peculiar to ourself."[112] The same principle applies to the elements of *literary taste*. Thus, in "The Education of Taste" (1919), taste is "an organization of immediate experiences obtained in literature."[113] In "Dante" (1929), the experience of a poem "is never repeated integrally," and yet it "would become destitute of significance if it did not survive in a larger whole of experience."[114] In *The Use of Poetry*, "the experience of poetry, as it develops in the conscious and mature person, is not merely the sum of the experiences of good poems. Education in poetry requires an organization of these experiences." And there is another stage, "one of reorganization," for a new experience means "a new pattern of poetry arranging itself in consequence." But one's taste in poetry "cannot be isolated from one's other interests and passions; it affects them and is affected by them."[115] In sum, "the real is the organized," and "this statement is metaphysics."[116]

The situation, then, is this: with Eliot philosophy terminates, somehow, in religion; but, though something is added, nothing is subtracted. And Eliot says: "To maintain the autonomy, and the disinterestedness, of every human activity, and to perceive it in relation to every other, require a considerable discipline."[117]

2

A Question of Language

Though it has long been known that Eliot was a student of philosophy, it has been assumed either that he left his philosophy in his dissertation or that with the supervention of religion he went blind in his philosophic eye. In this and the next chapter, I propose to consider these assumptions and certain of their consequences.

In a retrospective piece on Eliot in the *New Statesman* (8 January 1965) the unsigned author writes: "That in his literary criticism he was not a philosopher or aesthetician is hardly to his discredit—no first-rate critics ever have been." M. C. Bradbrook, in "Eliot's Critical Method" (1947), begins by remarking that "the influence of Mr. Eliot as a critic must surely be noted rather in the history of taste than in the history of ideas."[1] Hugh Kenner, in *The Invisible Poet* (1959), comparing Eliot's critical output with that of Coleridge, says: "Coleridge accumulated his millions of words more easily; he had ideas to lighten them"; and in *T. S. Eliot: A Collection of Critical Essays* (1962), explaining why he has included Blackmur's "In the Hope of Straightening Things Out," he says that the great merit of this essay is its "late protest" against treating Eliot's critical prose for its "ideas," for, Kenner says, "the critical prose was empirical."[2]

Philip Wheelwright, in "Eliot's Philosophical Themes" (1947), says: "There are for Eliot, I should judge, two supreme modes of apprehension—poetic and religious."[3] The mixture of these two modes constitutes Eliot's "philosophical" themes. In the same vein, Blackmur says that the criticism of I. A. Richards is a "more philosophical enterprise" than that of Eliot, for "Richards took instinctively to the twinning of science and poetry; Eliot twinned poetry and religion."[4] According to Richards, in *Coleridge on Imagination* (1934), Eliot is an antiphilosophic critic, for he exemplifies the literary prejudice against philosophic reflection on poetry and criticism.[5]

John Crowe Ransom, in "Criticism as Pure Speculation" (1941), speaks of certain theories of Eliot's as "the philosophy of the literary man"; and of Eliot's "special version of psychologistic theory" he says that he "would not answer for the conduct of a technical philosopher in assessing this theory."[6] René Wellek, in "The Criticism of T. S. Eliot" (1956), finds that "all of Eliot's criticism" is permeated by a "psychologistic emotional vocabulary."[7]

This is a curious situation, and one of long standing. And the consequence is that Eliot and his commentators have been talking at cross-purposes.

Blackmur helps to point this up. According to him, the "objective correlative" is not a "doctrine" but a "notion" or a "metaphor," and it is not meant to have any application outside of the *Hamlet* essay. As for Eliot's "own doctrine of poetry," it turns on what he says about "the triad of feeling, emotion, and sensibility." And after explaining what he understands by this triad, Blackmur says: "I think I depend only on the language as it is in the dictionary and in usage and *thereby* in Eliot's own use."[8]

That is the common assumption: Eliot's language is the language of popular usage, or of popular psychology. But on this assumption we cannot, I think, find a meaning for Eliot's language. Take, for example, the statement that "the emotion of art is impersonal," or the phrase "the objective 'poetic emotion.'"[9] What are we to make of emotion that is "impersonal" and "objective"?

To F. R. Leavis, Eliot's "doctrine of impersonality" is "a wholly arbitrary dictum."[10] Northrop Frye thinks that the word impersonal is "a figure of speech," and perhaps "deliberately paradoxical."[11] Frank Kermode speaks of Eliot's "highly personal impersonality."[12]

Or consider René Wellek's explanation that "the impersonality of the poet must be taken to mean that poetry is not a direct
transcript of experience."[13] Though there is something to that,
what Wellek calls "discontinuity"—the discontinuity between the
experience of the poet and his poetry—will not account for Eliot's
position, for "the principle upon which I insist," Eliot says, "is of
course the unity and continuity of feeling and objectivity."[14]

Feeling here is immediate experience or feeling. And though
with Eliot feeling is a larger term than emotion, let us for the time
being treat these terms as interchangeable (as Eliot himself tends
to do, and as common usage does). But, as Eliot says, we "must
accustom ourselves to 'feeling' which is not the feeling of psy-
chologists" but "a metaphysical use of the term feeling."[15]

According to Eliot, science arbitrarily divides experience
into two independent sides, subject and object regarded as externally related. The subject side, feeling, belongs to psychology, for
psychology, it is thought, deals with something more subjective
than other disciplines. Accordingly, psychology makes an object
of our feeling, but this is not the object *we* experience—not the
object for the experiencing subject. For the subject of experience, the "felt feeling" and the "objectified feeling" are one and
the same. Feeling, then, is both "felt" and "observed"; and, as
observed, it is an object. "So far as feelings are objects at all, they
exist on the same footing as other objects: they are equally public,
they are equally independent of consciousness, they are known
and are themselves not knowing."[16]

The difference, to restate it, is this. The feeling of psycholo-
gists is the adjective of a subject, the feeling of a subject about an
object, and this feeling is subjective and private, its only reality
being that of a consciousness. But in Eliot's metaphysical use,
feeling is self-transcendent: feeling becomes object (in and
through the medium of thought or intellect), and this "objectified
feeling" is a real object in the world of objects.

Let us see something of the use that Eliot makes of this
doctrine of feeling and object. In regard to poetry, he says that
"the feeling, or emotion, or vision resulting from the poem is
something quite different from the feeling or emotion or vision in
the mind of the poet";[17] a poem is "a presentation of feeling,"[18] or

poems are "statements of emotion,"[19] or the aim of the poet is "to state a vision."[20] The vision is the objectified feeling or emotion. Thus, speaking of "the artistic emotion presented by any episode of the Comedy," he says that "no emotion is contemplated by Dante purely in and by itself."[21]

According to Bradley, "every feeling . . . is partly perceptive," and "this perceptive side of feeling" is *"before us*, and in this sense is genuinely 'objective.'"[22] And Eliot in "The Perfect Critic": "Not only all knowledge, but all feeling, is in perception." Hence a literary critic "should have no emotions except those immediately provoked by a work of art—and these (as I have already hinted) are, when valid, perhaps not to be called emotions at all."[23]

Here, in "The Perfect Critic," is Eliot again: "The end of the enjoyment of poetry is a pure contemplation from which all the accidents of personal emotion are removed: thus we aim to see the object as it really is and find a meaning for the words of Arnold. And without a labor which is largely a labor of the intelligence, we are unable to attain that stage of vision *amor intellectualis Dei."*[24]

This last is apparently an allusion to Spinoza, who is mentioned earlier in the essay. But it might just as well be an allusion to Aristotle, who figures prominently in the essay. Thus Joachim, expounding Aristotle's use of *nous*, says that it is "the activity of thought in which the thinker . . . sees things as they ultimately are, and in that vision is at one with God."[25]

Obscurities of this sort are a feature of Eliot's critical prose; and if we are to give a proper account of the prose, we cannot altogether ignore them. To take another instance, in "Tradition and the Individual Talent" Eliot says, "I hinted, by an analogy," that "the mind of the poet is the shred of platinum," and that "the platinum itself is apparently unaffected; has remained . . . unchanged."[26] Later in the essay he hints at part of his meaning (hints at the meaning of his hint) by quoting from the *De Anima* the statement: "But the reason itself is something more divine, and not capable of being affected."

This sort of indirection is an integral part of Eliot's prose. The principle, it may be said, is that of analogy or metaphor: an identity of sorts among differences. Thus Spinoza is, like Bradley, a monist, and Aristotle is in some contexts "an epistemological monist."[27]

Eliot, in speaking of the apprehension of objects, uses such terms as "presentation," "perception," "vision," and "contemplation." The shortest way of elucidating this usage is by reference to the Greek word *theoria:* "a looking at, contemplation."

With Bradley, art, like philosophy, is a mode of "theoretic creation and contemplation": "mere seeing." In art as in philosophy, what matters is that something "should be *seen* to be realized"; "the end is the sight of the object, as such."[28]

As for religion, though it is essentially practical it has a theoretic or contemplative side, which Eliot in the passage quoted above represents as "that stage of vision *amor intellectualis Dei.*"[29]

Here, in the earlier Dante essay, is Eliot again:

> The mystical experience is supposed to be valuable because it is a pleasant state of unique intensity. But the true mystic is not satisfied merely by feeling; he must pretend at least that he *sees*, and the absorption into the divine is only the necessary, if paradoxical, limit of his contemplation. The poet does not aim to excite—that is not even a test of his success—but to set something down; the state of the reader is merely that reader's particular mode of perceiving what the poet has caught in words.[30]

Eliot's philosophy applies to objects of all types, to religious as well as to intellectual and aesthetic objects; and though these are different types of objects the structure of experience is the same for the mystic as for the poet and his reader. As Eliot says in the dissertation: "From first to last reality is experience, but experience would not (so far as we know) be possible without attention and the moment of objectivity." Experience is a whole, internally articulated into a subject and an object side, and these two sides are inseparable. Hence "there is always, in any existence worthy of us, a real object of attention."[31] Every experience, then, has an object, and otherwise it is mere passion, so that, according to this doctrine, "the true mystic . . . must pretend at least that he *sees*."

In the earlier Dante essay, speaking of the philosophic ingredient of Dante's poem ("the philosophy of Aristotle strained through the schools"), Eliot says that "we are not studying the philosophy, we *see* it." And he goes on to say that Dante deals with his philosophy "not as a theory (in the modern and not the Greek sense of the word) or as his own comment and reflection, but in terms of something *perceived.*"[32]

The question concerns the status of ideas in poetry, and Eliot is here transcribing Bradleyan doctrine. According to Bradley, ideas, in becoming poetry, have been transformed and have, as such, ceased to be there as ideas. That is, they have lost their logical status as true or false, and are there simply as matter of fact. Accordingly, we are not studying the philosophy, not treating it as argument and inquiring into its validity. Rather, as Bradley says, it is there "merely as perceived";[33] or, as Eliot expresses it, "we *see* it," or it is "something *perceived.*"

"We *see* it," Eliot says, and hints at his meaning by noting in parentheses the distinction between the modern and the Greek sense of theory. But it is the Greek sense as reinterpreted by Bradley. This is a frequent pattern in Eliot's critical prose.

Again, in "The Perfect Critic" Eliot says:

> If we are allowed to accept certain remarks of Pascal and Mr. Bertrand Russell about mathematics, we believe that the mathematician deals with objects—if he will permit us to call them objects—which directly affect his sensibility. And during a good part of history the philosopher endeavored to deal with objects which he believed to be of the same exactness as the mathematician's. Finally Hegel arrived, and if not perhaps the first, he was certainly the most prodigious exponent of emotional systematization, dealing with his emotions as if they were definite objects which had aroused those emotions.[34]

Eliot here seems to be appealing to Russell in order to dispraise Hegel, and by implication Anglo-Hegelians. But take the words "if he will permit us to call them objects." In the dissertation Eliot says that, according to Russell, universals or particulars may be known by direct acquaintance, but objects are inferred. "The entities (to use as non-committal a term as possible) which we know (by acquaintance) are not objects but means by which we apprehend objects, while the object is directly quite beyond the span of our knowledge. There are, in this interpretation, 'no such things' as objects, there are only experiences." And speaking of "the objects of mathematics," he says that the consequence of Russell's doctrine is that "numbers are not objects." Eliot has summarized this argument in "if he will permit us to call them objects."[35]

The mathematician "deals with objects . . . which directly affect his sensibility." The objects of mathematics are not self-supporting but, like other objects, are developed out of and depend upon immediate experience or feeling. In this sense, every object directly affects sensibility; for objects, as Eliot says, "cannot be merely contemplated, but must be *erlebt* (experienced)."[36] It is not only poets who "feel their thought"; for, as Bradley says, "ideas everywhere are only so far as they are felt."[37]

As for Hegel, he was "an exponent of emotional systematization, dealing with his emotions as if they were definite objects which had aroused those emotions."[38] With Hegel, emotion has no reference to an object. And Eliot goes on to compare Hegel with, among others, a seventeenth-century preacher. In "Lancelot Andrewes," "Andrewes's emotion is purely contemplative; it is not personal, it is wholly evoked by the object of contemplation, to which it is adequate; his emotion wholly contained in and explained by its object. . . . Donne is a 'personality' in a sense in which Andrewes is not: his sermons . . . are a 'means of self-expression.' He is constantly finding an object which shall be adequate to his feelings; Andrewes is wholly absorbed in the object and therefore responds with adequate emotion."[39]

Eliot discusses sermons, mathematics, philosophy, and poetry in terms of emotions and objects. Nor is this surprising in view of the fact that he is the author of a dissertation whose original title was "Experience and the Knowledge of Objects in the Philosophy of F. H. Bradley." Here in outline is the doctrine as Eliot gives it in his study of Bradley:

> Feeling is to be taken (*Appearance*, p. 419) "as a sort of confusion, and as a nebula which would grow distinct on closer scrutiny." That of which it is a confusion, and into which it can be analyzed, is (*Appearance*, p. 405) "speaking broadly . . . two great modes, perception and thought on the one side, and will and desire on the other side. Then there is the aesthetic attitude . . . and . . . plea-

sure and pain." Feeling is "the general state of the total soul not yet
at all differentiated into any of the preceding special aspects."[40]

There are difficulties. Thus emotions are objects; and, again,
objects arouse emotions and emotions, if valid, must have reference to objects. All that can be said at this point is that feeling
and object are only discriminated aspects of a whole of experience, and that feeling becomes object and object becomes feeling. Hence, as Eliot says, "the real situation is an experience
which can never be wholly defined as an object nor wholly
enjoyed as a feeling, but in which any of the observed constituents may take on the one or the other aspect."[41]

In speaking of the reaction of the critic to a work of art, Eliot
distinguishes between the "personal" and the "objective." In the
one, poetry is a stimulus to personal emotion ("all sorts of emotions which have nothing to do with that work of art"),[42] and in
the other, the emotion is relative to the work, is evoked and
explained by it.

This distinction may serve to bring out the difference between the psychological approach to aesthetics and Eliot's approach. The psychological interest is not in the object but in the
state of mind excited by the object, its pleasantness or unpleas-
antness, which is explained according to the laws of association.
In Eliot's approach, the interest is in the object, and the explanation of the state of mind is sought in the object.

In his chapter "The Psychologist's Treatment of Knowledge," Eliot writes: "What then as to the doctrine of Mr. Bradley
. . . that an emotion can be attended to? I believe this doctrine to
be correct. For on the theory which I have outlined above, pleasure as pure feeling is an abstraction, and in reality is always
partially objective: the emotion is really part of the object, and is
utlimately just as objective. Hence when the object, or complex
of objects, is recalled, the pleasure is recalled in the same way,
and is naturally recalled on the object side rather than on the
subject side: though it tends . . . to instate itself as an active
pleasure."[43] Eliot is speaking here of the feeling or emotion of
pleasure, and the doctrine he is alluding to has both a practical
and an aesthetic aspect.

Bradley holds that we can make an object of the feeling or emotion of pleasure—can have, that is, an idea of it—and that when we attend to an idea of pleasure our feeling may be pleasant, unpleasant, or indifferent. In other words, the idea of the feeling (of pleasure) is one thing, and what we feel in attending to it is another. Bradley's doctrine is that the feeling or emotion of pleasure is objectified in the sense that it becomes a part of the meaning of the object that gives us pleasure. Thus when we have an object before us, in perception or thought, our pleasure is contained and explained by the object.

Here, for instance, is Bradley in *Ethical Studies:*

> While being pleased by the contemplation of an object, you can transfer the pleasure, in idea, to that object, so that they form an integral whole. But then a new feeling must be excited by that whole in order to move you.[44]

Similarly:

> The child does not cry for the sugar on Tuesday because he remembers he had a pleasure on Monday, and thinks he should like another today; but because the feeling of sweet taste, now transferred as an idea to the sugar and made objective in it, is recalled in idea by its perception, and being recalled, excites a feeling which, against the felt absence of sweet taste, is felt as want, and accordingly moves.[45]

Bradley is dealing here with practical feeling (want or desire), and criticizing its explanation according to the psychology of association. But the doctrine applies, with a difference, to the theoretic pleasure of aesthetic contemplation, a pleasure arising from the perception of an objective meaning.

Often the only sign we have of Eliot's position is his criticism of other positions, nor is it always obvious what he is criticizing. This situation occurs throughout his critical prose, and we may offer an example of it here. In "The Perfect Critic" he writes:

> Mr. Symons . . . *is* the "impressionistic critic." He . . . would be said to expose a sensitive and cultivated mind—cultivated, that is, by the accumulation of a considerable variety of impressions from all the arts and several languages—before an "object"; and his criticism . . . would be said to exhibit to us, like the plate, the faithful

record of the impressions. . . . A record, we observe, which is also
an interpretation, a translation; . . . I do not say at once that this is
Mr. Symons; but it is the "impressionistic" critic, and the impressionistic critic is supposed to be Mr. Symons.[46]

That is an account of impressionistic criticism according to
the doctrine of sensationalism. According to this doctrine, as
Bradley describes it, knowledge is "the reception of outward impressions," the "simple record" of the facts conveyed through the
senses, the record being like "a passive print."[47] So Symons
"would be said to exhibit to us, like the plate, the faithful record
of the impressions."

Again, Bradley writes: "A feeling *is* at most; it is neither . . .
true nor false." If a feeling or a sensation is to be known or
understood, it must be an object for the intellect, and by intellect
is meant "that which separates (distinguishes), and at the same
time conjoins."[48] And Eliot: "The question is not whether Mr.
Symons' impressions are 'true' or 'false.' So far as you can isolate
the 'impression,' the pure feeling, it is, of course, neither true nor
false. The point is that you never rest at the pure feeling. . . . The
moment you try to put the impression into words, you . . . begin
to analyze and construct."[49]

In Hume's theory of knowledge, sensations or "impressions"
are the primary data of experience, and Eliot's language suggests
that of Hume. But with Eliot the only datum is immediate experience or feeling. Feeling in this sense is not one differentiated
aspect, but holds all aspects in one. And one never rests at the
pure feeling because there is no stage at which feeling is "merely
immediate"; in order that "it should be feeling at all, it must be
conscious, but so far as it is conscious, it ceases to be merely
feeling." In other words, feeling has "from first to last some objectivity"; and the transition from "the merely felt to the objectified" is the work of thought or intellect.[50] It is, as Eliot goes on
to say, "analysis and construction."

Later in the same essay Eliot writes: "But I believe that it is
always opportune to call attention to the torpid superstition that
appreciation is one thing, and 'intellectual' criticism something
else. Appreciation in popular psychology is one faculty, and
criticism another, an arid cleverness building theoretical scaffolds upon one's own perceptions or those of others."[51]

In "popular psychology," feeling and thought are separate faculties, and they are separate in the sense of being *exclusive*. That is also true of "popular epistemology," that is, "the popular theory of knowledge, from which our philosophies spring."[52] In the popular view, there is an external world independent of thought, and real because independent. Our knowledge of this world is divided into sensation and thought, as in the empirical school that derives from Locke, or into sensibility and understanding, as in the Kantian philosophy (as Eliot calls it). It will be convenient to illustrate the doctrine in question by quoting from Kant's *Introduction to Logic* (a book annotated by Coleridge).

According to Kant, sensibility and understanding are "distinct faculties," the one being the source of "intuitions" and the other of "concepts." Sensibility is "the faculty of *receptivity*," and understanding is "a faculty of *spontaneity*." Sensibility "only supplies the mere material for thought, while the understanding deals with this material, and brings it under concepts."[53]

The important point is that the material received by sensibility (sensations, feelings, impressions) is given independently of thought, the function of thought being to order and arrange this material. Thought is a purely formal exercise: it imposes a form on material external to it. Thus feeling and thought are exclusive, that is, externally related.

Now according to Eliot, "There is no greater mistake than to think that feeling and thought are exclusive—that those beings which think most and best are not also those capable of the most feeling."[54]

What is given in the experience of a poem is a felt unity, and in and by analysis and construction this vague totality is translated into an articulate whole of terms and relations. Thus our first experience of a poem is something we feel without as yet understanding it; then we begin to distinguish and relate the elements, to make distinct both the details and their connections; and in and through this process there emerges a definite structure. And this ideal or intellectual construction is the object we contemplate and enjoy.[55]

The error, Eliot says in the dissertation, "would consist in any sharp distinction between enjoyment and contemplation."[56] Similarly, in "The Frontiers of Criticism" (1956): "I must stress the point that I do not think of *enjoyment* and *understanding* as distinct activities—the one emotional and the other intellectual."[57]

In his posthumously published essay, "To Criticize the Critic" (1965), Eliot begins with a quotation from Bradley: "Criticism may be, what F. H. Bradley said of metaphysics, 'the finding of bad reasons for what we believe on instinct, but to find these reasons is no less an instinct.'" Eliot, in this essay, divides his critical prose into two classes: "the essays of generalization . . . and appreciations of individual authors." He is especially concerned—he returns to the point several times—that his "generalizations" should not be regarded as abstractions unrelated to his direct experience of poetry.

> But I am sure that my own theorizing has been epiphenomenal of my tastes, and that in so far as it is valid, it springs from direct experience of those authors who have profoundly influenced my own writing. I am aware, of course, that my "objective correlative" and my "dissociation of sensibility" must be attacked or defended on their own level of abstraction, and that I have done no more than indicate what I believe to have been their genesis. I am also aware that in accounting for them in this way I am now making a generalization about my generalizations.[58]

Eliot is generalizing about the relation of his theorizing and his direct experience of poetry—the relation (so to speak) of thought to immediate experience or feeling. But, though these are distinct, they are inseparable. Thus: "There is immediate experience, contrasted with ideal construction. . . . But we go on to find that no actual experience could be merely immediate, for if it were, we should certainly know nothing about it; and also that the line between the experienced, or the given, and the constructed can nowhere be clearly drawn."[59] Or, as he puts it in *The Use of Poetry and the Use of Criticism:* No theory can amount to much which is not founded upon a direct experience of good poetry; but on the other hand our direct experience of poetry involves a good deal of generalizing activity."[60]

The "objective correlative" and the "dissociation of sensibility" must be attacked or defended on their own level of abstraction—that is, on the level of theory. The theory has to do with thought, feeling, and object. And the difficulty is that we have to reckon with two views of thought and feeling: that of popular theory and that of Eliot's philosophy.

In general, the division of experience into independent elements externally related—a division which takes various forms—is the "dissociation of sensibility."[61] Sensibility in this usage is a "felt whole," or a "whole of feeling," or a "whole of experience"; and in the "unified sensibility" thought operates *within* this whole, is the elaboration and articulation of the whole—the making explicit of what was implicit.[62] In this philosophy, the only way in which feeling can be understood is to turn it into objects. And this is as true of a child frightened by a bogey as of the mathematician engaged upon a problem—for mathematics is "continuous with our ordinary tendency towards objectification."[63] It is also true of painting and music, of poetry and fiction, for the "only way of expressing emotion in the form of art is by finding an 'objective correlative.'"[64]

Eliot, besides being a difficult writer, is highly disconcerting. Thus he has done little to discourage the notion that he is an unphilosophic critic; indeed, if we attend to certain things he says *about* his work, as distinguished from what he says *in* it, he seems to go out of his way to encourage this notion. For instance, "I am too well aware of limitations of interest . . . and of incapacity for abstruse reasoning. . . . I have no general theory of my own."[65] Bradley sometimes writes in the same way, as when he says: "I regret that my incapacity for following abstract arguments has prevented me in great part from understanding the position he has here taken up."[66] Eliot, noting Bradley's habit of discomfiting an opponent with a sudden profession of ignorance, of inability to understand, or of incapacity for abstruse thought, says that this habit is not, as many conclude, all a mere pose, or simple irony, but the expression of a real modesty.[67] However it may be with Bradley, Eliot's repeated profession of incapacity for abstruse reasoning has been taken not as a pose or as irony but as an incapacity for abstruse reasoning. The consequence has been that Eliot and his commentators have been talking at cross-purposes, and it is perhaps well to look further into this situation, with the aim of showing just what the issue is.

Here, in *The Achievement of T. S. Eliot* (1935), is F. O.

Matthiessen: "Eliot is hardly more qualified for metaphysical speculation than Arnold was—he himself has spoken of his 'incapacity for abstruse reasoning'; in spite of his long training in philosophy, his mind is too heavily concrete, his insight too purely intuitive, to qualify him for sustained flight in the realm of pure logic." What Eliot discovered in "the philosopher Bradley (the author of *Appearance and Reality* and perhaps Eliot's chief master in prose style)" was "the quality of wisdom which 'consists largely of scepticism and uncynical disillusion.'" But it was his concern with "political and religious thought" that led him to "a much deeper understanding of the nature of art and its value for society than was possessed by the author of 'Tradition and the Individual Talent.'" "And that brings us once more to the very heart of Eliot's fundamental belief as an artist: the necessary union of intellect and emotion. He finds it in 'the consummate art' of the finest philosophic prose in our language, 'in which acute intellect and passionate feeling preserve a classic balance.' Such union, in which words are 'so close to the object' that the two become identified, as surely as in Donne or Baudelaire, is the chief attribute of great poetry as well."[68]

Eliot's fundamental belief as an artist is also his fundamental belief as a philosopher. But what Matthiessen is saying, if I understand him, is that this belief is an intuitive discovery of Eliot's, an insight he owes not to his philosophy but to his concern with political and religious thought.

As for word and object, Matthiessen is quoting from "Swinburne as Poet," where Eliot writes: "Language in a healthy state presents the object, is so close to the object that the two are identified."[69] That is a summary statement of the doctrine of word and object sketched in the dissertation. The process of translating feeling into object involves language, "because it is language which gives us objects rather than mere 'passions.' Or at least we have no objects without language."[70] "It must be emphasized, however, that there is properly speaking, no relation between the symbol and that which it symbolizes, because they are continuous."[71]

> Idea and phrase both denote realities, but the realities denoted are identical with the idea or the phrase. It is a mistake, I think, to treat

the word as something which barely points to the object, a sign-post which you leave behind on the road. . . . The phrase directs your attention to an object but the object is an object because it is also that object, because the mere hypothetical moment of objectivity is qualified by the characters of the phrase, which are real properties at once of the phrase and of the object.[72]

In short, "Language in a healthy state presents the object, is so close to the object that the two are identified."

It did not occur to Matthiessen that there was something in Eliot's prose that he was overlooking. He assumes that whatever Eliot's language means, its meaning is obvious, and everyone understands it. And that is the common practice: Eliot's commentators paraphrase his critical prose, largely in the language in which it is written, and then offer the paraphrase as an explanation of the language. But it is the language itself that must be explained. I am, therefore, trying to direct attention to a problem which Matthiessen overlooked and which commentators have continued to overlook.

Thus Mario Praz, in the Eliot issue of *Sewanee Review* (1966), addressing himself to those who speak of Eliot's "contributions . . . to criticism," says that "it seems necessary to warn that [Eliot], with typical Anglo-Saxon shyness, has waived any claim to systematic philosophical thought"; Eliot "does not want to indulge in 'speculations about aesthetics, for which [he has] neither the competence nor interest.'" Eliot is "an empirical critic"; "his real guide is not logic but intuition"; and his critical discoveries "take the shape of a myth or an image." Explaining how Eliot arrived at his concept of the metaphysical tradition, Praz says that Eliot's culture at the time "was not very extensive" and, in Eliot's mind, "the various elements of this little patrimony short-circuited into a poetic vision of genius"; and thus was born "the poetics of 'unified sensibility' or union of thought and sense."[73] According to Bradley, as quoted by Eliot: "But the union in all perception of thought with sense, the co-presence everywhere in all appearance of fact with ideality—this is the one foundation of truth."[74] As for the idea of the "objective correlative," it, Praz says, is "no less poetical" than the idea of a unified sensibility. There is much more to the same effect, all of which "throws considerable light on the empirical character of Eliot's criticism." But, Praz concludes, Eliot "has been anyhow a leader of taste," admired for his "earnestness and uprightness" and "also for the fundamental coherence in his apparent or actually substantial contradictions."[75]

Austin Warren, in the same issue of *Sewanee Review*, says that in "The Metaphysical Poets" Eliot "is not attempting some *a priori* thinking about *genres*: he is testing tentative hypotheses against specific cases." Warren has a good deal to say about the influence on Eliot of Irving Babbitt, and he introduces Ezra Pound and T. E. Hulme in discussing Eliot's view of imagery; but from "the British neo-Hegelian, F. H. Bradley, on whom Eliot wrote a Harvard dissertation," all that Eliot seems to have learned is a "cautious and elegant" style of prose.[76]

Frank Kermode, also in the same issue, says that "the objective correlative, a term probably developed from the 'object correlative' of Santayana, is an attempt . . . to purge [the image of romantic poetry] of any taint of simple expressiveness or rational communication," and that "the 'dissociation of sensibility' is an historical theory to explain the dearth of objective correlatives in a time when the artist . . . is working at the beginning of a dark age . . . in an ever-worsening climate of imagination." And he adds: "Such theories, as we now see, are highly personal versions of stock themes in the history of ideas of the period."[77]

What Kermode means by this last statement, as he explains in *Romantic Image*, is that the "dissociation of sensibility" is Eliot's version of "modern Symbolist aesthetics" as represented by Pound, Hulme, and Yeats. The aim of this aesthetics was "to restore to poetry a truth independent of the presumptuous intellect"; and though Eliot's attempt was "distinguished from the others by the accident of his personal concerns in theology, [it] is not essentially different from them." "Nor is his attitude difficult to understand; it is animated by a rich nostalgia for the great period of Anglican divinity . . . looking back, itself, to a vague past when the folly and arrogance of the intellect had not yet begun the process of dissociating Christianity."[78]

In this account, the intellect, which is opposed to the "image," is the agent of dissociation. Yet, according to Eliot, the unification of sensibility is the mark of "the intellectual poet";

moreover, "to express precise emotion requires as great intellectual power as to express precise thought." Thus *Agamemnon* and *Macbeth* are "as much works of the 'intellect' as the writings of Aristotle."[79] When Eliot praises the "intellectual poet" or speaks of poetry as the work of the "intellect," he means, according to Kermode, "the poet's special, anti-intellectual way of knowing truth."[80] As for the attempt to purge poetry of rational communication, Eliot says in the dissertation: "It is not true that the ideas of a great poet are in any sense arbitrary. . . . In really great imaginative work the connections are felt to be bound by as logical necessity as any connections to be found anywhere."[81] And in the preface to the *Anabasis* of St.-John Perse (a passage quoted by Kermode): "There is a logic of the imagination as well as a logic of concepts."

Murray Krieger, writing in *Southern Review* (1969), says: "Arnold may be seen as ultimately (or, rather, originally) responsible, not only for Eliot's . . . ideas on poetry and beliefs, but also for such other central doctrines in Eliot as the objective correlative and the unity of sensibility." Donald E. Stanford, writing in the same issue, quotes a passage from Hulme's "Lecture on Modern Poetry" and says: "Here is the basis for . . . Eliot's objective correlative." Further: "It is now generally recognized that as a literary critic Eliot was often inconsistent. Yvor Winters went into some detail on this subject twenty-five years ago in his *Kenyon Review* essay, 'T. S. Eliot: The Illusion of Reaction,' and more recently Mario Praz, in the Eliot issue of *Sewanee Review*, commenting on Eliot's inconsistencies refers to his method as 'intuitive' and 'empirical.' In the same issue Austin Warren . . ."[82]

What Winters set out to show was that Eliot's "intellectualism" is an "illusion." Nevertheless, Winters shows in his close examination of Eliot's language that if one neglects Bradley, Eliot's critical prose is largely unintelligible.

F. R. Leavis has performed the same unwitting service. Speaking of "Tradition and the Individual Talent," he says that "it was on this essay pre-eminently that was based Eliot's reputation as a thinker, a disciplined intelligence notably capable of rigorous, penetrating, and sustained thought." "Actually, the trenchancy and vigor are illusory and the essay is notable for its ambiguities, its logical inconsequences, its pseudo-precisions, its fallaciousness, and the aplomb of its equivocations and its specious cogency. Its offered compression and its technique in general for generating awed confusion help to explain why it should not have been found easy to deal with."[83]

The essay is indeed not easy to deal with, and it is well to have that said. But Leavis is confident of one thing: whatever the essay is saying, "the falsity and gratuitousness of its doctrine of impersonality are surely plain enough." Moreover, he finds in it an "ethos or case," that is, a failure of intelligence. "But when we recognize that the artist implicitly proposed is Flaubert, then the proposition becomes intelligible, if not acceptable." "Flaubert's opposing art to life . . . entails a self-contradiction: it portends an inner thwarting disorder . . . that has defeated intelligence in the artist." That gives us "Eliot's own case," for that is "what Eliot's theory of 'impersonality' logically points to—if it were a coherent theory, and could be said to point logically to anything."[84]

Eliot's philosophic theory, it may be, is false and gratuitous, but that is not the theory Leavis is talking about. Nor can it be made intelligible by reference to Flaubert. Eliot reads Flaubert as he reads other writers, in the light of his Bradleyan philosophy. Thus *Education Sentimentale* is "the labor of the intellect," the same quality of intellect as that of "Aeschylus and Shakespeare and Aristotle." Again, as we saw above, "idea and phrase both denote realities, but the realities denoted are identical with the idea or the phrase." So, speaking of Flaubert's idea of the small bourgeois in *Education Sentimentale*, he says: "It has there become so identified with the reality that you can no longer say what the idea is."[85]

3

Eliot and Bradley:
A Brief Review

It is accepted nowadays that F. H. Bradley ("the British neo-Hegelian") was an "influence" on Eliot, but at most only a marginal one. It is symptomatic of this situation that Bradley's name does not appear in the index to Herbert Howarth's *Notes on Some Figures behind T. S. Eliot* (1965); and though it occurs in the text, all that Howarth has to say about Eliot's dissertation is that "Dr. Anne C. Bolgan has examined Eliot's philosophical writing, and, if I understand her, interprets his view of 1916 as a belief that a man must fulfill his potentialities in action, and that by doing so he may extend God's creation."[1]

The allusion is to Bolgan's doctoral thesis, "What the Thunder Said: Mr. Eliot's Philosophical Writings" (Toronto, 1960), the object of which, as Bolgan explains it, is as follows:

> It is the specific objective of this dissertation to assert that every major critical concept which appears in Mr. Eliot's literary criticism—many of which initiated such stubborn controversies—emerges from his radical absorption in and criticism of Bradley's philosophy, and the content of my dissertation is but a demonstration of the way in which these notions and concepts originate in Bradley, are digested and recorded by Eliot as he writes his own Ph.D. dissertation between 1914 and 1916 and reappear beginning a year or two later, now in new, full, literary dress in Mr. Eliot's reviews and essays.

This chapter first appeared in *T. S. Eliot Review*,
volume 3, numbers 1 and 2 (1976), pages 29-58

If that is right, as I believe it is, Bradley is not a marginal but a central influence on Eliot as critic.

Howarth apparently did not think that Bolgan's assertion was worth reporting. Northrop Frye, who is listed as a member of the committee supervising Bolgan's work, is even more reticent. In *T. S. Eliot* (1963) he does not mention Bolgan's study, either in the text or in the bibliography. In his chapter on Eliot's criticism he remarks that "Eliot's first philosophical interest was in F. H. Bradley"; and of *Appearance and Reality* he says: "Thus what started out as a nineteenth-century idealist's problem about how far we can 'know reality' ends as a kind of mystical primer. In the Indian philosophy which Eliot next studied. . . ." And a few paragraphs later: "He finds in Christianity . . . a conception of the function and context of poetry."[2]

John D. Margolis, in *T. S. Eliot's Intellectual Development* (1972), reduces Bradley to a footnote, remarking that "there is hardly need here once again to examine Eliot's dissertation. . . . Despite Eliot's (possibly disingenuous) suggestion in the 1964 preface that the book's primary value is the insight it offered into the development of his prose style, a number of critics have fruitfully considered the impact of his study of Bradley." See especially, he says, Bolgan, "What the Thunder Said"; E. P. Bollier, "T. S. Eliot and F. H. Bradley: A Question of Influence" (1962); Hugh Kenner, *The Invisible Poet* (1959); J. Hillis Miller, *Poets of Reality* (1965); Kristian Smidt, *Poetry and Belief in the Work of T. S. Eliot* (1961); and George Whiteside, "T. S. Eliot's Dissertation" (1967).[3]

Margolis introduces his book with the statement that "as he himself well understood, T. S. Eliot's literary criticism was largely a consequence of his creative activity"; and he goes on to say that "his remarks . . . on literature . . . are more often valuable for the light they cast on Eliot's own thinking at the time than for the contributions they make to [the field] they concern." As for "Bradley's impact" on Eliot: "Bradley was unlikely to have exercised a direct religious influence. But 'of wisdom,' Eliot said, 'Bradley had a large share.' . . . That Eliot had imbibed Bradley's scepticism and disillusion was clear in his early poetry and prose; that he was now employing to his own ends that 'useful equipment for religious understanding' was evident throughout *For Lancelot Andrewes*."[4]

The view of Eliot as critic has not advanced beyond the point where F. O. Matthiessen left it. Margolis, it may be assumed, is registering the impression made on him by the writings he mentions in his footnote; and since that impression is more or less the general one, it may be useful to look at some of these, and certain other, writings.

Let us begin with Kristian Smidt's *Poetry and Belief in the Work of T. S. Eliot* (Oslo, 1949; rev. ed., London, 1961), the first extended inquiry into the philosophical background of Eliot's writings. Smidt, noting that "Eliot has repeatedly asserted that he has no capacity for abstruse thinking," says that "Eliot's limitations as a critic may have prevented him from becoming a theoretician of his art or a critic of the philosophical or purely scholarly type." His equipment consists of "sensibility and mastery of style," attributes of "the poetical *rather* than of the critical mind." And "that there should be inconsistencies and contradictions in a critic who avoids general aesthetic theories is only to be expected."[5]

Eliot's critical views, according to Smidt, are to be explained by reference to his "spiritual development" or his "individual needs." Thus, noting that "again and again Eliot points to the difference between art and belief," Smidt says:

> Very likely his own spiritual development partly accounts for his views. In his period of agnosticism he read Dante and found that Dante's ideas . . . would stand in the way of enjoyment if they had to be fully believed in. He could not fully believe in them, but nevertheless recognized the greatness of the poetry, helped, perhaps, by Santayana and Pound. So he not only decided that real belief was unnecessary but even that Dante need not have believed in these things himself. The theory of poetic belief which was indicated may not have originated with Eliot. But he probably found it congenial—as well as useful as a sort of defense around his poetry, enabling him to conceal himself in his works.[6]

Speaking of Eliot's conception of an "impersonal" poetry, Smidt says that it is "a phantom and an illusion," for "poetry is autobiographical." Though Eliot's conception "seems to owe something to *Appearance and Reality*," "it would seem that [it] at least partly originated in a revulsion from his own emotional freight at the time, and an intense distrust of the private and individual personality." So much for its origins. As for the theory itself, "In the process by which personal emotion and feeling become impersonal, the author assigns a large place to the intellect," but "the most important moment in the creation of a poem is removed from the sphere of reason . . . and transferred to a special artistic faculty." Eliot "comes close to accepting the idea of supernatural inspiration," and there is "actually a half-admission of belief in the divine inspiration of the poet." But this theory was "a difficult one to uphold consistently," and there are "statements which appear to contradict it"; and in any case by 1940 "he had changed his position and was no longer interested in elucidating his former views."[7]

Smidt's work has not been without its influence. Thus Grover Smith writes that, "as Kristian Smidt has shown," Eliot's doctrine about impersonality "seems almost mystical"; it "seems to have resulted from his disbelieving, with Bradley, that a man could have any personality worth expressing; it seems to have resulted from his inability to write poetry on any but these terms, from his shyness at the prospect of self-exposure."[8] Similarly, in "A Great Man Gone" (*Times Literary Supplement*, 7 January 1965): "Mr. Eliot was both a shy and a proud man, and some critics have thought that his insistence in early critical essays on the impersonality of poetic art . . . was partially a defense maneuvre, springing from an awareness of how thoroughly, even in his earliest work, he had unlocked his heart."

Though early critics had thought that Eliot's doctrine had something to do with Bradley, Bradley has now dropped out, and what is left may be called the "shyness" theory—a more popular theory, I believe, than, say, Leavis's "ethos or case" theory.

Of philosophic influences, Smidt says, the "most direct" and "incomparably the most important" was that of Bradley; yet Eliot "seems to have suffered a revulsion from Bradley's idealism." In the second of the essays for *The Monist* in 1916, Eliot "criticized Bradley's conception of the Absolute," and in the same essay "he denied even Bradley's idealism, especially his theory of 'finite centers.'" All the same, "Bradleyan ideas constantly occur in his poetry," and "Eliot's Christianity is strongly tinged with a monist philosophy."[9]

According to Smidt, in 1916, the year in which Eliot completed a dissertation defending Bradley's philosophy, he wrote an essay for *The Monist* in which he rejected the philosophy he defended. Since this is asserted without discussion, it will be well to take note of the essay in question, "Leibniz's Monads and Bradley's Finite Centers." Though Eliot in this essay criticizes the Absolute, he accepts and defends the doctrine of finite centers.

> "The one Absolute" knows itself and realizes itself in and through finite centers. "For rejecting a higher experience," Mr. Bradley says, "in which appearances are transformed, I can find no reason. . . ." But what we do know is that we are able to pass from one point of view to another, and that we are compelled to do so, and that the different aspects more or less hang together. For rejecting a higher experience there may be no reason. But that this higher experience explains the lower is at least open to doubt.[10]

Eliot, as I said, accepts the doctrine of finite centers—or, as he calls it, points of view—but rejects the Absolute; so in his dissertation he is critical of certain other aspects of Bradley's philosophy, psychological and logical. But this is the criticism of a disciple. His object in the dissertation is to defend Bradley's main positions, a defense in which the Absolute does not figure. In brief, what we have to deal with is Eliot's version of Bradley.

Though Smidt misreads the essay, the essay, it must be said, is extremely obscure. Indeed, taken apart from the dissertation, it is hardly intelligible—and the dissertation itself is a very obscure piece of philosophizing.

In the chapter on solipsism Eliot introduces a brief comparison between Leibniz's monads and Bradley's finite centers. Though these are not the same thing, Leibniz's aim "becomes more intelligible in the light of our 'finite centers.'" Thus Leibniz "made the error" of identifying a point of view with a "self" and again with the "phenomenal soul." But with Bradley "the finite center (or what I call the point of view) is not identical with the soul." (Though self and soul are not the same thing, Eliot and Bradley, for convenience, speak indifferently of self and soul.)

Now, Eliot says, "the assertion that 'the monads have no windows' in no wise entangles him in solipsism, for it means (or may be taken to mean) what Mr. Bradley means in saying that our knowledge of other finite centers is only through physical appearances within our own world." "And the pre-established harmony is unnecessary if we recognize that the monads are not wholly distinct, and that the subjective self is continuous with the self as object."[11] In the dissertation, then, Eliot criticizes and corrects Leibniz in the light of Bradley's finite centers.

The essay on Leibniz and Bradley is an expansion of this section; and though it contains a criticism of Bradley's Absolute, it is, with this difference, a restatement of the argument sketched above. Eliot speaks of finite centers as points of view, and in the *Monist* essay he says that the finite center "*is* immediate experience."[12] And this doctrine—the doctrine of immediate experience—is the basis of Eliot's dissertation, everything else being a development from it. Accordingly, though in the *Monist* essay Eliot gives the appearance of being equally critical of Bradley and Leibniz, he accepts and defends Bradley's doctrine of immediate experience—or finite centers or points of view.

Since most commentators represent Eliot and Bradley as solipsists, it is worth noting that the *Monist* essay restates the dissertation's argument against solipsism. If, as Eliot says there, Leibniz is read in the light of Bradley, his position "in no wise entangles him in solipsism." Eliot, then, did not think that Bradley was a solipsist. As for Bradley, though critics charged him with solipsism, "I cannot suppose," he says, "that those critics . . . can have much of an idea as to the position in which I stand."[13]

> Certainly I speak of my finite center, and with this an emphasis may be laid on the "my," and, with this, the road that leads to Solipsism once more seems opened. But it is forgotten here that my self, the self that I take as a thing which endures in time and which I go on to oppose to the world, is an ideal construction. It is a construction which is made on and from the present feeling of a finite center. . . . From the other side we naturally speak of the feeling center from which my self is developed, and with which it remains throughout continuous, as "its." And this expression is true so far as it means that this center is not directly one with others, and that the material and agency out of and by which my self is made, is to that

extent private. But we turn our truth into sheer error when we maintain that my self is an independent substantive, to which the rest of the world belongs somehow as an adjective, or to which other self-sufficient Reals are externally related. Such a position, as we have seen, cannot be defended. That foundation and agency from and by which my self is generated, and through which alone it persists, is one thing with the whole Universe. My self may rightly be called a necessary and even an indispensable element in the world. But its ultimate substantiality and closed privacy seem to be no more than false inferences.[14]

That is the position Eliot restates in the essay under discussion. Thus Leibniz, he says there, "refuses to recognize that the independence and isolation of the monads is only a relative and partial aspect."[15] That is, Leibniz does not see that the self is developed from the finite center, and that it is continuous with this background, and that through this background it is "one thing with the whole Universe." (The Universe appears in all finite centers, though each experiences it differently.)

The literary commentators who represent Bradley and Eliot as solipsists rely largely on the *Waste Land* note. Thus Smidt, illustrating Eliot's solipsism, quotes the lines

> We think of the key, each in his prison
> Thinking of the key, each confirms a prison

and observes that these lines are related, "in Eliot's own note, to Bradley's philosophy," and quotes the note, which ends with the words: "In brief, regarded as an existence which appears in a soul, the whole world for each is peculiar and private to that soul."[16]

Eliot had first used the passage he quotes as a *Waste Land* note in the essay on Leibniz and Bradley. The passage is taken from Bradley's discussion of communication between souls, and the point that Bradley is making there is that what "we are convinced of, is briefly this, that we understand and, again, are ourselves understood." But communication is indirect, and cannot work "save by the path of external appearance."[17] In other words, our knowledge of others is only through the mediation of symbols.

Though the verse seems to suggest solipsism, no inference can be drawn from it about Eliot's philosophic beliefs; and though the note, as Eliot quotes it, seems to support a solipsistic reading of the verse, it does not represent Bradley's position on solipsism.[18]

Eliot, then, in the essay on Leibniz and Bradley, is restating positions he takes in his dissertation. What is confusing is that, while basing his criticism of Leibniz on Bradley's finite centers, he says that Bradley's Absolute is as unnecessary as Leibniz's preestablished harmony. But this criticism of the Absolute must not be taken as a rejection of Bradley's philosophy.

For that matter, Bradley's attitude toward the Absolute is not a simple one. For instance:

> The immanence of the Absolute in finite centers, and of finite centers in the Absolute, I have always set down as inexplicable. Those for whom philosphy has to explain everything need therefore not trouble themselves with my views.[19]

Eliot holds that, though finite centers cohere, the manner of their coherence is inexplicable; and Bradley, while asserting that the coherence is owing to the Absolute, sets this down as inexplicable. It should be noted that the Absolute is not God.[20] Further, the Absolute never is, nor can be, experienced; it is, as Eliot expresses it, "a hypothetical limit of experience." And for Eliot, "the points at which [Bradley] *stops* are always important points."[21]

George Whiteside, in his essay on Eliot's dissertation, begins by saying: "I daresay only a handful of people have read the book. And no doubt only a handful ever will. The purpose of this article is to examine it for the benefit of anyone who wonders what is in it but has no time or inclination to read it." And at the end of the essay: "What has this survey of Eliot's dissertation taught us about him? Many things, but in my opinion one above all: that Eliot hungered for but lacked the sense that all things form a whole. The hunger made him embrace Bradleian monism, but the lack kept him unconvinced of it. This absence of conviction can explain why Eliot eventually gave up monism. And the hunger can account for his subsequent participation in the Christian unity."[22]

When it was that Eliot gave up "monism" we are not told, nor are we told what that is supposed to mean. "For this belief justified his life-long doctrine of the impersonality of art." Similarly, "This is Eliot's life-long notion of tradition. It is a notion of Bradley's."[23]

Speaking of Eliot's definition of "idea," Whiteside says: "He was attached to it. Why? Love of language was one motive. . . . But he had an even greater motive, I think, and that was his desire to believe that imagined things are realities external to the imaginer. . . . So Eliot wanted to believe. . . . I think it was to assure himself that his poems were not just personal that Eliot worked out his definition of the word *idea*."[24]

The main thesis concerns what Eliot "wanted to believe" about immediate experience. "Clearly he wanted to believe it," but he "refused to believe in an Absolute," and "to embrace Bradleian monism yet feel obliged to reject its ultimate underpinning . . . led him, I think, to despair. . . . Why couldn't he convince himself? And why did he feel obliged to reject the Absolute?"[25]

The answer is withheld until later in the essay, where, resuming his argument, Whiteside writes: "Was Eliot's faith in the wholeness of experience genuine? I mean: he said he believed in its wholeness, but did he feel it is a whole? No, I said. . . . Now I will give two reasons. . . . First, he rejected Bradley's Absolute. . . . From these sentences one might conclude that Eliot did not believe immediate experience coheres without the aid of the Absolute. But second, he said we cannot know how it coheres, what it is like: he called it 'the bag of gold at the end of the rainbow' (p. 151). But such bags of gold do not exist, so his metaphor suggests that he felt it—the whole of experience shared by all—is a fiction. For these reasons I suggest Eliot *said* it is a whole and shared but was inclined to *feel* it is in pieces and private, and this feeling kept him from being convinced of what he said. . . . I think he clung to it, without genuine conviction, only because he wanted desperately to fight off this feeling which he had: the feeling that experience is unshared, i.e., that solipsism—solipsism as regards experience—is correct."[26]

"Was Eliot a solipsist as regards objects? . . . Therefore, though Eliot . . . said he was not a solipsist as regards objects, his philosophy led to such solipsism, in my opinion. And in spite of what he . . . said, I think he felt it led to such solipsism. For there is despair in his endorsement of Bradley's solipsistic statement that each soul's 'whole world . . . is peculiar and private to that soul.'" In a footnote, Whiteside adds that Eliot quoted Bradley's "solipsistic statement" both in the notes to *The Waste Land* and in the essay on Leibniz and Bradley, and that "in both places he endorses the words and shows despair in the endorsement."[27]

We have, as I said, to deal with Eliot's version of Bradley; and though Eliot has certain criticisms to make of Bradley, "I believe," he says, "that all of the conclusions that I have reached are in substantial agreement with *Appearance and Reality*."[28]

Whiteside, I believe, misconstrues the passage that contains the words "the bag of gold at the end of the rainbow." With Eliot, no clear line can be drawn between the given and the constructed, so that no knowledge is immediate in the sense of excluding mediation. But radical empiricists "assume that we have an 'immediate' knowledge of a mysterious flux," and criticists "assume that we know sense-data, or universals, immediately." But "we have no direct (immediate) knowledge of anything: the 'immediately given' is the bag of gold at the end of the rainbow."[29]

In "Eeldrop and Apoplex," Eeldrop ("in private life a bank clerk") says: "The essential is, that our philosophy should spring from our point of view and not return upon itself to explain our point of view. A philosophy about intuition is somewhat less likely to be intuitive than any other."[30] Eeldrop is speaking about Bergson; and in the dissertation Eliot distinguishes Bradley's view of experience from that of Bergson (as well as from that of William James). He says that the "*élan vital* . . . is abstracted from experience, for it is only in departing from immediate experience that we are aware of such a process."[31] The *élan vital*, that is, is a construction out of experience, and this construction is treated as though it were an independent fact, a datum.

With Bradley, philosophy springs from our point of view (immediate experience), and it does not return to explain our point of view, because that is inexplicable. Thus, as we saw earlier, "the relation . . . of immediate experience . . . to those contents which transcend it, must be taken as fact. It can neither be explained nor even (to speak properly) described, since description necessarily means translation into objective terms and relations."[32]

The *élan vital* is supposed to be grasped by intuition, by an apprehension that is immediate or direct—as contrasted with knowing that is discursive or relational. But the *élan vital*, Eliot says in the dissertation, is an "ideal construction from experience." Hence, as Eeldrop says, "Bergson is an intellectualist" (not an intuitionist). And in *The Sacred Wood*, "Bergsonism itself is an intellectual construction."[33]

Eliot construes Bergson (as he does Leibniz) in the light of Bradley—in the light, that is, of immediate experience (finite centers or points of view) and its transcendence.

According to Smidt, Eliot's "despair of metaphysics," a despair caused "by the loss or lack of a philosophy," is manifested in intricate ways in his early poems.[34] This same despair, according to Whiteside, is manifested in the dissertation. Others find it in "A Prediction in Regard to Three English Authors" (Henry James, Sir James Frazer, and F. H. Bradley). Thus Hugh Kenner writes that in 1924 Eliot presented Bradley as a potential influence "whose philosophy can operate . . . only 'upon sensibility through the intellect,' " and he adds that "it cannot even be believed in." (At the same time, "the 1916 thesis . . . is evidence for his unqualified ingestion of certain perspectives of Bradley's which we do not discover him ever to have repudiated.")[35]

There are several matters here that require clarification, beginning with Eliot's "despair of metaphysics." In the dissertation he writes:

> And if anyone assert that immediate experience, at either the beginning or end of our journey, is annihilation and utter night, I cordially agree. That Mr. Bradley himself would accept this interpretation of his "positive non-distinguished non-relational whole" is not to be presumed. But the ultimate nature of the Absolute does not come within the scope of the present paper. It is with some of the intermediate steps that the following chapters are concerned.[36]

In "A Prediction" Eliot returns to the sentiment of "annihilation and utter night." Speaking of "the total effect" of Bradley's philosophy "upon a sensibility," he says:

> Once you accept his theory of the nature of the judgment, and it is as plausible a theory as any, you are led by his arid and highly sensitive eloquence (no English philosopher has ever written finer

English) to something which, according to your temperament, will be resignation or despair—the bewildered despair of wondering why you ever wanted anything, and what it was that you wanted, since this philosophy seems to give you everything that you ask and yet render it not worth wanting.[37]

Once you *accept* Bradley's theory of the judgment, you are led by the argument to resignation or despair. In the dissertation he says: "I accept Bradley's definition of a judgment as the predication of an idea of reality, and I agree that this idea is one whole."[38] Indeed, this philosophy "seems to give you everything that you ask." And if its effect "upon a sensibility" is resignation and despair, in the dissertation it is "annihilation and utter night," and the dissertation is a defense of Bradley's philosophy.

"A Prediction" appeared in *Vanity Fair* in 1924 (and in *Nouvelle Revue Française* in 1923). In the *Criterion* (1924), in a note on Bradley's death signed "Crites," Eliot says of Bradley's writings that "they perform that mysterious and complete operation which transmutes not one department of thought only, but the whole intellectual and emotional tone of [one's] being." And it is "not for his achievements in his time" that Bradley is to be honored; "I am engaged with the future."[39]

In "Francis Herbert Bradley" (1927) Eliot says: "Of wisdom Bradley had a large share; wisdom consists largely of scepticism and uncynical disillusion; and of these Bradley had a large share. And scepticism and disillusion are a useful equipment for religious understanding; and of that Bradley had a share too."[40]

According to Smidt, Eliot's "metaphysical scepticism" led him to deny Bradley's philosophy;[41] and Kenner, speaking of Bradley's "*metaphysical* scepticism," says that it is "the unsettling conviction that abstruse thought, carried on for determinate ends, is mereticious."[42] If one is going to speak of Bradley's position as "*metaphysical* scepticism," that term must not be taken to mean scepticism of metaphysics. Though Bradley was, as he said, something of a sceptic, his scepticism was coupled with an addiction to metaphysics.[43]

E. P. Bollier has examined in some detail the effect of Bradley's "scepticism" on Eliot. The important sense of the term is what Bradley calls "theoretical scepticism"; and as Bollier notes, Bradley was not in this sense a sceptic, nor was Eliot.

By "theoretical scepticism" Bradley means scepticism of metaphysics: the assumption that knowledge of reality is impossible or, if possible in some degree, is practically useless.[44] The source of this scepticism is the doubt or denial of "the existence of a criterion" of reality. But, Bradley holds, we possess such a criterion: "theoretical consistency" or the "idea of system"; and though the knowledge this gives of reality is general and incomplete, it is positive, is true so far as it goes, and is enough "to save us from mere [theoretical] scepticism."[45]

Though metaphysical speculation, Bradley says, led him "neither to scepticism nor to pessimism," for most students, he supposed, metaphysics is likely to end in "theoretical scepticism."

> By theoretical scepticism I certainly do not understand a positive doctrine about our knowledge and its necessary limits. . . . I mean by scepticism the mere denial of any known satisfactory doctrine, together with the personal despair of any future attainment. [Or, as he also says, "the denial or doubt with regard to the existence *de facto* for me of that which satisfies intellectually."] And I must admit that with many persons this may be the intelligent outcome of a sincere metaphysical endeavor.[46]

It might seem that Bradley is here providing Eliot with the scenario for "A Prediction," which seems to echo Bradley's words; but Eliot says there that Bradley's philosophy "seems to give you everything that you ask"; that is, it is a "satisfactory doctrine," a doctrine that "satisfies intellectually." And if the effect of the doctrine upon Eliot's temperament was disillusion and despair, that effect, as we have seen, can coexist with a defense of the doctrine that caused it.[47]

As Bollier notes, Eliot's "scepticism" did not prevent him from affirming that the human intellect can arrive "at something outside ourselves, which may provisionally be called truth," nor did it prevent him from "employing ideals and ideas as if they were to some extent true." He also notes that the theories formulated in *The Sacred Wood* spring directly from Bradley's philosophy: the idea of an impersonal poetry, of tradition, of literature as an ideal order, of the objective correlative, of sensuous thought or felt thought, of the distinction between poetry and philosophy, and much else.[48]

Bollier's primary concern, however, is not with Eliot's literary theories but with the influence of Bradley's "scepticism" on Eliot's religious development. And he finds that this influence is "more profound and paradoxical" than critics have thought, for it provided the "intellectual rationale" for Eliot's conversion to Christianity.[49]

To generalize Bollier's argument, Bradley's philosophy, or Eliot's version of it, stands in the background of Eliot's religious thought. Philosophy is, and must remain, intellectual—the theoretical criterion is in theory supreme. But the intellect has its limitations, and these are in principle insuperable. Thought or truth is not, and never can be, the same as reality, which is something more and other than thought or truth. The ultimate reality is an experience in which being and knowing are one. Now thought as judgment is the predication of an idea of reality (under the form of an object or objects). The predicate is about the subject, and is therefore different from it; and this difference is essential to judgment. There is, in other words, a "dualism" of "that" and "what," of "fact and ideality," of "existence and idea." Though thought seeks to overcome this dualism and attain to reality, it can never succeed, without losing its character as thought (relational and discursive). As Bradley says of thought or truth, "It implies that dualism which, involved in truth's essence, for ever stands between it and its goal."[50]

In "The Hollow Men,"

> *Between the idea*
> *and the reality*
> *Between the motion and the act*
> *Falls the Shadow*
> > *For thine is the Kingdom*

Philosophically, everyone inhabits the world of appearance, for reality is known only through its appearances, though without its appearances there would be no reality. But with Eliot reality has two contexts.

With Bradley, though the Absolute is immanent in finite centers and finite centers are immanent in the Absolute, the manner of this coherence is "inexplicable." The point at which

Bradley stops thus leaves space for mystery, wonder, and doubt.[51] For Eliot, the problem posed by Bradley is resolved by the Incarnation. As Bollier expresses it,

> Incarnation, . . . that miraculous fact which somehow unites the multiplicity of finite experiences with the almost felt and almost intellectually comprehensible whole:
>> *The hint half guessèd, the gift half understood*
>>> *is Incarnation.*
>> *Here the impossible union*
>> *Of spheres of existence is actual,*
>> *Here the past and future*
>> *Are conquered and reconciled. . . .*[52]

Adrian Cunningham, in "Continuity and Coherence in Eliot's Religious Thought," also argues that the growth toward a religious position does not reverse any previous assumptions: "The religious question is posed by the insufficiency of the pattern already established and . . . the religious answer does not cancel or radically alter that pattern but validates it at the points where it would otherwise break down."[53]

Though Cunningham also discusses in this connection the influence of Babbitt, Hulme, and Maurras, they are, it seems to me, "external" influences. Certainly, the problem that occupied Eliot was first posed for him by Bradley. Thus in the dissertation, "the life of a soul does not consist in the contemplation of one consistent world but in the painful task of unifying (to a greater or less extent) jarring and incompatible ones, and passing, when possible, from two or more discordant viewpoints to a higher which shall somehow include and transmute them."[54] Moreover, Cunningham sometimes confuses Maurras with Bradley. Thus he attributes Eliot's remarks that religion and culture are "different aspects of the same thing" and that culture is "essentially the incarnation (so to speak) of the religion of a people" to "the influence of Maurras."[55] What is overlooked is Eliot's statement that "to put the matter in this way may throw light on my reservations concerning the word *relation*."[56] At the time of that statement (1948), Eliot was still thinking of the problem in terms of his philosophy, or in terms not incompatible with it.

J. Hillis Miller, though he refers twice to "the refutation of solipsism in *Knowledge and Experience*," writes that "the notion of man's imprisonment in . . . his own 'finite center' is . . . pervasive and fundamental in the dissertation." Thus "the self can never encounter anything other than itself. . . . Just this notion of the validity of subjectivism is expressed in the passage from Bradley's *Appearance and Reality* which is cited in the notes to 'The Waste Land' and in one of the essays on Leibniz published in *The Monist*."[57]

Virtually everything that Miller has to say is based directly or indirectly on Eliot's "subjectivism" or "subjective idealism."[58] He divides Eliot's development into two main periods, idealist and Christian. In the first of these he discovers two stages, the earlier of which is "subjective idealism" and the later "collective idealism" (or "collective subjectivism"). Though in both stages "everything is subjective," there is a "reversal from individualism to collectivism"; that is, for a "private mind" Eliot substituted a "collective mind" (or a "collective consciousness"). Then comes "the reversal which makes him a Christian." And "Eliot can only become a Christian when he ceases to be an idealist," though "traces of idealist thinking still remain in his later prose."

"Only the poetry written prior to 'Gerontion' and 'The Waste Land' remains limited to the assumptions of subjective idealism." During this stage, the poet inhabits a "subjective space" (or a "mental space"). Instead of seeking to escape from its prison, the self explores the contents of "the inner world of the isolated ego." But this proved to be unsatisfactory. And now there is "a turning inside-out of the enclosed sphere of the self," and the poet enters a "collective consciousness." Thus, "without abandoning his subjectivist assumptions," Eliot "seems to have freed himself triumphantly from the prison of his ego."

But "this triumph is really defeat," for he is still "within the same prison." To escape, two steps are necessary. The poet must first recognize "the sterility of idealist thought"; and this step is taken in "The Hollow Men," which shows "the emptiness of collective idealism" and is also "an eloquent analysis of the vacuity of subjective idealism." The second step is "another turning inside-out of the mind, a reversal which recognizes that time, nature, other people, and God are external to the self";[59] and this step is taken in "Ash Wednesday."

Miller's procedure is largely deductive. Thus, since Eliot could not become a Christian without ceasing to be an idealist, the "hollow men" must be idealists, both subjective and collective. Bishop Berkeley aside, the trouble is that Eliot was not a subjective idealist and there is no transformation of subjective idealism into "what might be called a 'collective idealism.' "[60]

With Eliot, every experience is both personal and objective. What Miller seems to have done is to construe the one aspect as subjective idealism and the other as collective idealism, and then to deduce for each of them a theory of poetry. In one theory, poetry is the fusion of elements in the private ego, and in the other it is the fusion of elements in the collective consciousness. The first theory stresses "the way authentic art is the expression of the artist's personality." Since this theory "presupposes the isolation of each ego from the others," it presented "a problem of communication," and Eliot found the solution for this problem in the "emotive image": "emotive images" have a "magical power" of breaking through "the opaque walls of the self to communicate the incommunicable." This "idea of the miraculous power of verbal images is codified in the concept of the objective correlative." The second theory "seems to follow naturally from the failure of the first theory to provide a way out of the prison of the isolated ego." In this theory, "impersonality is achieved by a turning inside-out of the enclosed sphere of the self." And "if the effect of the platinum is *quasi* magical, the fusion of the elements is no less so."

The first theory was codified in the *Hamlet* essay (1919) and the second theory was worked out in "Tradition and the Individual Talent" (1919). In *The Waste Land*, where both theories are reflected, Eliot managed "to reconcile his impersonal theory of art with the idea that art is self-expressive." Miller, in his discussion of the first theory, refers to the criticism of 1932, 1945, 1953, and 1956. But the second theory is "the basis of most of Eliot's literary criticism." That is, in principle, correct. And it may be noted here that Eliot, writing in 1963, said: "I do not repudiate 'Tradition and the Individual Talent.' "[61]

In the Christian period there is "a new definition of the role of poetry." Though a statement in "Poetry and Drama" (1951) suggests that ultimately poetry is to be seen in a Christian context, Eliot never worked this out. What is to be remarked is that in this essay Eliot is still talking of poetry in terms of feeling or emotion and its intensification. In any case, "poetry is, of course, not to be defined by its uses."[62]

Richard Wollheim, in "Eliot, Bradley and Immediate Experience," writes: "A philosophical critic, he has also been a student of academic philosophy. . . . The question therefore arises, to what extent are there present in Eliot's . . . criticism ideas and thoughts that are strictly philosophical: and if there are such ideas, do they manifestly affect the direction in which the writing goes?"[63]

Wollheim, it seems to me, does something less than justice to the question. For instance: "Is there not something disturbing in the fact that a critic who has always been comparatively indifferent to the unity of a work of art should, in his doctrine of tradition, insist so emphatically, so unrealistically, on the unity of art as a whole?"[64]

The unity of a work of art, as we shall see, is a recurrent theme in Eliot's criticism, and the unity of art as a whole is merely a larger type of the same kind of unity. On this point, I am happy to say, Miller is quite right when he observes that "Eliot's view of the concept of organic unity . . . may be seen as operating as a basis of judgment in all the contexts of his criticism," from "the single poem, to the *oeuvre* of a writer, to the literature of Europe, to the whole of which that literature is a part."

With Bradley, as Wollheim might have explained, "organic unity" is a metaphor for the idea of system or an individual whole, a whole that is more than the sum of its parts. This idea occurs everywhere in Eliot's prose. For instance, the "meaning of a word . . . is . . . more than the sum of the meanings."[65] Similarly, "These parts [of a poem] can form a whole which is more than the sum of its parts."[66] So culture "is not merely the sum of several activities," for "these things added together do not constitute the culture"; "a culture is more than the assemblage of its arts, customs, and religious beliefs. These things all act upon each other, and fully to understand one you have to understand all."[67]

Of the objective correlative, Wollheim says that this critical theory was elicited by Eliot "at one remove, or two, from the theory of Immediate Experience."[68] But the critical theory is surely Bradleyan doctrine, though it was left to Eliot to develop the aesthetic implications of the doctrine. Wollheim returned to the subject in "Eliot and F. H. Bradley: An Account,"[69] and as a consequence we have a very fine analysis of *Knowledge and Experience*—in addition to the excellent critical account of Bradley's thought in *F. H. Bradley*.

Wollheim, however, is sceptical of attempts to trace the influence of Eliot's philosophical writing on his literary work "in points of detail," and he confines himself "to suggesting three very general tendencies that are to be found in Eliot's writing, particularly his critical writing, and that also occur in Bradley": the impersonal theory of poetry, the objective correlative, and the dissociation of sensibility. But to go "beyond such generalities seems to me a most hazardous and uncertain undertaking."[70]

One of the hazards is that criticism is likely, "overtly or covertly, to reverse the enterprise and to find itself using the poetry and the criticism as a gloss on, or as a key to, the philosophy." That is apparently a reference to the inferences that have been drawn from the *Waste Land* verse and note on Eliot's and Bradley's "solipsism."[71] More centrally, the dissertation is "a painfully dark work," and in the critical writing one has to reckon with Eliot's "irony" and with his "habit of toying with ideas." There is, further, the question of the status of Eliot's critical ideas: Are they strictly philosophical or are they merely analogues of the philosophy? Again, were they "transmitted from Bradley to Eliot" or were they merely "reinforced in Eliot by his reading of Bradley"? Finally, there is "some obscurity how this critical theory is to be connected with those parts of the philosophy which it seems to parallel."[72]

The problem for us, to put it simply, is finding a meaning for the language of the critical prose, and we cannot do that, I believe, without reference to the philosophy. At the same time, if we try to say exactly what the relation is between the literary theory and the philosophy, we meet problems of various kinds. The only thing to be done with them is to show what they are—to exhibit, in other words, the character of Eliot's critical prose: his habits of prose composition, his "style."

Let us take a fresh example. With Eliot, ideas have no purely psychological existence; and Wollheim, in his discussion of this doctrine, quotes Eliot to the effect that "the idea as you try to grasp it as an object, either identifies itself with the reality or melts back in the other direction into a different reality, the reality of its physiological basis." Here, in the dissertation, is Eliot again: "What . . . has Lipps in mind as the field of psychology? Simply, I think, the old chimera, 'states of consciousness,' meanings torn from their reference."[73] And in the critical prose: "Dante helps us to provide a criticism of M. Valéry's 'modern poet' who attempts 'to produce in us a *state*.' A state, in itself, is nothing whatever."[74]

Eliot construes Dante in the light of his philosophy, and then says that *Dante* helps us to provide a criticism of Valéry. Indirection or misdirection?

In Eliot's early criticism, Mowbray Allan writes in *T. S. Eliot's Impersonal Theory of Poetry* (1974), "we find phrases or even whole passages in a kind of metaphysical vocabulary that suggest, darkly, the presence of an underlying theory. That this theory remained largely esoteric is due, I think, to a deliberate decision on Eliot's part." Allan's purpose is "by beginning with Eliot's thesis on F. H. Bradley" "to identify and explicate Eliot's basic critical concepts."[75]

On whether Eliot abandoned idealism, Allan writes that "before reaching the point at which (in Miller's view) Eliot should have succeeded in rejecting idealism, an even more important change had occurred in his critical approach: he had purified his critical vocabulary of metaphysical assumptions, if not entirely, at least well enough so that it does not imply any one philosophical position."[76]

Though there is no "one philosophical position," Allan finds, in the later as in the earlier criticism, a "fundamental adherence to idealism." For instance, "This is a perfect expression, in the year 1935, of the idealism of Eliot's thesis as applied to literary criticism." He also notes that in "The Three Voices of Poetry" (1956) Eliot is still applying "Bradley's concept of 'immediate experience' " to literary criticism.[77]

"Did Eliot's acceptance of Christianity alter his attitude to the soul?" Though there was a change in attitude, this change was of "a limited nature," and "it by no means caused a simple reversal of Eliot's critical position," for "at the end, as at the beginning, the great central theme of Eliot's criticism is to affirm the primacy of the aim 'to see the object as in itself it really is.' "[78] In other words, Eliot never abandoned his criticism of psychology and of the representational theory of knowledge. Indeed, much of Allan's book is devoted to tracing the part this theme plays in Eliot's thought, including his sociological thought.

Though Allan is very good at identifying the critical use that Eliot makes of his philosophy, he is not always successful in his explications. For example, "And shortly after completing his thesis, Eliot in two essays pointed out the shortcomings of Leibniz's theory of the soul (and of Bradley's by implication, since Eliot found Bradley's finite centers essentially similar to Leibniz's monads), compared with Aristotle's theory of the soul."[79] But Eliot, as I have tried to show, corrects Leibniz's monads in the light of Bradley's finite centers. Similarly, Eliot in his early criticism held "a strictly Aristotelian theory of the soul."[80] But this, too, seems to me a misconstruction of the essays referred to. Again, "Of the literary essays of the early period, 'Tradition and the Individual Talent' is the most Aristotelian." The reason given is that Eliot there denies "the substantial unity of the soul."[81] In Eliot's interpretation of Aristotle (as in Zabarella's) the soul or mind is not a substance (a thing with its adjectives), and so far Aristotle's position is not unlike that of Bradley. But the literary essay is throughout based on Bradley.

Allan takes a very broad view of Eliot's "idealism," and as a consequence he tends to offer us multiple choices. For example, "It will have been noticed that the Platonic view of knowledge, once purged of prejudice against sensation, is very suggestive of the concept of the 'objective correlative' "; "Aristotle's reduction of movement . . . to sensation . . . amounts, if applied to literary criticism, to almost the same thing as the concept of the objective correlative"; "The importance that, in the early criticism, Eliot attributed to sensation can be explained as due to the influence of Bradley, as well as of Aristotle"; "So far as we explain it by influence, it is to that of Gourmont that I should attribute the remarkable sensationalism of Eliot's criticism"; "We have observed that the position Eliot took in his thesis can be understood as an attempt to fuse together behaviorism and subjective idealism, giving a result like Spinozism."[82]

Eliot's doctrine of sensation is an important part of his critical theory and practice, but we are left in the dark as to what that doctrine is. It should be noted that, in regard to sensation and thought, Eliot is a critic of "a vast number of systems, both idealistic and realistic."[83]

In the "Conclusion" we are told that "Eliot's critical theory is remarkably Hegelian," though "of course, the influence of Hegel would be mostly indirect, through Bradley." Further, "We may say, then, that if Eliot's critical theory is in the Romantic tradition, his critical practice is *an effort to escape from that theory*"— that is, from subjectivism. Insofar as he succeeded, he did so by supplementing the Romantic tradition "with the sanity of earlier criticism." Allan seems bent on blurring his own argument, and even on discounting it. Thus he ends by saying that "we ought to consider our examination of Eliot's theoretical writings as merely a preface to . . . his appreciations of individual authors."[84]

It is fitting to end this chapter on the same note with which we began. Thus Graham Hough writes:

> It is well known that Eliot began his intellectual career as a philosopher, writing a doctoral dissertation on F. H. Bradley. It is slightly less well known that when he ultimately published this work, in 1964, he professed himself unable to understand what he had been talking about. None the less . . . Mowbray Allan's study . . . finds the influence of Bradley to be the strongest and most continuous guiding thread. For this he makes a good case. To search for the philosophical foundations of Eliot's criticism may of course be a mistaken endeavor. What we find may turn out to be not the skeletal structure of a living organism, but a few large dry bones belonging to a previous state of affairs altogether.[85]

4

The Invisible Critic

Though it has been established that Bradley was an "influence" on Eliot, the nature of the influence—its character and extent—remains uncertain. It will therefore be well to take note of Hugh Kenner's treatment of the question in *The Invisible Poet: T. S. Eliot*. Kenner, whose examination of the criticism is limited to the years 1917–1921, says: "The topics, at this distance, matter less than Eliot's increasingly discernible pattern of interests and perceptions." Eliot began with an "intuitive poetic method" which, during the five years mentioned, was "brought to fruition . . . under the auspices of an idealist philosophy," and thereafter "he wrote little more prose of concentrated urgency."[1]

Kenner is concerned primarily with the poetry, and with the criticism for the light it throws on what the poet was thinking about at the time he wrote his poetry. Though that is a legitimate use of the criticism, it is rather restricted. In any case, according to Kenner, "the critical prose was empirical,"[2] though "naturally, a few odds and ends of what the plain reader of Bradley would call Bradleyan 'doctrines' do turn up in Eliot's writings."[3]

Owing to the elusiveness of Bradley's thought and the difficulty of paraphrasing it (it is "as a coloring, not as a body of doctrine, that he stays in the mind"), Kenner prefers to speak not of "doctrines" but of "Bradleyan deposits in Eliot's sensibility," of "stain," of "color," of "tonal influence."[4] Where the poetry is concerned, that seems to me exactly the right language, for the poetry, as Kenner observes, does not traffic in "ideas." But the idea of such a poetry is based on Bradley's doctrines, and though the doctrines may be obscure, they are everywhere in the critical prose. And that, in a way, is the trouble, for what is present everywhere is present nowhere in particular. For our present purpose, it will be enough to give some indications of this, leaving a more detailed discussion of the doctrines to later chapters.

In "Bradley" Kenner is concerned with the poet, and we hear that "Eliot's sense of poetry, of personality, and of history are all congruent with Bradley's philosophy";[5] but in "Criticism" we hear very little of this philosophy, though Bradley is mentioned several times, once in a footnote. And it is as a footnote that he figures in the chapter.

These chapters, then, tell rather different tales. In his discussion of Eliot's sense of poetry Kenner refers repeatedly to Bradley's doctrine of immediate experience. For instance, he notes in this connection that the "dissociation of sensibility" and the "unified sensibility" have something to do with this doctrine; but the "objective correlative" is one of Eliot's "incidental remarks," a notion that occurred to him in the course of trying to explain the difference between the soliloquies of Macbeth and Hamlet.[6] But the "objective correlative" *is* the doctrine of immediate experience, in its aesthetic aspect. Kenner's account is thus curiously incoherent. (It is as if the critic did not know what the poet was doing, and, further, as if the critic's right hand did not know what the left hand was doing.)

Kenner says of the statement about the "objective correlative": "This makes perhaps a more general claim than Eliot intended; he could hardly have foreseen its misapplication to the job of the lyric poet, preoccupied as he was with simply explaining why *Hamlet* is 'the Mona Lisa of literature.' Like Matthew Arnold, he has a dangerous gift of phrase." And he goes on: "For he was not devising a dangling interdependent system of abstractions, like Alexander Calder, but writing *ad hoc*. . . . Each review is an occasion to think something out as he goes along."[7]

Though the phrase "objective correlative" occurs only in the *Hamlet* essay, the idea is present everywhere in the critical prose—the idea, that is, of art as the objectification of feeling. For instance, in "Cyril Tourneur," though the emotions expressed in

The Revenger's Tragedy have "objective equivalents," they "exceed the object"; and in the *Hamlet* essay Hamlet's emotion, and Shakespeare's, lacks an "adequate equivalent."[8] Similarly, in "The Possibility of a Poetic Drama" "permanent literature is always a presentation: either a presentation of thought, or a presentation of feeling by a statement of events in human action or objects in the external world"; and in the essay on *Hamlet* "the only way of expressing emotion in the form of art is by finding an 'objective correlative'; . . . a set of objects, a situation, a chain of events which shall be the formula of that *particular* emotion."[9]

As for its misapplication to the lyric, Eliot is speaking of the only way of expressing emotion *in the form of art*, and the lyric is a form of art. Thus in "William Blake" he says of the *Songs of Innocence and of Experience* that "the emotions are presented in an extremely simplified, abstract form." Similarly, in "In Memoriam," a poet "can express his feelings as fully through a dramatic, as through a lyric form."[10] It applies perhaps in the first place to the lyric and by extension to the drama—or, more generally, as in Eliot's essay on generic criticism, to "the three voices of poetry."

Kenner's chief exhibit of the critic's debt to Bradley is "Tradition and the Individual Talent." But here, too, he takes away with one hand what he gives with the other. In "Bradley," Eliot's study of Bradley "solved his *critical* problem, providing him with a point of view towards history and so with the scenario for his most comprehensive essay," an essay that "concludes a train of thought which can be traced through earlier *Egoist* articles to its origins in the Bradley thesis three years earlier"; but in "Criticism" this essay "has been investigated with too much solemnity, as though it were Eliot's 'theory of poetry.' It is not that; it is a meditation on how the old is related to the new, the extensive summation of many *obiter dicta*."[11]

If this essay is not Eliot's "theory of poetry," it is based on Bradleyan doctrines, some of which Kenner identifies. Thus he notes that "the poet's or anyone else's personality (here Bradley asserts himself vigorously) is a working fiction." Similarly, quoting Eliot's "the whole of literature has a simultaneous existence and composes a simultaneous order," he remarks that Bradley's mind "lies behind" that statement. Again, Eliot writes that "whoever has approved this idea of order . . . will not find it preposterous that the past should be altered by the present as the present is directed by the past," and here Kenner cites Bradley's "the past and future vary, and they have to vary, with the changes of the present."[12] That, it may be noted, is something of a paradox, as the word "preposterous" suggests, for in the popular view the past is external to the present (is independent of it, and real because it is independent), so that, in this view, to speak of the past as altered by the present is "preposterous." But with Bradley the past is an "ideal construction . . . based on and . . . inseparable from present feeling and perception."[13] "And so the past varies with the present, and can never do otherwise, since it is always the present upon which it rests. This present is pre-supposed by it, and is its necessary preconception."[14]

But Kenner takes the essay too lightly. For instance, he says that "its understatement of the role of creative imagination reflects the fact that the readers of *The Egoist* needed no incitement on that score."[15] What it reflects is an "odd and end" of Bradleyan doctrine, for, as Bradley says, "My act never is creative"; and Eliot says: "I am careful not to talk of the creative activity of mind, a phrase meaningless in metaphysics."[16]

The point raised by Kenner has been noticed by others. Thus Northrop Frye writes: "A curious, and to me regrettable, feature of Eliot's critical theory is his avoidance of the term 'imagination,' except in the phrase 'auditory imagination' at the furthest remove from the poetic product."[17]

Eliot, as we have seen, tends to speak of imaginative literature as the work of the intellect, a position that can be brought out by reference to Kant. Kant speaks of the reproduction and association of impressions as "imagination," and "imagination" is separate from "understanding." But Kant's "synthesis of the imagination" is for Eliot a discursive activity (differentiation and integration). It is "thinking in images," but thought on this level is inexplicit—not, as in conceptual thinking, explicit. With Eliot, imagination is a form of thought.[18]

As for Eliot's "theory of poetry," its essence is given in what he says about the "transforming catalyst," but Kenner has nothing to say of this, presumably because he takes Eliot's language to be merely figurative. But in fact it is, for all its indirection, a transcription of Bradleyan doctrine.

In "Criticism" Kenner is concerned with the book reviews that Eliot wrote during the years 1917–1921; of the pieces that do not fall into this category, only one is discussed, "Tradition and the Individual Talent." It is, then, largely with the critic as book reviewer that the chapter is concerned. Kenner writes:

> The elimination of book-reviewing paraphernalia from the familiar selected volumes has led readers to suppose that the author chose his angles of approach, and that the essays were conceived as chapters in a comprehensive critical message delivered by Mr. Eliot to posterity. . . . It is worth emphasizing that, with numerically insignificant exceptions . . . Eliot's essays, both the few that have been collected and the hundreds that have not, were commissioned by editors who sent something along for review.[19]

Though the essays appear in a somewhat different light when seen as book reviews, Kenner makes altogether too much of this. As Eliot has suggested, *The Sacred Wood* is "something more than a mere collection of essays and reviews."[20] In general, nothing is to be inferred about *what* Eliot says in his critical writing from the fact that it is said in a review. Take, for instance, "The Perfect Critic." Though it originated as a review of *Studies in Elizabethan Drama* by Arthur Symons, it makes no mention of Elizabethan drama; Eliot used the occasion to consider "how far criticism is 'feeling' and how far 'thought,' and what sort of 'thought' is permitted."[21] Indeed, the reviews are, in a way, extensions of the dissertation—applications and developments of philosophic principles. As Eric Thompson says, Eliot's "practical criticism is, perhaps, theoretical criticism, an instrument, mainly, for elucidating literary principles"—these principles deriving from the "metaphysical perspective" of the dissertation.[22] Kenner writes:

> For the subject, the thing thrust beneath the reviewer's scrutiny, is everything. Deliverances of principle occur only as some nexus in the anatomizing of the subject requires them, and, like the famous statement about the objective correlative, they come with great pregnancy precisely because they are not major premises to an

argument but generalizations forced upward into visibility by the pressures of some particular instance.[23]

That is well said, except that the principles are not empirical generalizations but the premises of Eliot's literary argument.

Thus in the dissertation Eliot divides fiction into two types, "creative" and "critical"—though "this difference should not be insisted upon, for the author may shift from a creative to a critical point of view and back at any moment." In a footnote he adds that "the combination of criticism and creation is found perhaps in such writers as Molière and Stendhal: whilst the characters of Balzac and Dostoevsky are much more nearly lived through simply."[24] In "Ben Jonson," quoting a passage from *The Silent Woman*, he says: "The 'satire' is merely a medium for the essential emotion. Jonson's drama is only incidentally satire, because it is only incidentally a criticism upon the actual world. It is not satire in the way in which the work of Swift or the work of Molière may be called satire. . . . The important thing is that if fiction can be divided into creative fiction and critical fiction, Jonson's is creative."[25] This shows the characteristic relation of principle to argument, though it is not always so evident.

Though Kenner speaks of "Ben Jonson" as one of Eliot's "classic essays," it is not one of the reviews that he discusses. But those he discusses tell pretty much the same story. In his discussion of Eliot's review of *Selections from Swinburne*, quoting a remark of Eliot's he says: "This leads Eliot to a confident affirmation of considerable scope: 'Language in a healthy state presents the object, is so close to the object that the two are identified.'"[26] But, as we have seen, that is not, as Kenner presents it, an empirical generalization but a statement of principle worked out in the dissertation.

Again, discussing Eliot's review of Kipling's *The Years Between*, Kenner writes:

He is persuading himself to undertake a more than superficial notice. Comparison and analysis, then: the tools of criticism. And the comparison—at first sight unlikely—is with Swinburne. They are alike in their use of sound, which they use for oratorical purposes, to persuade. . . . So far, a routine piece of review-making; but at this juncture a cogent generalization suggests itself:

And like the orator they are personal: not by revelation, but by throwing themselves in and gesturing the emotion of the moment. The emotion is not "there" simply, coldly independent of the author, of the audience, there and for ever like Shakespeare's and Aeschylus' emotions: it is present so long only as the author is on the platform and compels you to feel it.

I look down at his feet: but that's a fable.

If that thou be'st a devil, I cannot kill thee,

is "there," cold and indifferent.

Nothing is better, I well think,
Than love; the hidden well-water
Is not so delicate a drink.

This was well seen of me and her.

(to take from one of Swinburne's poems which most resembles a statement); or

The end of it's sitting and thinking
And dreaming of hell-fires to see—

these are not statements of emotion, but ways of stimulating a particular response in the reader.

Kenner continues: "This distinction is something gained; without the exercise of reviewing Kipling it might never have been concretely achieved. Four months later it irrupts into another review, and we have the paragraph on the 'objective correlative,' which, one may conjecture, might never have been written if the problem of defining Kipling's use of sound had not arisen four months earlier."[27]

Though Kenner offers no discussion of the distinction, if one is to see what Eliot sees in the verses one must do as Eliot does— bring the distinction with one. I am not saying there is no difference between the verses but only that the difference cannot be expressed in terms of popular psychology. As Eliot says, "The prejudice [is] that feeling is something subjective and private."[28] But with Eliot, emotions are objects, and "whatever is made an object is public."[29] Accordingly, the "presentation is really 'there,' "[30] for "what is presented is really the object, and this is not presented as a [mental] presentation, but as real."[31] Thus "we stand before a beautiful painting, and . . . the painting . . . is an object independent of us."[32] So, in *The Use of Poetry and the Use of Criticism*, the poem's existence is "somewhere between the writer and the reader; it has a reality which is not simply the reality of what the writer is trying to 'express,' or of his experience of writing it, or of the experience of the reader or of the writer as reader."[33] In short, it is "independent of the author, of the audience."

Eliot, as he has said, often repeats himself[34] (so that if we are to show the critical use he makes of his philosophy we can hardly avoid a certain amount of repetition). In the Kipling review, Kipling is not so much the poet as the orator. And in "Rudyard Kipling" (1941) the poem is for Kipling "something which is intended to *act* . . . to elicit the same response from all readers"; he does not aim at making something which shall "first of all *be*, something which in consequence will have the capability of exciting, within a limited range, a considerable variety of responses from different readers."[35] The experience of a poem is in this respect like every other experience: it "implies the existence of something independent of the experience, something capable, therefore, of being experienced differently."[36]

Kenner, speaking of the Kipling review, says that another of its "incidental remarks" is that "cohension is imposed . . . by a point of view," and there is a footnote explaining that "point of view" is a "Bradleyan notion," and that it is present in *The Waste Land*.[37] In the review Eliot writes:

> Swinburne and Mr. Kipling have these and such concepts; some poets, like Shakespeare or Dante or Villon, and some novelists, like Mr. Conrad, have, in contrast to ideas or concepts, points of view, or "worlds"—what are incorrectly called "philosophies." Mr. Conrad is very germane to the question. . . . [He] has no ideas, but he has a point of view, a "world"; it can hardly be defined, but it pervades his work and is unmistakable. . . .
>
> And this is why both Swinburne's and Mr. Kipling's verse . . . appear to lack cohesion. . . . There is no point of view to hold them together.[38]

With Eliot, "the world is a construction out of finite centers."[39] The finite center ("what I call the point of view") *is* immediate experience; and from this felt background there is developed a multiplicity of worlds, including those of "poetry and general fiction," not to speak of "the entire region of the arts."[40] The world of an artist is "a whole world of feeling, and the object is simply that world so far as objectified," and "the object is inseparable from the point of view."[41]

If each review is an occasion to think something out as he goes along, he seems in his reviews to be thinking out the same thing, or some aspect of it. Thus Henry James "did not provide us with 'ideas,' but with another world of thought and feeling."[42] And speaking of James's "escape from Ideas" he says: "Englishmen . . . like to refer to France as the Home of Ideas; a phrase which, if we could twist it into truth . . . ought to mean that in France ideas are very severely looked after; not allowed to stray, but preserved for the inspection of civic pride in a Jardin des Plantes, and frugally dispatched on occasions of public necessity. . . . In England ideas run wild and pasture on the emotions."[43]

Ideas, like facts, are context-bound, so that without the implication of a system in which it belongs the idea is not an idea at all. If an idea is taken out of its context, it loses what was definite and gains what is indefinite. It loses, in other words, its *intellectual* character and takes on an emotional or a rhetorical one.[44] It becomes the "idea-emotion" or the "undigested 'idea,' " something that is neither "clear thinking" nor "clear statement of particular objects." Again, the moment an idea "has been transferred from its pure state . . . it has lost contact with art" (in the sense here of clear thought, as in Bradley's *Principles of Logic* or Russell's essay "Denoting"); it "can remain pure only by being stated simply in the form of a general truth."[45]

That throws light on Eliot's "general form" of statement, a procedure for using his philosophy without popularizing it. It also explains why, though the philosophy pervades the critical prose and is unmistakable, it can hardly be defined. But to pursue that is to turn in a circle.

Kenner, discussing Eliot's review of *Essays in Romantic Literature* by George Wyndham, says:

Eliot contrasts Wyndham with Leonardo. . . . "Leonardo turned to art or science, and each was what it was and not another thing. . . . He lived in no fairyland, but his mind went out and became a part of things." This was so because Leonardo conducted his life impersonally (like a self-possessed alien in London): "he had no father to speak of, he was hardly a citizen, and he had no stake in the community. . . . George Wyndham was Gentry. He was chivalrous, the world was an adventure of himself." This leads to an important formulation:

What is permanent and valuable in Romanticism is curiosity . . . a curiosity which recognizes that any life, if accurately penetrated, is interesting and always strange. Romanticism is a short cut to the strangeness without the reality, and it leads its disciples only back upon themselves.

And "the only cure for Romanticism is to analyze it."[46]

Leonardo's mind "went out and became a part of things." This was so because, as Eliot says in the dissertation, "to inspect living mind, you must look nowhere but in the world outside."[47] Leonardo is a classicist. Romanticism, on the other hand, is self-centered, and the self inhabits a solipsistic world. Here Eliot's analysis is based on Bradley's account of the psychological self or soul. According to Bradley, we may, for certain limited purposes, take "my self or soul as a separate thing, and . . . regard everything that happens to it as its psychical states." And so far as we are true to this idea, "I can experience nothing beyond my own states," for "all the world is merely a state of my self."[48] So Romanticism "leads its disciples only back upon themselves," and for George Wyndham "the world was an adventure of himself."

In "The Function of Criticism" Eliot writes:

Those of us who find ourselves supporting what Mr. Murry calls Classicism believe that men cannot get on without giving allegiance to something outside themselves. I am aware that "outside" and "inside" are terms which provide unlimited opportunity for quibbling, and that no psychologist would tolerate a discussion which shuffled such base coinage; but I will presume that Mr. Murry and myself can agree that for our purpose these counters are adequate, and concur in disregarding the admonitions of our psychological friends. If you find that you have to imagine it as outside, then it is outside.[49]

"Our psychological friends" are the behaviorists, who serve here as stand-ins for Eliot. But though Eliot is, like the behaviorists, a critic of introspection, that is as far as the agreement extends. In the dissertation, "the distinction between inner and outer . . . cannot stand," for "if the real world means the world of real objects," "the real world is not inside or outside; it is not presented in consciousness or to consciousness . . . for as presented it is not in or to consciousness at all: it simply is."[50]

Classicism ("outside") and Romanticism ("inside") pre-suppose the division of experience into mental and extramental, ideal and real, subjective and objective. But in Eliot's theory this distinction is, as he says, "unnecessary."[51] Accordingly, we can only say that Eliot's position is neither subjective nor objective, in the ordinary use of these terms, but idealist, in Eliot's use of the term.[52]

Bradley, as Kenner notes, is a critic of the "atomistic view of things";[53] he is also a critic of psychological atomism. And Eliot, in his review of I. A. Richards's *Science and Poetry*, observes that " 'interests,' for Mr. Richards, tend to be atomic units."[54] In the same review, "There is a certain discrepancy between the size of his problems and the size of his solutions. . . . If one is going to consider philosophically the nature of Belief, it is as dangerous to be a scientist as to be a theologian; the scientist, still more—in our time—than the theologian, will be prejudiced as to the nature of Truth. Mr. Richards is apt to ask a supra-scientific question, and to give a merely scientific answer."[55] So with Leibniz, "theology and physics join forces . . . to rob metaphysics of its due." In *The Use of Poetry*: "As for psychology and linguistics, that is his field and not mine."[56] But for Eliot, psychology is not independent of metaphysics. Further, "meaning . . . does not as such form an object for psychology"; and "we may point out that criticism . . . is other than psychology in that it includes at every point a refer-ence to a real world . . . which in psychology is inadmissible."[57]

To take a rather elaborate example of Eliot's indirections, in a *Criterion* review of *Reason and Romanticism* by Herbert Read and *Messages* by Ramon Fernandez, he begins by remarking that "in our time the most vigorous critical minds are philosophical minds," and that Read and Fernandez are critics of this type, though they go about their work in different ways: "M. Fernan-dez as a psychologist, Mr. Read as a metaphysician. Mr. Read is interested . . . in metaphysical and logical truth; M. Fernandez is

interested . . . in *personality*."[58] The important point for his purpose, Eliot says, is that Fernandez's position is based on

> what I choose to call a *Cartesian* point of view. M. Fernandez
> [builds] . . . on the fact of *one's own existence* as the primary reality.
> And the question . . . is whether M. Fernandez, by positing *per-
> sonality* as the ultimate, the fundamental reality in the universe, is
> really supporting or undermining that "moral hierarchy" of which
> he, as well as Mr. Read, is so stout a champion.[59]

Further:

> M. Fernandez . . . has to assume a theory of reality which seems to
> be that of traditional psychology. The Mind seems to have for M.
> Fernandez a primary reality, psychology seems to take precedence
> over ontology. The Aristotelian commentator Zabarella, observes:
>
> *Dicamus quod intellectus seipsum intelligit, quatenus supra suam
> operationem reflectitur, dum alia intelligit, cognoscit enim se intel-
> ligere, proinde cognoscit se habere naturam talem, quae est apta fieri
> omnia. . . . (Let us say that, since intellect comprehends itself, to
> whatever extent it is reflected beyond its own workings, for while it is
> comprehending other things it is learning to comprehend itself, just
> so it recognizes that it has an open nature, capable of becoming all
> things.)*
>
> and on the other hand we find in Watson's *Behaviorism* the follow-
> ing definition of personality:
>
> *The sum of activities that can be discovered by actual observation of
> behavior over a long enough term to give reliable information. In
> other words, personality is but the end product of our habit systems.*
>
> The last definition is a little unsatisfactory, because one wonders
> what is a "long enough" term to give "reliable" information. There
> is, however, a certain agreement between Aristotle and Professor
> Watson (though Professor Watson may not think so): they are both,
> I think, in disaccord (by implication) with M. Fernandez. "Person-
> ality" for both Aristotle and Professor Watson, refers to something
> outside.[60]

That is, I believe, Eliot's most explicit discussion of
"personality"—explicit for Eliot. And though he carries on the
discussion entirely by indirection, he is restating Bradley's doctrine that the self is not "an ultimately given fact."[61]

In traditional psychology—Locke, say, or the Russell of *The Problems of Philosophy*—the self is supposed to be a datum, something of which we have direct experience. There is, according to Locke, a sort of inner consciousness whereby we are aware of the internal operations of our minds. So, according to Russell (as quoted by Eliot, who notes the resemblance to Locke): "We have acquaintance in sensation with the data of the outer senses, and in introspection with the data of what may be called the inner sense—thoughts, feelings, desires, etc."[62] But for Eliot "there is properly no such thing as internal perception," and "the self . . . is not given as a direct experience. . . . The self is a construction."[63] Further, it is a construction whose meaning is inconsistent, so that it is appearance and not reality—not in this sense ultimate.

If, Bradley says, you start from "the absolute reality of your self," solipsism "must demonstrably follow."[64] The question is, then, whether Fernandez is supporting or undermining the "moral hierarchy" of which he, like Read, is a champion.[65] As Eliot restates it, "M. Fernandez is in danger of being an idealist without ideals; Mr. Read of being a realist without real objects. Both are struggling to find an objective truth; both are encumbered by the wipings of psychology."[66]

Again, Eliot writes: "M. Fernandez is in a sense with Bergson, with the pragmatists, with those who have reached a certain degree of sophistication about 'the nature of truth': for Mr. Read, I imagine, there is, or there should be, no 'nature' of truth, there is only truth and error."[67]

In the preface to *Knowledge and Experience* Eliot speaks of his work as a "study of the theory of knowledge according to the philosophy of Francis Herbert Bradley"; but in the text he says: "In a metaphysic such as Mr. Bradley's, certainly, there can be no place for a theory of knowledge"[68]—or, as Bradley puts it, "There can be really no such thing as the theory of cognition."[69] What is meant is epistemology as a special science, distinct from but involving both psychology and logic. The point is discussed by Harold Joachim in *The Nature of Truth*.[70]

Alluding to a review of Read's book in the *Times*, Eliot says:

The critic of the *Times* . . . quotes the following passage from Mr. Read's book:

The criticism of revealed religion has been operative not only on the empirical plane . . . but also on the psychological plane. A religion like Christianity is built up largely on unconscious symbols. . . . The effect of experimental science has been to destroy the unconsciousness of these symbols; it understands them and therefore equates them with conscious equivalents, which are no longer symbols and which on that account no longer compel the imagination.

. . . Mr. Read has here got himself into a muddle. . . . Mr. Read . . . is throwing away a trick to M. Fernandez. Why should Mr. Read take the psychological plane so seriously; and what does he mean by unconscious symbols? If we are unconscious that a symbol is a symbol, then is it a symbol at all? and the moment we become conscious that it is a symbol, is it any longer a symbol?[71]

In the dissertation, criticizing certain remarks of Bradley's which seem to suggest that ideas are mental signs or symbols, Eliot says:

In what sense is an idea a sign? This seems a most treacherous statement. A sign has its existence beside its content, and it is just this separate existence—the fact that the sign might be misinterpreted or simply not recognized as a sign at all, which makes it a sign and not an identity. Take some of the examples of sign which Bradley mentions. A flower may become the sign or symbol of an emotion; the fox is the symbol of cunning. . . . Now does an idea refer to reality as fox refers to cunning? The quality to which the fox or the flower refers is something known or knowable otherwise than through the fox or the flower. . . . A flower may be the sign of an idea, but how can an idea be the *sign* of a reality? Such a view would surely lead us to a representational theory of knowledge.[72]

Eliot is using the terms "sign" and "symbol" in the sense of represent, stand for, refer to—in the sense these terms bear in the representational theory of knowlege. Though there are various versions of this theory (one of which is to be found in the *De Interpretatione* of Aristotle), let us consider Locke's version, or so much of it as is necessary for our present purpose.

By an "idea" Locke means "whatsoever the mind perceives in itself, or is the immediate *object* of perception, thought, or understanding." And "the mind knows not things immediately, but by the intervention of the *ideas* it has of them." The mind, then, knows its "ideas" directly, and everything else it knows mediately, through the representative function of its "ideas."

The first point Eliot makes is that if "fox" is to refer me to cunning, I must recognize "fox" as a separate existence. But I am not aware of "ideas" in that way. When I look at an object, I do not see the physical process that underlies my seeing—I do not see rods and cones or the inverted image on my retina. It is the same with the mental events that are said to accompany the physical process. Whatever this psychological machinery may be, it is not *what* I see. I am not, then, aware of an "idea" as a separate existence, an "idea" which intervenes between the object and my perception of it, and through which, as through a symbol, I apprehend the object.

The second point is that if "fox" is to symbolize cunning, cunning must be known or knowable independently of "fox." But it is only through "fox"—through my "idea"—that I am able, for the first time, to know cunning—to know the fact my "idea" represents.

A third condition is that if "fox" is to symbolize cunning for me, I must know the connection whereby "fox" refers me to cunning, and I must know it as a particular case of a principle belonging to an established system of symbolism, founded perhaps on a literary or an artistic convention. Without such a principle, I would have no way of relating "fox" to cunning: "fox" might mean for me not cunning but speed. In Locke's theory no such scheme of symbolism is presupposed, so that in this respect also "ideas" fail as mental signs or symbols.[73]

Eliot says of symbols that "so far as they refer to their objects they are not themselves known, and so far as they are made objects of knowledge they no longer refer to objects"[74]—or as in the *Criterion* review, if we are unconscious that a symbol is a symbol, it is not a symbol at all; and the moment we become conscious that it is a symbol, it is no longer a symbol.

Again:

I believe myself in sympathy with both Mr. Read and M. Fernandez, and out of sympathy with the critic of the former in the *Times*, in the conception of Intelligence. . . . [To this critic] Mr. Read must naturally seem to have a "bias towards intellectualism." "Intellectualism" is a pejorative flung at Aristotle—and at St. Thomas—by those who have not taken the trouble to acquaint themselves with the sense of the texts. Similarly, the same critic, objecting simultaneously to Mr. Read and to St. Thomas, comments:

> *To a modern mind the word "intelligence" does not connote the faculty or act of "simple apprehension of truth." To a modern mind that act or faculty is "intuition." Whether we know as much as we ought to know about intuition may be doubted, but we shall not increase our knowledge by calling it intelligence.*

> To this it may be replied, that we only complicate our ignorance by calling it "intuition," and that for anyone who has devoted even a little attention to St. Thomas, or to Aristotle, the term "intelligence" is adequate. *Intelligibilia se habent ad intellectum sicut sensibilia ad sensum*: they may be, and sometimes are, grasped immediately by inspection; and to insist on another faculty "intuition" is merely to demand a more potent and thuriferous ju-ju. And I think that M. Fernandez, as well as Mr. Read, will be on the side of what we call "the intelligence."[75]

This passage led John Middleton Murry to assume that Eliot was a Thomist in epistemology, and there ensued in the pages of *Criterion* a debate about the terms "intuition" and "intelligence," the participants being Father M. C. D'Arcy, Ramon Fernandez, Charles Mauron, and Eliot. Eliot, in his reply to Murry, writes:

> Mr. Murry asks me whether I accept the Thomist theory of Knowledge? Well, I have very strong leanings towards it, first because it happens to have a great deal in common with another theory of knowledge which I know better, that of Aristotle. But Mr. Murry's own knowledge of theories of knowledge seems curiously limited. He divides theories of knowledge into three kinds: the physical (I suppose he means physiological?), the psychological, and the *metaphysical*. The last type, which includes that of Aquinas, he dismisses summarily, for, says he, "it has singularly little reference to the actual process of knowing in human experience." One must conclude that Mr. Murry is dismissing with the same condemnation such modern theories of knowledge as those of Meinong, and Husserl, and that which Mr. Russell holds or once held. . . . How such freaks came to be . . . Mr. Murry does not tell us. But . . . there are still thinking human beings who are not quite convinced that psychology is the key to the universe.[76]

We shall return to Murry's attitude toward *metaphysical* theories of knowledge. What may be noted here is that in the dissertation Eliot is a critic of Meinong and Russell, and he also discusses the relation of physiology to epistemology.[77] Husserl, like Eliot and Bradley, is a critic of psychologism. But Joachim and Bosanquet are critics of Husserl's conception of pure logic (as well as Russell's).[78] Their point, to put it in Eliot's language, is that "meaning cannot be merely contemplated, but must be *erlebt* (experienced)."[79] In other words, the realm of the intelligible is not self-supporting but depends upon and is developed out of immediate experience or feeling.

As for Aristotle, it is worth noting that Bradley, speaking of his debt to Hegel's "doctrine of Feeling, as a vague *continuum* below relations," says: "My knowledge of the history of modern psychology does not, I regret, enable me to say how far Hegel has followed others, as, I presume, he has followed Aristotle."[80] If, Joachim says, one pressed to the full certain implications in Aristotle—not the Aristotle of the representative theory of knowledge—one would reach a conception of knowledge like the one he expounds[81]—the conception of what Eliot calls a "sound idealism," and not, as Bradley says, "what is called sometimes 'Idealism.' "[82]

Though Eliot's conception of intelligence is in certain respects like Aristotle's, it is also different from it. With Aristotle, the mind has a power of intuitive as well as discursive thought: a power of intellectual insight or conceptual apprehension whereby it grasps, directly and immediately, certain intelligibles which it proceeds to analyze and to express in the form of definitions.[83] But with Eliot the mind has no special function of intuition; its operation is throughout discursive. But it has an intuitive aspect: "a feature of immediacy," as Bradley says, in the sense that all its terms are given in immediate experience or feeling.[84]

"Mr. Murry suggests," Eliot writes, "that I must mean one of two things: either I deny 'intuition' altogether, or I affirm 'intuition' to be a form of 'intelligence.' I certainly do not mean the former; I do not at all wish to expunge the word 'intuition' from the dictionary."[85] "I can now make a little clearer what, in my rough and ready way, I mean by 'being on the side of what we call the intelligence.' I mean that intuition must have its place in a world of discourse; there may be room for intuitions both at the top and the bottom, or at the beginning and the end; but that intuition must always be tested, and capable of test, in a whole of experience in which intellect plays a large part."[86]

A "whole of experience" is "a felt whole in which there are moments of knowledge." There is "immediate experience" at "the beginning [and] end of our journey." Though this is a "timeless unity," we are forced to think of it in temporal terms.[87] At the beginning there is an immediate experience below relations; then comes the world of objects ("the intellectual middle space"); and at the end is an immediate experience above relations and exclusive of them.[88]

The trouble is, as Eliot says, that "one has the difficulty of having to use the same words for different things."[89] "Intuition" means immediate experience: a direct or immediate awareness, an awareness without mediation or independent of mediation (the Kantian "faculty 'intuition' ": the sensibility that is the source of intuitions; or Russell's acquaintance, in sensation and feeling, with external and internal data). Now, though with Eliot no experience is merely immediate, in the sense of being prior to or independent of thought, intuition, in the sense of the immediacy of feeling, is an inseparable aspect of knowledge, at all stages and at every level.

But intuitive feeling is not knowing in the sense of understanding. Knowledge is knowledge of objects, and an object is something internally distinguished and related; but the form of feeling is nonrelational, so that feeling cannot possibly express or understand anything relational. And this objection, Bradley says, would seem to be fatal to the claims of intuition; for "even if your intuition is a fact, it is not an *understanding* of the self or of the world."[90]

Intuitive feeling is "a being and knowing in one." There is no internal distinction of subject and object, of knowing and known; and, if so, there is no cognition, no object to be known and no one to know it. An intuition, then, can hardly be the explanation of anything; it is rather something that must itself be explained or understood. And to do that we must make an object of it, and what we have then is a judgment, which is a mediated experience and not an intuition. Judgments are true or false as they cohere or are discrepant with a system of judgments. Intuitions, as Joachim says, must endure "the test of mediation"; and apart from such a test they are mere experiences, neither true nor false.[91]

"And just this depreciation of intelligence . . . and this exaltation of intuition . . . is . . . what leads Mr. Murry into making mistakes about his own intuitions."[92] According to Murry, "the true poet starts with an ineradicable faith in intuition," for intuition is "a finer means of attaining truth" than conceptual thinking.[93] This position, Eliot says, leads Murry to make poetry a substitute for science and philosophy, and for religion, too. But that is not being "on the side of intelligence."[94]

In *The Use of Poetry*, "it is when he [the poet] philosophizes upon his own *poetic* insight that he is apt to go wrong. A great deal of the weakness of modern poetry is accounted for in a few pages of Mr. Richards's short essay, *Science and Poetry*; and although he has there D. H. Lawrence under specific examination, a good deal of what he says applies to the Romantic generation as well. 'To distinguish,' he says, 'an intuition of an emotion from an intuition *by* it, is not always easy.' "[95] With Eliot (we are not concerned here with Richards's meaning), emotions are objects and, like other objects, they are felt or intuited as well as contemplated; but "they are known and are themselves not knowing."[96]

Aristotle, Watson, Aquinas, Meinong, Husserl, Russell, and Richards—all indirections. Eliot not only trails a coat behind him but trails a coat behind his coat. His philosophy is a metaphysical philosophy, and for the "modern mind" metaphysics is an impossible subject—and what is more, a useless one. What Eliot has done, then, is, as he says, to "preserve in cryptogram certain notions which, if expressed directly, would be destined to immediate obloquy, followed by perpetual oblivion."[97]

5

The Mind of the Poet

Eliot writes in such a way as to use his philosophy without exposing it; and the consequence is that his critical prose is marked by
hints, suggestions, analogies, ambiguities, indirections, and
misdirections—and in this sense, it may be said, the prose is
style-bound.

In "Tradition and the Individual Talent," for instance, "this
essay," he says, "proposes to halt at the frontier of metaphysics or
mysticism, and confine itself to such practical conclusions as can
be applied by the responsible person interested in poetry."[1] For
Eliot, though mysticism is, like speculative thought, a permanent
impulse of human nature, they are not the same thing.[2] But for
the modern mind, as represented, say, by Bertrand Russell,
metaphysics is a form of mysticism, an attitude toward reality
based on emotion and supported by a logical facade. Its chief
modern practitioners, as Russell points out, have been Hegel and
his followers.[3] So Hegel, Eliot says, was an exponent of "emotional systematization." Similarly, "Coleridge's metaphysical
interest was quite genuine, and was, like most metaphysical
interest, an affair of his emotions,"[4] and "we owe to Coleridge as
much as to anybody our enjoyment of the doubtful benefits of
German Idealism"; still, "he establishes literary criticism as a part
of philosophy."[5]

As for his dissertation on Bradley, he can present it "only as a
curiosity of biographical interest, which shows . . . how closely

my own prose style was formed on that of Bradley and how little it has changed in all these years."[6] Whatever is to be said about the "prose style," the style of thought is certainly that of Bradley, and it changed very little.[7]

We must, before proceeding, take note of certain internal complications. For Eliot, psychology reduces to physiology. When in the dissertation he speaks of "real" and "ideal" elements, the real elements have a physiological basis, and these elements are self-transcendent. Bradley, on the other hand, even when he is writing metaphysics, employs the language of psychology—speaks, that is, of psychical states and events. But with Bradley every psychical fact is included under feeling, if considered merely as such and as existing immediately. Thus the self in the sense of the "this-mine" is a felt unity, or it is the psychical self as "*only* the felt." Psychical states have two aspects: existence and content. The content is referred beyond its existence, and whatever is not thus transcended constitutes my "exclusive self," my "private experience," my "private self," my "private personality."[8]

There are, then, several sets of terms, diverse expressions of the same principles; and in what follows we must sometimes use one set and sometimes another. To note another complication, Bradley writes: "We cannot always be laboring to express at once the complementary aspects of the whole. We are forced, to suit our varying purpose, from time to time to make statements which, as they are made, contradict one the other."[9] And Eliot: "In short, we can only discuss experience from one side and then from the other, correcting these partial views."[10]

Take, to begin with, Eliot's statement that poetry is not "an expression of personality, but an escape from personality."[11] "Escape" here means the transcendence of the self—the self in Bradley's sense of my "private self" or my "private personality." The self in this usage is the "this-mine" (or the "this-here" or the "this-me"). Every element in the "this-mine" may at one time or another refer itself to something beyond, and in this process of transcendence there is a negation of other elements. The residue, which is merely felt and not transcended, is the "subjective" or "merely personal"; and it is "subjective" because it is irrelevant to the purpose in hand: it is not subordinate to an "ideal whole," whatever that whole may be. In the construction of a poem, then, whatever sensations, images, and ideas do not subserve the poem in question are "merely personal." In this sense, what happens, as Eliot says, is a "continual surrender of himself as he is at the moment to something which is more valuable," a "continual self-sacrifice," a "continual extinction of personality."[12]

"It is," Eliot continues, "in this depersonalization that art may be said to approach the condition of science."[13] The process of transcendence and negation is "ideality." This being the mainspring of experience,[14] it belongs, Bradley says, to everything serious in life: to morality, logic, and aesthetics; and when art is what it should be, it belongs as much to art as to morality and logic.

Eliot says "approach" because, as he remarks elsewhere, "both in creation and enjoyment much always enters which is, from the point of view of 'Art,' irrelevant"[15]—subjective and personal. Still, he is "concerned with literary *perfection*";[16] and "the more perfect the artist, the more completely separate in him will be the man who suffers and the mind which creates."[17]

In the dissertation, "a work of imagination is never simply personal. So far as we consider it as *only* personal—i.e. significant only to the author—we explain it not as imagination but as the product of pathological conditions. Thus we are tempted to explain a poem of Mallarmé as we explain dreams, as due to morbid physiological activity."[18]

In general, the notion of the I, the self, the personality as something separate and definite, as the exclusive individual, though useful and even necessary for practical life, is theoretically untenable. The self is a unity of experience, and the principle of unity is the mind, or a mind—a mind in its experiences.[19]

In "Tradition and the Individual Talent," "the mind of the poet" is a "transforming catalyst," or it is a "medium" in which experiences "combine in peculiar and unexpected ways." In "The Metaphysical Poets," experiences are "compelled into unity by the operation of the poet's mind," and "in the mind of the poet these experiences are always forming new wholes."[20]

Bradley, in "Association and Thought," brings this process under two laws: the law of redintegration (Bradley's version of association) and the law of fusion (blending or coalescence). He says:

> Can we . . . find a principle which underlies the two laws we have just set forth? I think we can. . . . Every mental element (to use a metaphor) strives to make itself a whole or to lose itself in one, and it will not have its company assigned to it by mere conjunction in presentation. Each struggles to develop itself by the weapon of identity, which gives strength by coalescence and enlargement by recall. And this effort to succeed by association with like characters may bring loss of life to the single member. To speak more strictly, each element tends . . . by means of fusion and redintegration to give itself a context through identity of content, and in the result which is so made the element may not survive in a distinguishable form.[21]

What counts, Eliot says, is "the intensity of the artistic process."[22] As Bradley puts it, "Where different elements . . . have any feature the same they may unite wholly or partially. The more wholly they unite the more their differences are destroyed, with a transfer of strength to the result."[23] The point is that the intensity of the experience is not the sum of its elements but derives from the process in which the elements are fused and transformed. As Eliot says: "For it is not the 'greatness,' the intensity, of the emotions, the components, but the intensity of the artistic process, the pressure, so to speak, under which the fusion takes place, that counts."[24]

We may call it, Bradley says, "the law of Individuation," and "our psychology would, I think, find it a key to unlock several puzzles. The failure of psychology with regard to the creative imagination can, I think, in part, be so removed."[25]

Though we can see that the critical prose has a philosophic basis, if we try to show the exact relation between the two we meet intolerable complications, complications of style as well as doctrine, Bradley's style as well as Eliot's.

Take what Bradley calls redintegration. This is Bradley's term for "association": the reproduction and extension of experience. And Bradley is at pains to distinguish his version of "association" from that of the English empirical school. His most extensive critique of the empirical version is given in the chapter of his *Principles of Logic* titled "The Theory of Association of Ideas," where he objects to "association" as psychology, as logic, and as metaphysics.[26]

One difficulty is that, though Bradley regards psychology and logic as special sciences, and as such independent in a restricted sense of metaphysics, his treatment of these sciences is based on his metaphysics—on the doctrine of immediate experience (feeling) and on that of ideality (thought). Thus the "idea of immediate experience . . . is necessary, I would insist, both for psychology and for metaphysics."[27]

This ambiguity appears in his treatment of fusion and redintegration. Thus in "Association and Thought" he presents fusion and redintegration as psychological laws—subject to the principle of identity. In *Principles of Logic* he deals with redintegration, and to some extent with fusion, from the point of view of logic. These laws also hold in metaphysics. Thus he says, speaking of immediate experience or feeling, "Nor do I see reason to doubt that the laws of Redintegration and also of Fusion (if we admit such a law) will hold in this field."[28]

In "Association and Thought" Bradley is writing psychology, and he presents fusion and redintegration as psychological laws. But, as he says, in his account of these laws he resorts to metaphor and fiction. Thus, speaking of the way in which every mental element struggles toward a whole by means of fusion and redintegration, he says: "The reader may dismiss this statement as mere 'transcendentalism'; but . . . it is strict empirical psychology, a mere general statement of the way in which events do happen. . . . But we must remember that our law perhaps to some extent uses a scientific fiction. It is convenient to speak of the movement of each element, but we must not assert (or deny) that in reality the element can do or be anything—unless, indeed, we are prepared to make psychology a battle field for metaphysicians.[29]

The fiction is "psychological Atomism," which underlies the theory of association of ideas. In this theory, the mind is a complex of mutually exclusive elements, each a separate and independent unit; and the theory has become a "metaphysical doctrine," a doctrine as to "the ultimate constituents of mind."[30] For

Bradley, these elements are abstractions from a whole of experience, and anything so abstracted and treated as independent is an unreal fiction.

If, Bradley says, speaking of the movement of each element to form a whole by fusion and redintegration, "we like to call the movement an *ideal* process, this may distinguish it from what by comparison is *mechanical*."[31] In the empirical version, sensations and images are separate and distinct existences, and association means a mechanical conjunction of particular existences. "And they have absolutely no internal bond of connection. There is no ground common to the different units, which could serve as a real basis for their union. Universality and identity are derided as fictions."[32]

In Bradley's version everything depends on identity and the association of universals—on ideality. Identity is identity of content; and "any process . . . which preserves identity of ideal content is thought and is objective." And Bradley adds, referring to his *Principles of Logic*, "Thought is certainly a function of analysis and synthesis."[33]

Fusion and redintegration are ideal operations; and in Bradley's explanatory psychology these operations develop into the functions of analysis and synthesis. Speaking of these functions, Bradley says: "They are two different sides of one operation, and you can never have one without having the other"; and again: "Analysis is the synthesis of the whole which it divides, and synthesis the analysis of the whole which it constructs. The two processes are one."[34]

The distinctive principle of the mind is thought, and thought in discriminating connects and in connecting discriminates. This process always operates within a whole. "Every such whole must qualify and be qualified by its terms. And, where the whole is different, the terms that qualify it and contribute to it must so far be different, and so far therefore by becoming elements in a fresh unity the terms must be altered."[35] That is, stated in its most general form, the principle according to which experiences are always forming new wholes.

Consider now Eliot's "suggestive analogy" of the chemical compound. Bradley in his notes to "The Theory of Association of Ideas" discusses the doctrine of "the chemistry of ideas." According to this doctrine, there is a chemical union or compound of mental elements which results in a product that is not analyzable into its component parts. But the fact of such a union, Bradley says, has not been shown to exist, and in any case it would not be the right way to state the fact; for "no psychical state, as a unity, can be wholly resolved into the mere compounding of units— even 'chemically.' "[36] This is not, then, Bradley's doctrine. Nor is it Eliot's. Accordingly, we must not take Eliot's analogy as referring to "the chemistry of ideas."

The doctrine, to restate it, is this: The elements are fused and transformed, and in the process they lose, wholly or partially, their self-identity, so that they have no existence apart from the whole. The key terms are transformation ("those are pearls that were his eyes") and organization, in the sense of an individual whole, a whole without separate or separable parts.

"The experience, you will notice, the elements which enter the presence of the transforming catalyst, are of two kinds: emotions and feelings."[37]

Bradley writes: "What I feel, that surely I may still feel, though I also and at the same time make it into an object before me." The feeling remains as the background against which the object stands, and feeling and object are continuous. Now, Bradley says, "Take an emotional whole such as despondency or anger or ennui." One part of the emotion "consists already of objects, of perceptions and ideas before my mind," but "there are other felt elements which cannot be said to be before my mind"; and "the whole emotion being one," these felt elements are "united with these objects before my mind."[38]

Eliot says of a work of art: "It may be formed out of one emotion, or may be a combination of several; and various feelings . . . may be added to compose the final result." Similarly, "This is, so to speak, the structural emotion, provided by the drama. But the whole effect, the dominant tone, is due to the fact that a number of floating feelings, having an affinity to this emotion by no means superficially evident, have combined with it to give us a new art emotion."[39] As he explains in the dissertation, quoting Bradley: "There are features in feeling (this is the point) which already in a sense belong to and are one with their object, since the emotion contains and unites both its aspects."[40]

"The business of the poet is not to find new emotions, but to use the ordinary ones and, in working them up into poetry, to express feelings which are not in actual emotions at all."[41]

The "process of the transmutation of emotion" goes on, more or less, all the time. As Bradley says, any ordinary emotion in becoming an object undergoes transformation, so that "the emotion we attend to is, taken strictly, never precisely the same thing as the emotion which we feel."[42] For one thing, there is the alteration by addition of elements from the background of feeling; and, for another, the object side of the emotion is enlarged by internal development or by addition of elements from the outside. Further, the emotion as object becomes a subordinate element in a new unity of feeling, in which it may be combined with other emotions.

Thus in "Philip Massinger": "The poetic drama must have an emotional unity, let the emotion be whatever you like. It must have a dominant tone; and if this be strong enough, the most heterogeneous emotions may be made to reinforce it"—the whole pattern having "the properties of a chemical compound."[43] Or as in "John Ford": The "unity and significance of pattern [is] . . . a unity springing from the depth and coherence of a number of emotions and feelings."[44]

Again, Eliot writes:

> It is not in his personal emotions, the emotions provoked by particular events in his life, that the poet is in any way remarkable or interesting. His particular emotions may be simple, or crude, or flat. The emotion in his poetry will be a very complex thing. . . . And emotions which he has never experienced will serve his turn as well as those familiar to him. Consequently, we must believe that "emotion recollected in tranquillity" is an inexact formula. For it is neither emotion, nor recollection, nor, without distortion of meaning, tranquillity. It is a concentration, and a new thing resulting from the concentration, of a very great number of experiences which to the practical and active person would not seem to be experiences at all; it is a concentration which does not happen consciously or of deliberation. These experiences are not "recollected," and they finally unite in an atmosphere which is "tranquil" only in that it is a passive attending upon the event. Of course this is not quite the whole story. There is a great deal, in the writing of poetry, which must be conscious and deliberate.[45]

Let us begin with recollection, about which Eliot has something to say in the dissertation. For instance, the "natural view" of memory is "simply a tissue of contradiction"; memory is not "simply a restoration of the past"; and of the view that to "recall feeling . . . is merely to live it over," he says that this "is not a case of memory at all" but of "hallucination." "In short, it appears that the past in the sense in which it is supposed to be recalled, in popular psychology, simply never existed; the past lived over is not memory, and the past remembered was never lived."[46]

The practical, conclusion to be drawn from this is, as he says in "Tradition and the Individual Talent," to "divert interest from the poet to the poetry."[47] He returns to this point in *The Use of Poetry and the Use of Criticism*, where, quoting Arnold on the greatness of Wordsworth's poetry, he says:

> One way of testing it is to ask why other poets are great. Can we say that Shakespeare's poetry is great because of the extraordinary power with which Shakespeare feels estimable feelings, and because of the extraordinary power with which he makes us share them? I enjoy Shakespeare's poetry to the full extent of my capacity for enjoying poetry; but I have not the slightest approach to certainty that I share Shakespeare's feelings; nor am I very much concerned to know whether I do or not. In short, Arnold's account seems to me to err in putting the emphasis upon the poet's feelings, instead of upon the poetry.[48]

The emotion in a Wordsworth poem is not the emotion that Wordsworth the man experienced, nor in reading the poem do we, as has commonly been supposed, relive the life of the poet. The emotion that Wordsworth experienced was a psychical event, that is, a particular existence which arose and perished. And as Bradley says of such particular existences, "they can never have more than one life; when they are dead they are done with."[49] Accordingly, Wordsworth could not have reinstated the perished emotion except in hallucination.

The key here is Bradley's distinction of existence and meaning. Existence is phenomenal existence: "that which appears in the series of events that occur in space and time."[50] And the states and changes of mind that we call feelings and emotions are temporal occurrences. Further, the dominant character of such occurrences is their "particularness."[51] Meaning, on the other hand, is universal: "a meaning, an ideal content which is distinct from its existence as a psychical occurrence"[52]—though without the occurrence there could be no meaning.

Here, in "The Dry Salvages," is Eliot:

> We had the experience but missed the meaning,
> And approach to the meaning restores the experience
> In a different form, beyond any meaning
> We can assign to happiness. I have said before
> That the past experience revived in the meaning
> Is not the experience of one life only
> But of many generations–not forgetting
> Something that is probably ineffable.

We must confine ourselves here to the distinction and relation of experience and meaning. The meaning is the experience in a *different* form: it is used apart from the experience, and is combined with the meanings of other experiences, not all necessarily those of the poet. And this enlarged and enriched meaning has its life in the poem and not in the history of the poet. Accordingly, in reading Wordsworth or Shakespeare (or Eliot) we do not have the slightest approach to certainty that we are sharing the feelings of the author, or that in reading his poems we are reliving his life.

Eliot has stated and restated this position. For instance, in a 1927 review of *The Problems of the Shakespeare Sonnets* by J. M. Robertson he approves of Robertson's reticence about the "autobiographical" element, and goes on to say:

> I believe that experience, for the poet, is a very different thing from experience for the stockbroker. A love affair, successful or fatal, might cause a successful or bad investment: it cannot, without a great many other and alien experiences of which the ordinary man is incapable, cause good poetry. Nowhere is the public, in general, more at fault than in its decipherings of the meaning of poems according to some "experience." A fine poem which appears to be the record of a particular experience may be the work of a man who has never had that experience; a poem which *is* the record of a particular experience may bear no trace of that or of any experience. About good poetry, the public (including often critics and experts) is usually quite wrong: the experience it sees behind the

poem is its own, not the poet's. I do not say that poetry is not "autobiographical": but this autobiography is written by a foreign man in a foreign tongue, which can never be translated.[53]

Eliot's point may be brought out in the following way. Memory, for Eliot, is not a special faculty, any more than imagination is. Memory is an ideal construction based on present feeling, and in this respect it does not differ from imagination or inference. Moreover, the past comes to us in imagination and inference as well as in memory. Thus we may recall mailing a letter yesterday; or we may imagine how we might have done so, though we know that we did not; or though we cannot remember mailing the letter, we can perhaps prove that it happened.[54] Now Wordsworth could not have looked into his mind and extracted for inspection a naked memory, memory as distinct from perception, imagination, inference, or dream. These experiences have no separate being; they exist only relative to one another, and, further, they interpenetrate one another. Thus there is perception in memory, memory in imagination, and imagination in dream.[55] (Compare, in *The Use of Poetry*, Eliot's statement that "there is so much memory in imagination that if you are to distinguish between imagination and fancy in Coleridge's way you must define the difference between memory in imagination and memory in fancy.")[56] The memory is fused and transmuted, and this memory was never lived, nor is it recollected.

Let us return to the distinction between experience and meaning. An emotion, as we have seen, is a psychical fact, and psychical facts are particular existences. What the experience leaves behind is an ideal content, a meaning; and it is the meaning, not the experience, that is reproduced. And the meaning is a universal.

Thus Bradley in *Principles of Logic*: "I maintain that all association is between universals. . . . Every kind of reproduction . . . takes place by virtue of identity *plus* the connection of universals. 'And do you really,' there may here come a protest, 'do you really believe this holds good with emotions?' . . . I reply without hesitation that I believe it is so."[57] The old feeling has perished, and the new feeling is the meaning of the old feeling now reparticularized in a new psychological context.

And, so far as mere reproduction goes, nothing but the universal could ever be called up. It is the *fresh presentation* which adds detail to the reproduced element. This new perception re-particularizes the universal, and does so in a way which will not be the old way, and in many cases will be strikingly different. But such re-particularization . . . is *not* association, and is *not* reproduction. For though the new particular feeling . . . is no doubt the *result* of reproduction, yet *it* never was associated, and *it* can not have been reproduced, since it exists now for the first time.[58]

And Eliot in *The Use of Poetry*: "What is the experience that the poet is so bursting to communicate? By the time it has settled down into a poem it may be so different from the original experience as to be hardly recognizable. The 'experience' in question may be the result of a fusion of feelings so numerous, and ultimately so obscure in their origins, that even if there be communication of them, the poet may hardly be aware of what he is communicating; and what is there to be communicated was not in existence before the poem was completed."[59]

"The emotion of art is impersonal."[60] True, the poet "starts from . . . his own emotions," but what constitutes life for a poet is "the struggle . . . to transmute his personal and private agonies into something rich and strange, something universal and impersonal."[61] Eliot hints at his meaning in "A Dialogue on Dramatic Poetry," where he remarks that Aristotle hit on "some of the universals."[62] Though Eliot, like Aristotle, thinks of poetry in terms of emotions, with Eliot emotions are universals. To speak more strictly, since both the old and the new feeling exist only as particularized, emotions are concrete universals. And that is a considerable novelty.

It is interesting to note that in *The Transcendence of the Ego* Jean-Paul Sartre writes: "My emotions and my states, my ego itself, ceases to be my exclusive property. To be precise: up to now a radical distinction has been made between the objectivity of a spatio-temporal thing or of an external truth, and the subjectivity of psychical 'states.' . . . Psychological understanding occurred by analogy. [Husserl's] phenomenology has come to teach us that *states* are objects, that an emotion as such (a love or a hatred) is a transcendent object and cannot shrink into the interior unity of a 'consciousness.'"[63] This "profound and novel conception," as Sartre calls it, is also Eliot's and Bradley's.

The organization of experience "does not happen consciously or of deliberation" but is "a passive attending upon the event—though that is not the "whole story." In the dissertation, speaking of "the transition from the merely felt to the objectified," Eliot says: "It is neither wholly unconscious nor capricious, but is more or less a willed change."[64] These statements say the same thing in different ways. Indeed, he goes on, in the dissertation, to consider the "more fundamental aspect of the question,"[65] that is, the way in which feelings are united with objects, the emotion containing and uniting both its aspects.

Eliot's "passive attending upon the event" has troubled commentators, some dismissing it as mystification and others seeking to explain it away. But Eliot is here transcribing philosophic doctrine.

Ideality, as Bradley says, is the common mark of experience, and this process is specialized in morality, logic, and aesthetics. Thus the poet, like the thinker, must "follow the object" and must "co-operate" in its development. Though this implies will, the experiences that come to us (an unexpected perception or a sudden and surprising thought) are not all the effect of will. Similarly, thought cannot make its materials but depends upon prior distinctions and antecedent connections which seem largely to grow up apart from thinking in the proper sense, nor can it by itself re-create the past or procreate the given present or the future. "And," Bradley says, "it may be said to wait on and to follow a course of events which it is powerless to make."[66] But, he continues:

> When, in order to create a work of art, a man has to keep down (so far as is necessary) what is merely particular to himself, that does not mean either that the work makes itself without him, or that it is not different because he in particular has made it. . . . When that is called "objective," the meaning is not that the individual's will makes no difference. The meaning is that whatever in him is irrelevant to the issue, is suppressed as *merely* "subjective." . . . The ideal movement of the object itself, which I follow, does not make itself. In the first place apart from individual minds there is no

object anywhere. In the second place, so far as I in particular am concerned, the process . . . demands my personal self-realization. If you took that away, the objective process would not exist in me at all.[67]

Eliot has "preserved" this doctrine in other and later contexts, for instance, in a "Commentary" in the *Criterion*. "And as no great art is explicable simply by the society of its time, so it is not fully explicable simply by the personality of its author: in the greatest poetry there is always a hint of something behind, something impersonal, something in relation to which the author has been no more than the passive (if not always pure) medium"[68]— not always "pure" because, as we have seen, much always enters which is, from the point of view of "Art," irrelevant.

Eliot's use of the term "personality" seems to be at odds with itself. Thus great art is not fully explicable simply by the personality of its author. In "Tradition and the Individual Talent," on the other hand, "the poet has, not a 'personality' to express, but a particular medium, which is only a medium and not a personality."[69] Though this usage is puzzling, it is not inconsistent, for we have to reckon with two contexts, that of popular psychology and that of Eliot's philosophy.

In the dissertation he writes: "With regard to objects, I have reached the conclusion that all objects are non-mental; and with regard to mental activity, I conclude that we find only physiological activity or logical activity, both independent of, and more fundamental than what we call the activity of mind."[70]

The tendency of experiences to form a whole is, in principle, a logical activity—though we need not go into that here. The activity, it is enough to note here, is an objective process that works in and through individual minds, which use it and, in a sense, make it their own, the individual minds being the particular mediums in which the process becomes self-conscious. The process is a single activity with two inseparable sides, subjective and objective. But, as Bradley says: "The merely 'subjective' does *not* mean what is personal";[71] and Eliot: "To be 'subjective' is not to be mental."[72] The allusion is to the mental experience studied by the psychologist, the mental being what is personal (subjective and private): states of mind abstracted from their objects. But for Eliot there is, in this sense, "nothing mental."[73] Similarly, Bradley writes: "And the individual, as so isolated, I agree, can do nothing, for indeed he is nothing. My real personal self which orders my world is in truth inseparably one with the Universe. Behind me the absolute reality works through and in union with myself."[74] In Eliot's version there is "something behind," an objective process with which the author is personally engaged, and must be engaged if he is to realize himself as an artist.[75]

To introduce a bit of chronology, "Tradition and the Individual Talent" was published in 1919 and the "Commentary" in *Criterion* in 1932. In 1956, in "The Frontiers of Criticism," Eliot writes: "I am even prepared to suggest that there is, in all great art, something which must remain unaccountable however complete might be our knowledge of the poet, and that that is what matters most. When the poem has been made, something new has happened, something that cannot be explained by *anything that went before*. That, I believe, is what we mean by 'creation.'"[76]

It is the same theme, and the style is also the same. Eliot in this essay (lecture) is a critic of causal explanation: explanation by origins or genetic explanation. And in developing his criticism he resorts to a "suggestive analogy," in this instance a passage of Jung's quoted by Father Victor White, O.P., in his book *God and the Unconscious*. The substance of the passage concerns two types of explanation: the mechanistic, which is purely causal, and the energetic, which is in essence final. And Eliot goes on to speak of the entelechy of a poem, remarking that it is a long time since he has employed such terms with assurance, an allusion apparently to the *Monist* essay on Leibniz, where he discusses the meaning that entelechy has for Leibniz and Aristotle, concluding that with Leibniz the term is merely figurative.[77]

There is no need to discuss this particular indirection—to show by quotation how Eliot uses Jung's passage to express his own point of view. It is enough to note that, as Bradley says, the mechanistic view has no application to "the interpretation of mind."[78] The mind is not a thing in space but an activity: not a *kinesis* but an *energeia*.[79] Or, to use a more familar term, the mind—the power of knowing—is a "spiritual" activity. Though knowing occurs in the world of time and event, it transcends this world. As Eliot says in *The Four Quartets*, "To be conscious is not to be in time." Knowing, that is, is not an "inner" (psychical) event nor is it an "outer" (external) event. To quote Eliot again, it is "not inside or outside" but "simply is."

As for something "unaccountable," it has two meanings. Thus Eliot, speaking of the "process of realization of a world," says: "I should never admit that the situation was due to the subject side any more than to the object side, or that the notion of activity was ultimately possible at all."[80] The activity is the activity of thought, and this notion, Bradley holds, when it is examined, turns out to be inconsistent, so that "thought is not intelligible."[81] It is, accordingly, not ultimate; it is appearance and not reality.

That does not mean, however, that thought is not real; indeed, there is nothing more real than thought. But thought is not a subjective faculty: not a power inhering in and originated by individual subjects. Nor is it formal: it is not an abstract form imposed on a matter external to it, the matter remaining the same before and after the exercise of thought.[82] Rather, as Eliot says in "Tradition and the Individual Talent," "the mind digest[s] and transmute[s] . . . its material."[83] What, so to speak, goes in at one end comes out at the other transformed, so that "something new has happened, something that cannot be wholly explained by *anything that went before*."

Here, in his treatise on history, is Bradley:

> There are results for which no "genetic development" will account, or give a reason, however much it may "explain" them; and processes again (as we see, for example, in the case of many works of art) the elements of which defy distinction, because indissolubly fused within particular personalities by a flame, which mixes the substance of the elements with the nature of the vessel that holds them, and which itself is the new-birth of an individual soul. Hence they are not natural growths but creations; and if we like to call them miracles, we may.[84]

This account is as obscure as Eliot's, if not more so. Moreover, there is the same problem of language, as in Bradley's use of "particular personalities." And since we are concerned with the style as well as the thought, it is perhaps worth offering another example of Bradley's style. In the same work he writes:

If to say that all "knowledge comes from experience" is to utter no more than "an empty tautology," then it must be a similar tautology to assert that all experience is personal experience. The teaching that it is impossible for a man to transcend his consciousness is not unfamiliar to our ears; and we have learnt the lesson (important or otherwise) that we can only know the things which we can know, and that our world will never be wider than the world which will be ours.[85]

Later in his argument he returns to the same topic. Discussing how, starting with a given world, this world is transformed into something new, he writes:

> But the mind is such a unity that it holds a contradiction in itself until the divided elements cohere, are solved and blended into another consciousness, a fresh system, a new world—new, and which contains the old in a transformed shape.
> And this is why (to begin with "personal") the personality is wanted; for that is no less than the principle of synthesis which makes this new world.[86]

With Bradley, it is the mind that is the principle of synthesis. And "personality" here means mind, a process that is both "inside" and "outside"; as "inside," it is self-conscious, and in this sense it is personal, or, as Bradley says elsewhere, the "particular personality." To be a mind is to be a self-conscious subject of experience, a medium for a process that is rooted in the nature of things, objective and impersonal.[87]

We come now to "the mind of Europe." Eliot, in "Tradition and the Individual Talent," speaking of "the obvious fact that art never improves, but that the material of art is never quite the same," says of the poet:

> He must be aware that the mind of Europe—the mind of his own country—a mind which he learns in time to be much more important than his own private mind—is a mind which changes, and that this change is a development which abandons nothing *en route*, which does not superannuate either Shakespeare, or Homer, or the rock drawing of the Magdalenian draughtsmen. That this development, refinement perhaps, complication certainly, is not, from the point of view of the artist, any improvement. Perhaps not even an improvement from the point of view of the psychologist or not to the extent which we imagine; perhaps only in the end based upon a

complication in economics and machinery. But the difference between the present and the past is that the conscious present is an awareness of the past in a way and to an extent which the past's awareness of itself cannot show.[88]

To start with the last point, here is Bradley writing about "the concrete development of the historical mind": "In that ceaseless process which differentiates itself only as a means to integration, and which integrates itself only with the result of a fuller differentiation, the consciousness of the earlier stage of humanity is never the consciousness of a later development. The knowledge it has of itself is partial and false when compared with the epoch of an intenser realization. And . . . we see that it is a hope doomed only to disappointment, when the present expects in the mind of the past to find the views and beliefs of the present."[89] The consciousness of the present differs from that of the past because it is the past transformed. Thus "each stage is the qualitative new-birth of an organic, and more than an organic, unity, which resumes its lower developments in a fresh integration."[90] The historical mind is more than organic; but, as with an organism, there is a continual "reorganization," so that each stage "contains the old in a transformed shape." That suggests why "the mind of Europe" abandons nothing *en route*. Again, history is "a progress not only in the sense of that which increases in quantity, but in the sense of that which develops or evolves itself, is essentially the same in stages of growth which are diverse in quality."[91] The stages of history are not external to one another but are diverse aspects of a single process. Finally, though there is development, the process is essentially the same in its different stages, so that in this sense there is not any improvement. The process is an identity in diversity, and it is the process of "a mind which is . . . more than the mind of this or that man."[92]

What, one wonders, would constitute an improvement for the psychologist? The allusion seems to be to the notion that the early or primitive mind is prelogical, a notion shared by certain anthropologists. Thus Eliot in his introduction to *Savonarola: A Dramatic Poem*: "M. Lévy-Bruhl . . . invents an elaborate 'prelogism' to account for the savage's identification of himself with his totem, where it is not certain that the savage, except so far as he had mental processes similar to our own, had any mental process at all."[93] In the dissertation: "When we turn to inspect a lower stage of mind, child or animal, or our own when it is least active, we do not find one or another of these elements into which we analyze the developed consciousness, but we find them all at a lower stage. We do not find feeling without thought, or presentation without reflection: we find both feeling and thought, presentation, redintegration and abstraction, all at a lower stage. And if this is the case, such study of primitive consciousness seems futile; for we find in our knowing exactly the same constituents, in a clearer and more apprehensible form."[94]

There is some improvement, but not to the extent which we imagine. For "the intellect," Bradley says, "would never have appeared on the scene, if it had not been present and active from the first."[95] The laws of fusion and redintegration operate from the very first, and thought proper is a development from this ground of "preceding ideality."[96] Hence "all stages of mind" can be interpreted as "the growth of one single principle," first unconscious or inexplicit and then conscious or explicit.[97]

The mind of Europe, in Eliot's account, is something which changes in the sense of a development which is not any improvement. Change implies something which changes and which is the same at the end as at the beginning; and yet if it were not different at the end from what it was at the beginning there would be no development. Now identity and continuity are always ideal, so that the only permanence is that of ideality; and without permanence, as we have just seen, there could be no change.[98] The identity is expressed in and through its differences—its later and earlier stages—though it is nothing apart from its differences.

Accordingly, the "historical sense involves a perception, not only of the pastness of the past, but of its presence"; and the poet lives in what is "not merely the present, but the present moment of the past."[99]

Again, the "historical sense" is "a sense of the timeless as well as of the temporal and of the timeless and of the temporal together."[100] Actually, every experience has two inseparable sides, existence and content, particular and universal—for "an identity of content in different contexts is and must be an universal."[101] What we experience is always an ideal content, and though it is experienced under particular conditions, the conditions are not an element in the content. Thus beauty, Bradley says, has "a certain existence" in time, but it "transcends the lapse of time and the flux of change, and it everywhere in this sense is eternal."[102] So, according to Joachim, though a work of art is manifested through "temporal processes and under temporal conditions," it is "a thing of transcendent value," for beauty is "eternal."[103] Similarly, Eliot writes in *The Use of Poetry*, history teaches us to see the relation of poetry to "the conditions of its time and place"; but if we regard the history of criticism not merely as "a catalogue of successive notions about poetry" but as a process of "readjustment" and "readaptation," it may help us to discover what changes and what does not change—"what is permanent and eternal in poetry." For though the criticism of every age makes "particular responses to particular situations," there is always "some permanent element in common"; but "every effort to formulate the common element is limited by the limitations of particular men in particular places and at particular times; and these limitations become manifest in the perspective of history."[104]

It is, as we have seen, only the permanent that can change. And another aspect of Eliot's idea of order is that what comes later may determine what comers earlier.

Thus, speaking of the literature of Europe, the existing monuments, he says, form an "ideal order" among themselves, which is modified by the introduction of the new work of art among them; for order to persist, "the *whole* existing order" must be altered and readjusted. "Whoever has approved this idea of order . . . will not find it preposterous that the past should be altered by the present as much as the present is directed by the past."[105]

Eliot restates the general idea in *The Use of Poetry*, where education in poetry is said to be not merely "the sum of the experiences" of poems but an "organization" of these experiences; and there is also a "reorganization" occasioned by meeting something new, "a new pattern of poetry arranging itself in consequence."[106] In the mind of the critic, as in that of the poet, experiences are always forming new wholes.

Nowhere, Bradley writes, do we find "substances fixed and

rigid"; they are "ideal wholes of content, standing on a ceaselessly renewed basis of two-sided change," "unities for ever created and destroyed." Or they are, as Joachim calls them, "significant wholes," wholes of meaning, the parts of which are meanings. And such wholes are common to knowledge, art, and conduct.[107]

According to Joachim, a science, as an organized whole of knowledge, is not "a *sum, aggregate, collection*, or *class* of single truths," each of which has its meaning by itself and is what it is in the science as outside it, any more than the Choral Symphony is "a *collection* of beautiful sounds," or *Othello* "an *aggregate* of fine ideas," or a painting by Rembrandt "a *sum* of colors and lines." Further, the development of a science is not an affair of adding some elements and dropping others; rather, when a new discovery is made, the science undergoes a modification which is akin to the organic growth of a living thing. Thus the mathematical mind was not left unaltered by the discovery of the differential calculus but its "entire character" was changed.[108] It is the same with conduct, which is an organized system of purposes. Thus, according to Bosanquet, a difference in purpose does not mean a new suggestion or an additional idea "tacked on, so to speak, without affecting the organized system"; there is a "dislocation" and "rearrangement" of "the whole system," a "transformation" and "reorganization" of views, attitudes, and perceptions, so that it is not the case that the new element concerns "only the future and not the present or the past."[109]

Eliot, making the same point, says that "any explanation in terms of 'because' (a term made necessary by the weakness of human conceiving) can be only misleading unless we turn it about the other way as well."[110] It is assumed that the cause precedes the effect; but in the process described above, though the later stage is determined by the earlier, the earlier is also determined by the later. (Past and future determine each other in the same way: since the elements have "a simultaneous existence" and compose "a simultaneous order,"[111] there is no temporal before and after; instead, there is mutual implication of elements within a whole that is always "present.")[112]

"And the poet who is aware of this [that the past is altered by the present as much as the present is altered by the past] will be aware of great difficulties and responsibilities."

In a peculiar sense he will be aware also that he must inevitably be judged by the standards of the past. I say judged, not amputated, by them; not judged to be as good as, or worse or better than, the dead; and certainly not judged by the canons of dead critics. It is a judgment, a comparison, in which two things are measured by each other. To conform merely would be for the new work not really to conform at all; it would not be new, and would therefore not be a work of art. . . . We say: it appears to conform, and is perhaps individual, or it appears individual, and may conform; but we are hardly likely to find that it is one and not the other.[113]

Comparison is a type of judgment, and every judgment exhibits an identity in difference or difference in identity. It is not a judgment of better or worse but of the same and different; and it cannot be different unless it is the same—conforms; but it cannot merely conform because without difference there is no identity. As Eliot says, "Identity, we have learned, is nowhere bare identity, but must be identity in diversity."[114] It cannot conform without being individual, and it cannot be individual without conforming.

If, Eliot says, we were self-critical in our criticism, one of the facts that would come to light would be our tendency to dwell upon "the poet's difference from his predecessors," the tendency to praise a poet for those aspects of his work in which "we pretend to find what is individual"; but if we approach a poet "without this prejudice," we shall find that "the most individual parts of his work" may be those in which the dead poets, his ancestors, assert their immortality most vigorously.[115]

The "prejudice" is "a preconception as to the self," that is, "the identification of it with the particular self"; or it is what is called "individualism," because "selves are 'individual' in the sense of exclusive of other selves." And "every community of men" is a "collection" of particular selves, the same in the collection as out of it. But apart from the community, no such selves exist.[116] It is the "common mind" within him that makes the individual what he is. Further, "If this is true of the social consciousness in its various forms, it is true certainly no less of that common mind which is more than social. In art, in science and in religion, the individual by himself remains still an abstraction."[117]

Bradley treats this theme at considerable length in *Ethical Studies*; and what he says of the social community applies to artistic, scientific, and religious communities, the difference being that these last do not, like the social community, have a visible enbodiment, but are invisible communities.

The artistic community is a real community—an "organic whole," though "a better theory tells us it is *more* than organic."[118] But it must not be forgotten that "the principle may be there and may be our basis or our goal, without our knowing anything about it."[119] However, if it is to be realized, the members must be aware of themselves, and aware of themselves as members. In other words, the common mind must be "self-conscious" in its members. And this saves the truth of individualism, for it means that its "self-consciousness" in him is "his own individuality."[120]

Eliot, in "The Function of Criticism"—this essay is "an application of the principles" expressed in "Tradition and the Individual Talent"—writes:

> I thought of literature then, as I think of it now . . . not as a collection of the writings of individuals, but as "organic wholes," as systems in relation to which, and only in relation to which, individual works of literary art, and the works of individual artists, have their significance. . . . A common inheritance and a common cause unite artists consciously or unconsciously: it must be admitted that the union is mostly unconscious. Between the true artists of any time there is, I believe, an unconscious community. And, as our instincts of tidiness imperatively command us not to leave to the haphazard of unconsciousness what we can attempt to do consciously, we are forced to conclude that what happens unconsciously we could bring about, and form into a purpose, if we made a conscious attempt. The second-rate artist, of course, cannot afford to surrender himself to any common action; for his chief task is the assertion of all the trifling differences which are his distinction.[121]

The second-rate artist is the "this-me" regarded as an existent in time and space, a particular self constituted by marks and relations that differentiate him from other particular selves. But the particular is not the individual. There is "something outside of the artist . . . to which he must surrender and sacrifice himself."[122] In this negation and transcendence he specifies in himself the common mind, and in this way he reaches "his own individuality."[123]

Eliot employs his principles in a variety of contexts. Thus in "Literature and the Modern World" (1935):

> A man is both an individual and a member. Instead of "individual" I shall use the word "person." His *personality* is unique and not to be violated; but he is equally created to be a *member* of society. When society is conceived as merely a sum of individuals, you get the chaos of liberal democracy. When the person is wholly subordinated to society, you get the dehumanization of fascism or communism. The extremes, however, may meet. For what liberal democracy really recognizes is a sum, not of persons, but of individuals: that is to say, not the variety and uniqueness of persons, but the purely material individuation of the old-fashioned or Democritean atom. And this is a disrespect to the person. For the person is no longer a person if wholly isolated from the community; and the community is no longer a community if it does not consist of persons. A man is not himself unless he is a member; and he cannot be a member unless he is also something alone. Man's membership and his solitude must be taken together. There are moments . . . when a man may be nearly crushed by the terrible awareness of his isolation from every other human being; and I pity him if he finds himself only alone with himself and his meanness and futility, alone without God. . . .
>
> Now all this may sound perfectly irrelevant to my subject; but it is not so. This same balance ought to exist, on its plane, in the activity of the artist. For the artist cannot devote himself truly to any cause unless by that devotion he is also most truly being, and becoming, himself.[124]

As Bradley puts it, "apart from my life in it, my knowledge of it, and devotion to it, I am not myself."[125] The devotion of the artist, like that of the scientist, is to something that is more than social. No doubt art and science do as a rule lead indirectly to the welfare of others, but that is not enough to make them social. Each aims at a single end of its own. And if that were not true, the artist, as such, and the inquirer, as such, would have to consider ends falling outside of art and inquiry. But it is the moral duty of the inquirer simply to inquire and of the artist simply to produce the best work of art; and these pursuits as ends in themselves and not merely as means are approved as morally desirable.[126]

Again, in a "Commentary" in *Criterion* (1932):

> The craving for some passionate *conviction*, and for a living organic society, assumes odd and often extremely dangerous forms. Man must have something to which he is ready to sacrifice himself; he must, if necessary, sacrifice himself, but he must not be sacrificed. I question whether Communism would leave the individual in possession of enough of himself to sacrifice. Where willingness towards self-sacrifice is deficient . . . it is usually that men as individuals do not feel that they are being called upon to sacrifice themselves for anything in which they have an essential interest, but are merely being sacrificed to alien interests: and when I say "interests," I do not mean only material interests, but ideal interests without which the man feels that he would be less himself. But what, I wonder, is this mass-identity into which our individual consciousnesses are to be merged? Admitted that the ordinary mediocre man maintains his petty and not wholly real individuality by subterfuges and expedients: by money, social position, public distinctions, skill at games and other irrelevances that distinguish him from his neighbor. The Buddhist may become merged in nirvana; but that is a voluntary extinction, accomplished by the most arduous self-discipline, not a salvation from individuality imposed upon him by society.[127]

Our concern here is only with the philosophic ingredients. Thus "the not wholly real individuality" is the "this-me," the particular or private self. As for "ideal interests without which the man feels that he would be less himself," it is, Bradley writes, the identification of my self with "objective interests" that "makes me myself," and "in realizing them I realize myself, and can do so only by realizing them."[128]

"What," Bradley asks, "is self-sacrifice?" It is, he says, summarizing a long discussion of this theme, the identification with the ideal, or it implies the identification with an object. And this demands "the suppression of the self in some form; and so, though self-realization, it yet at the same time is self-sacrifice." The effort to realize the object entails the "negation of our private existence."[129]

In the dissertation, "I am I," Eliot writes, "only in relation to objects."[130] Similarly:

All of Valéry's poetry . . . is impersonal in the sense that personal emotion, personal experience, is extended and completed in something impersonal—not in the sense of something divorced from personal experience and passion. No good poetry is the latter; indeed, the virtue, the marvel of Lucretius is the passionate act by which he annihilates himself in a system and unites himself with it, gaining something greater than himself. Such surrender requires great concentration. But to those who like to preserve themselves in their limited "personalities," and to have the emotions and notions of these petty personalities flattered by constant repetition rather than extended and transformed by the poet's superior organization, neither Lucretius nor Valéry, nor any other excellent poet, can ever be really acceptable and comprehensible.[131]

Again:

We do tend, I think, to organize our tastes in various arts into a whole; we aim in the end at a theory of life, or a view of life, and so far as we are conscious, to terminate our enjoyment of the arts in a philosophy, and our philosophy in a religion—in such a way that the personal to oneself is fused and completed in the impersonal and general, not extinguished, but enriched, expanded, developed, and more itself by becoming more something not itself.[132]

Finally:

What we find when we read Lucretius or Dante is that the poet has effected a fusion between that philosophy and his natural feelings, so that the philosophy becomes real and the feelings become elevated, intensified and dignified.[133]

Though what has been said here is not the "whole story," it is, like the "whole story," all in the idiom of Bradley. If that is not obvious, it is because Eliot chose to preserve his philosophy in cryptogram. For one thing, the philosophy is a *metaphysical* philosophy. ("That metaphysics should approve itself to common sense is indeed out of the question. For neither in its processes nor in its results can it expect, or even hope, to be generally intelligible.")[134] For another, Eliot, when he is not the poet criticizing poetry in order to create poetry, is the man of letters writing polite literature; and to introduce technical philosophy into such writing would be a violation of literary propriety, about which Eliot tended to be rather scrupulous.[135]

In any case, we have to do with a paradox. Eliot's critical prose, it has often been noted, is characterized by a lack of definiteness, is elusive, is marked by a certain evasiveness. So it is. And yet it is based on definite doctrines, and there is a curious precision in the way that the prose transcribes the doctrines without exposing them. Still, the prose remains elusive and evasive, for the doctrines themselves are abstruse. But that is another and separate matter, which falls outside the present inquiry.

6

Taste and Theory

"But I am certain of one thing," Eliot writes in "To Criticize the Critic": "that I have written best about writers who have influenced my own poetry. And I say 'writers' and not 'poets,' because I include F. H. Bradley, whose works—I might say whose personality as manifest in his works—affected me profoundly."[1]

What attracted Eliot in the philosophic personality was, presumably, the mixture of modesty and irony, the gift for language, and the intense addiction to an intellectual passion.[2] As for the philosophy, though it gets into the poetry, its chief influence is on Eliot's idea of poetry, and for that we must go to the critical prose.

Speaking of the first period of his criticism, he says:

> In *The Egoist* appeared an essay called *Tradition and the Individual Talent*, which still enjoys immense popularity among those editors who prepare anthological text-books for American college students. There were then two influences which are not so incongruous as might at first sight appear: that of Irving Babbitt and that of Ezra Pound. The influence of Pound at that time may be detected in references to Remy de Gourmont, in my papers on Henry James, an author whom Pound much admired. . . . The influence of Babbitt (with an infusion later of T. E. Hulme and of the more literary essays of Charles Maurras) is apparent in my recurrent theme of Classicism versus Romanticism.[3]

These writers were no doubt influences, but their influence is not apparent in the essay with which (by implication) they are associated. And indeed they had nothing to do with Eliot's literary theory, which is a philosophic aesthetics. We shall deal with Gourmont later. In philosophy, Hulme, as is well known, was a disciple of Bergson; but Bergson must not be confused with Bradley. If Pound, Babbitt, and Maurras had a definite philosophy, it was not that of *Knowledge and Experience*.

It is the facile treatment of "influences" that compels us to be pedantic, but we cannot understand the critical prose if we ignore the language in which it is written—unless it is supposed that Eliot's meaning is to be grasped by an intuitive understanding of his mind.

Take, for example, the theme of Classicism versus Romanticism. In "Experiment in Criticism," expressing his dissatisfaction with Babbitt's use of these terms, he says: "Everyone who writes about these two abstractions believes that he knows what the words mean; actually they mean something a little different for each observer, and merely mean to mean the same things."[4] Similarly, in *The Use of Poetry and the Use of Criticism*, commenting on Rivière's use of the term "Romanticism," the danger is, he says, "it is a term which is constantly changing in different contexts."[5] And in the dissertation: "Now in any use of a word which symbolizes an abstraction the actual object of attention, I submit, is exceedingly variable: there is not simply one determinate object in various contexts, but the object varies with the context."[6]

Eliot draws "an important line of demarcation between the essays of generalization (such as *Tradition and the Individual Talent*) and appreciations of individual authors." In the latter category he makes a distinction between the essays on Elizabethan and Jacobean drama and such later essays as those on Tennyson and Byron; it is the earlier work in which he continues to have the most confidence and which he thinks has the best chance of survival. In the former category he mentions, besides the piece already noted, an essay dealing with "the function of criticism," and the generalizing phrases "objective correlative" and "dissociation of sensibility." The generalizations "had their origin in my sensibility" and have been "epiphenomenal of my tastes"; they may be accounted for as "conceptual symbols for emotional preferences," "attempts to summarize, in conceptual form, direct and intense experience of the poetry I have found most congenial."[7]

We have already observed that Eliot is here generalizing about his generalizations in terms of his philosophy. Thus, as he says in the dissertation: "Knowledge is based upon and developed out of feeling"; it is this "felt background against which we project our theories, and with reference to which our speculations have their use."[8] But Eliot gives no indication of the variety and extent of his generalizations (the use he makes of his philosophy).

Let us begin with "In Memoriam," since that is one of the essays he mentions. In this piece, after some remarks on Tennyson's metrical accomplishments, he comes to his main interest: Tennyson's religious attitude. Quoting some verses in which Tennyson speaks of God and nature, he says: "That strange abstraction, 'Nature,' becomes a real god or goddess, perhaps more real, at moments, to Tennyson than God ('*Are God and Nature then at strife?*')."[9] It is not irrelevant to note that this is a theme of Bradley's: "Nature" is an abstraction; and Bradley, in his discussion of this abstraction, considers whether "Nature" is "an object of possible worship."[10]

"Tennyson," Eliot says, "is distressed by the idea of a mechanical universe; he is naturally, in lamenting his friend, teased by the hope of immortality and reunion beyond death. Yet the renewal craved for seems at best but a continuance, or a substitute for the joys of friendship upon earth. His desire for immortality never is quite the desire for Eternal Life; his concern is for the loss of man rather than for the gain of God."[11] Bradley, in his analysis of "the desire for immortality," finds much confusion and self-deception in this desire. But to keep to the point—what is in the mind of the man who hopes for reunion after death is "to remain much what I am now" or "to continue to be much what I am."[12] That is, in part, Eliot's point. It is, to be sure, a small point, but it is the principle of the thing that counts.

Apparently Tennyson's contemporaries, once they had accepted *In Memoriam*, regarded it as a message of hope and reassurance to their rather fading Christian faith. It happens now and then that a poet by some strange accident expresses the mood of his generation, at the same time that he is expressing a mood of his own which is quite remote from that of his generation. This is not a question of insincerity: there is an amalgam of yielding and opposition below the level of consciousness. Tennyson himself, on the conscious level of the man . . . consistently asserted a convinced, if somewhat sketchy, Christian belief."[13]

That may be taken as a comment on *The Waste Land* as well as on Tennyson's poem. And Eliot is explaining the matter in terms of his philosophy. The amalgam below the level of consciousness (it will be recognized from our earlier discussion) is the theory that "the identity of religion and culture remains on the unconscious level, upon which we have superimposed a conscious structure wherein religion and culture are contrasted and can be opposed." This theory, that religion and culture are "aspects of one unity" and, also, "two different and contrasted things," here foreshadowed in the essay on Tennyson, was not to be elaborated until twelve years later, when Eliot published his notes on the definition of culture.

In the essay on Byron, summarizing his impression of *Don Juan*, he writes:

> What puts the last cantos of *Don Juan* at the head of Byron's work is, I think, that the subject matter gave him at last an adequate object for a genuine emotion. The emotion is hatred of hypocrisy; and if it was reinforced by more personal and petty feelings, the feelings of the man who as a boy had known the humiliation of shabby lodgings with an eccentric mother, who at fifteen had been clumsy and unattractive and unable to dance with Mary Chaworth, who remained oddly alien among the society that he knew so well—this mixture of the origin of his attitude towards English society only gives it greater intensity.[14]

If the style, as is evident, has changed very little, the reason is that the philosophy was assimilated to the point where it became a habit of thought.

I will give an instance or two from the later Dante essay (first published as a book). Discussing Canto XXX of the *Purgatorio* (the meeting with Beatrice), Eliot observes "how skillfully Dante expresses the recrudescence of an ancient passion in a new emotion, in a new situation, which comprehends, enlarges, and gives meaning to it. . . . And in the dialogue that follows we see the passionate conflict of the old feelings with the new."[15] The analysis is inseparable from the theory—is indeed a particularized statement of the theory.

Eliot, as we have seen, can be exceedingly cryptic. Thus, speaking of the *Vita Nuova:*

> I find in it an account of a particular kind of experience: that is, of something which had actual experience (the experience of the "confession" in the modern sense) *and* intellectual and imaginative experience (the experience of thought and the experience of dream) as its materials, and which became a third kind. . . . If you have that sense of intellectual and spiritual realities that Dante had, then a form of expression like the *Vita Nuova* cannot be classed either as "truth" or "fiction."[16]

The "third kind," it must be, is what in the dissertation he calls "a *real* fiction,"[17] something which is neither "truth" nor "fiction."

Though the generalizations are not so thick in the later as in the earlier work, the same theory is present throughout; and taste and theory in the *literary* criticism cannot, as a rule, be treated apart.

We may consider in this connection the essay on Philip Massinger. In this essay (a combination of two reviews) Eliot is concerned with showing the inferiority of Massinger to his elder contemporaries ("The next period is the period of Milton . . . ; and this period is initiated by Massinger.").[18] What he finds wanting in Massinger is the capacity for "perceiving, registering, and digesting impressions"; the "gift for combining, for fusing into a single phrase, two or more diverse impressions"; the "perpetual slight alteration of language, words perpetually *eingeschachtelt* into meanings."[19] That is the language of "Tradition and the Individual Talent" applied to the question of verbal poetry. It is illustrated by copious quotation, which Eliot is most admired for. Similarly, discussing Massinger's indebtedness to Shakespeare, he says: "The good poet welds his theft into a whole of feeling which is unique, utterly different from that from which it was torn; the bad poet throws it into something which has no cohesion."[20] ("A whole of feeling" is, of course, Bradley's language; or, as Bradley also puts it, "a felt whole . . . as in a work of art.")[21] In regard to dramatic form, Massinger is a dramatist who "welds together parts . . . remote from unity." He also fails at characterization; for "a character, to be living, must be conceived from some emotional unity," that is, "of parts that are felt together"[22]—or, as Bradley gives it, "a many felt in one."[23] To give one last instance: "Romantic drama tended . . . toward what is sometimes called the 'typical,' but which is not truly typical; for the *typical* figure in a drama is always particularized—an individual."[24] The type, the universal, exists only as particularized— is a concrete universal.

Eliot, noting that other critics before him had recognized Massinger's inferiority, says: "These critics have left in their work an undissolved residuum of their own good taste, which, however impeccable, is something that requires our faith. The principles which animate this taste remain unexplained."[25] Eliot's language, in this essay and others, is evidence of the principles that animate his own taste.

Eliot returns to the theme of "the Unities" in *The Use of Poetry*–"the fundamental question of 'unities,'" as Bradley calls it.[26] Eliot supports, in principle, Sidney's strictures on Elizabethan drama, and he brings in Aristotle, quoting Butcher on the unity of action. It seems to be a standard academic discussion, except for certain peculiarities. "The doctrine of *Unity of Sentiment*, in fact, happens to be right"; and "the Elizabethan drama did tend to approach that *unity of feeling* which Sidney desires." This is "a slightly larger term than Unity of Action"; it comprises the "unification of all the elements," including "the emotions to be unified."[27]

This leads to a larger generalization:

> But my point is simply that the unities differ radically from human legislation in that they are laws of nature, and a law of nature, even when it is a law of human nature, is quite another thing from a human law. The kind of literary law in which Aristotle was interested was not law that he laid down, but law that he discovered. The laws (*not* rules) of unity of place and time remain valid in that every play which observes them *in so far as its material* allows is in that respect and degree superior to plays which observe them less. . . . This is not to establish another law. There *is* no other law possible. . . . Furthermore, we must observe that the Unities are not three separate laws. They are three aspects of one law.[28]

The theme here is the laws of thought (identity, contradiction, and excluded middle), which are also the laws of being. These are laws, not rules, because they state the fundamental conditions of both being and knowing. (Every special inquirer, if he is to know anything at all, must know these laws, though he need not be directly concerned with them.) In idealist logic (Bradley, Bosanquet, Joachim, Nettleship), the laws of thought are construed as wholes or unities, each of which is an identity in difference (the whole or unity is an identity and the parts are differences within it). And, as Bradley says, "a study of the principal forms of unity in difference would not leave much outside it."[29]

Though Eliot is aware that the unities of place and time are not Aristotelian doctrine, the unities, for him, are "three aspects of one law," for, according to Bradley, "space or time . . . is . . . an instance of the one principle of identity in difference."[30] Works of art are another. As Eliot says: "Poetry . . . create[s] a variety of wholes composed of intellectual and emotional constituents."[31]

These wholes, as Bradley says, cannot be "explained"; and Eliot says, "By *understanding* I do not mean *explanation*"[32]— that is, analysis based on the category of whole and parts. Everything, it is assumed, is either simple or complex; and the complex is explained by resolving it into its simple elements, and then, by another and separate operation, reconstructing the complex from its elements—a procedure that disintegrates and explains away the wholeness or unity.[33]

Thus Bradley: "You cannot always apply in actual experience that coarse notion of the whole as the sum of its parts into which the school of 'experience' so delights to torture phenomena." It is in the light of this notion that the empirical school analyzes "the *composition* of Mind."[34] Similarly, criticizing Russell's analysis of an emotion: "Let us agree that our state is a unity. Now the question is whether this unity consists in a relation or relations. Given the terms and the relations (whatever these are) . . . , and given nothing else, have you got, or can you reconstitute, the emotional fact?" The answer is that a "felt whole" cannot be described in this way. And the same thing is true, Bradley goes on to say, in "the instance of some product of fine art."[35]

So Eliot in the dissertation quotes the following sentence from a textbook of Titchener's: "The psychologist seeks, first of all, to analyze *mental experience* into its simplest elements"[36] (Eliot's italics). And in the earlier Dante essay: "Shakespeare takes a character apparently controlled by a simple emotion, and analyzes the character and the emotion itself. The emotion is split up into its constituents—and perhaps destroyed in the process."[37]

What is left out in such analysis is feeling ("diversity and unity in one whole");[38] terms and relations are but features and aspects of feeling, and taken apart from feeling they are empty abstractions. They cannot, accordingly, describe or reconstitute an emotion, which is a specialization of feeling.[39]

In "The Metaphysical Poets" Eliot writes: "Johnson has hit, perhaps by accident, on one side of their peculiarities, when he observed that their attempts were always analytic; he would not agree that, after the dissociation, they put the material together again in a new unity."[40]

Johnson hit on one side of the process. But "analysis and synthesis," Bradley says, "are essentially one," and "performing one operation we find that we have also accomplished the other."[41]

Again:

> Johnson, who employed the term "metaphysical poets," apparently having Donne, Cleveland, and Cowley chiefly in mind, remarks of them that "the most heterogeneous ideas are yoked by violence together." The force of this impeachment lies in the failure of the conjunction, the fact that often the ideas are yoked but not united; and if we are to judge of styles of poetry by their abuse, enough examples may be found in Cleveland to justify Johnson's condemnation. But a degree of heterogeneity of material compelled into unity by the operation of the poet's mind is omnipresent in poetry.[42]

There must be *some* diversity (otherwise there would be mere being, or nothingness)[43]. two or more elements that constitute a unity, or two or more differences in and of an identity.[44] As for "yoked but not united," that summarizes Bradley's various arguments that no bare conjunction of elements can constitute a unity. Nor is such an arrangement intelligible. The conjunction is a unit, standing between the other units, and there must be another conjunction to link these two sets of units, and so on in infinite regress.[45]

Consider the question of explanation in literary study. Literary scholarship is based on the application of formal logic to the analysis of a literary work, and from this point of view a literary work is a whole in the sense of the sum of its parts.[46] Thus the belief in the explanatory value of sources and influences assumes that the elements apart and the elements together are the same; and by investigating what a poem is made of, and the way in which its materials are ordered and arranged, we seek to explain the poem. But we also think of a poem as a work of the creative imagination, and regarded in this light, a poem, we feel, is in some sense more than the sum of its parts. The question is, In what sense? Well, a poem, it is said, is an organic unity. But this, we hear, is only a metaphor, though what is supposed to follow is not made clear. Or one reads in a textbook on linguistics: "The old axiom of Euclid, 'the whole is equal to the sum of all its parts,' does not apply to *organized* wholes. An organized whole is always *greater* than the sum of all its parts, because it is equal to the sum of its parts *plus the way they are organized*."[47] But from Bradley's point of view, that begs the question. Of course, linguistics, a special discipline, is, like other such disciplines, free to use whatever working ideas serve its limited purposes. Similarly, "In literary criticism," Eliot says, "we are constantly using terms which we cannot define, and defining other things by them."[48]

Let us consider "Milton II," where Eliot says of Milton's poetry: "The emphasis is on the sound, not the vision, upon the word, not the idea; and in the end it is the unique versification that is the most certain sign of Milton's intellectual mastership."[49]

The organization of sound is, like other kinds of organization, the work of the intellect, for it is the intellect, not sense or feeling, that analyzes and constructs. Since in Milton's versification this operation shows "exceptional energy," it is "more conclusive evidence of his intellectual power than is his grasp of any *ideas* that he borrowed or invented."⁵⁰

What Eliot does not explain is that thought on this level is inexplicit rather than explicit. It is, however, still thought, still in principle intellectual activity, an operation mediate and discursive. What is great in Milton's work is the "unique versification." Milton's verse is "especially refractory to yielding up its secrets to the examination of the single line," for the "full beauty of the line is found in its context." That is the mark of its "unique pattern."⁵¹

Bradley discusses the notion of uniqueness at considerable length. In the sense that is relevant here, uniqueness means "individuality or self-containedness": "A thing which is self-contained is unique."⁵²

Milton's versification is not unique just because it is unlike any other versification, or because it is not an instance or example of a kind or class of versification. These are only the negative aspects of its uniqueness, and it is unique in this negative way because of something positive. Thus in the essay on Massinger, speaking of the gift "for combining, for fusing into a single phrase, two or more diverse impressions," Eliot cites Shakespeare's "in her strong toil of grace" and remarks that this phrase is "such a fusion. . . . ; the resultant is one and is unique."⁵³ More generally, a poem is "unique" because it has "cohesion"; and this, as he explains, means the ability "to perform that slight alteration of *all* the elements in the world of a play or a story, so that this world is complete in itself."⁵⁴ Or, as he says in the *Hamlet* essay, "self-complete."⁵⁵ Milton's versification is unique because, to borrow from the later Dante essay, the elements are "transformed in the whole."⁵⁶ The consequence is that the full beauty of the line is found only in its context.

A poem is an individual whole; and such a whole, being self-contained, does not refer to anything else, so that a poem does not in this sense say something but *is* something. But this is to anticipate a discussion that must be left till later.

The two Milton essays (1936, 1947) are of a piece with the rest of the critical prose: same theory, same criteria. Thus in "Milton I": with Shakespeare, "the combinations of words offer perpetual novelty; they enlarge the meaning of the individual words joined." But with Milton, "the separate words [are not] developed in significance" but are "merely combined."[57]

> The sun to me is dark
> And silent as the moon,
> When she deserts the night
> Hid in her vacant interlunar cave.

Here interlunar is certainly a stroke of genius, but is merely combined with "vacant" and "cave," rather than giving and receiving life from them. Thus it is not so unfair, as it might at first appear, to say that Milton writes English like a dead language.[58]

In a dead language the words are fixed in their meaning; or, as Eliot puts it, Milton's language is "conventional"[59]: the words are used with their ordinary meaning. But, as he observes in the dissertation, in really great imaginative work "terms are used with more or other than their normal meaning."[60]

We are trying to show that the two Milton essays are of a piece with the rest of the critical prose. In particular, they are an extension of the argument of "The Metaphysical Poets," the elements of which appear in other reviews written at that time, collected and uncollected. Eliot during this period was engaged with the Elizabethan and Jacobean poets, and his reviews show his preoccupation with the formula that would define this poetry and distinguish it from the poetry of subsequent periods. What happened was that "in the seventeenth century a dissociation of sensibility set in . . . ; and this dissociation . . . was aggravated by the influence of . . . Milton and Dryden."[61] Eliot mentions this theory in both of the Milton essays, thus linking the essays with the theory. The main argument is given in "Milton I," and is restated in brief form in "Milton II," with the qualification that what is great in Milton's work is the versification.

In "Milton I," comparing Milton with Shakespeare, he finds that in "the verse of Shakespeare . . . the auditory imagination and the imagination of the other senses are more nearly fused, and fused together with the thought." In Milton's verse this quality of sensuous thought shows itself in the organization of the sound. But the sound in Milton's verse is one thing, and the thought another. Moreover, there is "the hypertrophy of the

auditory imagination at the expense of the visual and the tactile."
Milton's sensuousness is all in the sound, the "*noise.*" And the
complication of sound is "joined" to the thought, which is "simplified" and "abstract" (it is "not a particular ploughman,
milkmaid, and shepherd that Milton sees . . . ; the sensuous effect of these verses is entirely on the ear, and is joined to the
concepts of ploughman, milkmaid, and shepherd"). The consequence is that there is a "dislocation" of sense and thought, so
that "the inner meaning is separated from the surface, and tends
to become something occult," or there is an "interruption between the surface . . . and the core." It is, accordingly, necessary
to read Milton's verse in "two different ways, first solely for the
sound, and second for the sense."[62]

We must turn here to Eliot's doctrine of sensation and
thought as given in the thesis on Bradley. "I have argued . . . that
a 'sensation of color' is a loose expression for a perception of a
colored something. . . . The sensation, I maintain, is always a
way of being conscious of an object."[63] Or sensations "refer" to
objects.

Anything that refers to something other than itself is a symbol, and sensations (or sensory images) are symbols. If I tell you
about some Florida oranges a friend sent me for Christmas, in
thinking of these objects you use whatever sensations (of color,
shape, taste) your experience has provided you with; and different people, and you at different times, will use sensations that
differ in various ways. The oranges are the common point of
reference of all these sensations, but the meaning of the oranges
(a kind of fruit) is distinct from the sensations. We experience the
meaning through the sensations that refer to it.[64]

The white sheet of paper on my desk is an object, and the
object "exists only in a context of experience, of experience with
which it is continuous." If I attend to the object, "sensations
organize themselves around a (logical) point of attention" (a
sheet of writing paper). Eliot uses the term meaning in two ways:
meaning as reference and meaning as object. Further, the sensations are the "real meaning" and the point of attention is the
"logical meaning." Between these two aspects (real and ideal,
particulars and universal) is "mutual reference and implication":

the meaning would not be that meaning without those sensations, and the sensations would not be those sensations without that meaning.[65]

A sensation is always the sensation *of* an object, but the sensation itself is not an object. "A sensation is certainly an object in the sense that it is the object to which it refers; but when we are aware of an object, the sensations through which we come into contact with it do not persist alongside it as independent objects." Thus "the picture which certain masses of color 'imply' is just as 'objective' as the color-sensations, but not objective in the same way; the cognition of the picture means a transition to a different plane of reality. The color-masses have thus transcended themselves, and ceased to be simply objects."[66]

Sensation and meaning are continuous, or as Eliot expresses it in the essay on Milton, "fused." With Shakespeare, the imagination of the senses is fused with the thought. But with Milton we become aware of the sound as an independent object, alongside the object as meaning. Further, since the sound is exploited at the expense of the other senses, there are few sensations with which to qualify and determine the meaning, the result being that the "inner meaning" is separated from the surface, and tends to become something "occult."

Sensations or images are symbols. A symbol always refers to something other than itself; and if it does not refer to one object, it refers to some other object. Just as there are no "floating" ideas, there are no "floating" symbols.

In the Milton essay, Eliot compares Milton with Dante, as well as with Shakespeare, and we quote the following passage from the later Dante essay:

> I do not recommend, in first reading the first canto of the *Inferno*, worrying about the identity of the Leopard, the Lion, or the She-Wolf. It is really better, at the start, not to know or care what they do mean. What we should consider is not so much the meaning of the images, but the reverse process, that which led a man having an idea to express it in images. We have to consider the type of mind which by nature and *practice* tended to express itself in allegory: and for a competent poet, allegory means *clear visual images*. And clear visual images are given much more intensity by having a meaning—we do not need to know what that meaning is, but in our

awareness of the image we must be aware that the meaning is there too. Allegory is only one poetic method, but it is a method which has very great advantages.[67]

No image exists in isolation; and though we may not know to what meaning the image refers, the image always carries a meaning; and the intensity is a function of the fusion of image and meaning.

Let us look briefly at "Swinburne as Poet," where Eliot employs the same argument as in "Milton I," though with a somewhat different twist. He is analyzing the quality of "diffuseness" in Swinburne's poetry, and he quotes some verses of Campion and Shelley in which the words have "a sound-value and at the same time a coherent and comprehensible meaning, and the two things—the musical value and meaning—are two things, not one." (Though sound and meaning are continuous, they are distinct: two things, not one). But in Swinburne "the meaning and the sound are one thing."

> He uses the most general word, because his emotion is never particular, never in direct line of vision, never focused; it is emotion reinforced, not by intensification, but by expansion.
>
> > *There lived a singer in France of old*
> > *By the tideless dolorous midland sea.*
> > *In a land of sand and ruin and gold*
> > *There shone one woman, and none but she.*
>
> You see that Provence is the merest point of diffusion here. Swinburne defines the place by the most general word, which has for him its own value. "Gold," "ruin," "dolorous": it is not merely the sound that he wants, but the vague associations of idea that the words give him. He has not his eye on a particular place. . . . It is, in fact, the word that gives him the thrill, not the object. When you take to pieces any verse of Swinburne, you find always that the object was not there—only the word.[68]

This raises a question about the relation of the critical theory and the philosophy. Thus Richard Wollheim, commenting on the Swinburne essay: "Once again there is some obscurity how this critical theory is to be connected with the philosophy that it seems to parallel: for instance, with such a view as that the symbol 'is continuous with that which it symbolizes.' . . . For what in the critical theory is asserted as a perfection or something to be aimed at, in the philosophical theory is asserted as a necessary fact."[69]

Though there is this obscurity, the critical theory is not inconsistent with the philosophy. For instance, "It is essential to the doctrine which I have sketched that the symbol or sign be not arbitrarily amputated from the object which it symbolizes, as for practical purposes, it is isolated. . . . No symbol, I maintain, is ever a mere symbol, but is continuous with that which it symbolizes. Without words, no object."[70] The key lies in the phrase "for practical purposes." But first we must say something about word and object.

When Eliot speaks of the word or phrase, he means the sound or written marks: "the 'word,' the written sign, or the *vox pretereo nihil.*"[71] The word is constituted of elements of sensation, but the word must be distinguished from the sensations or images discussed above. The latter are "particular perceptions," but there is nothing in perception that corresponds with the word.[72] Thus the word "sunset" is a way of organizing "a set of experiences," the sensations or images through which we enjoy the sunset. The word directs attention to the meaning, but it is not itself a (reference) meaning; or the word denotes the meaning, but it is not a qualification or determination of the meaning.[73]

Objects, then, exist for us in two ways: as "we *intend* an object" and as "we experience an object." In practice, we tend to substitute the verbal symbol for the experience of the object, to handle and use objects "by symbols which merely denote them," forgetting that "their reality is as much in their [real] meaning as in their denotation," and taking it for granted that "they simply are."[74]

This is not unlike Husserl's theory. With Husserl, the mere intention or denotation is an empty awareness, which is filled in with the help of images; and these real elements are distinguished from the meaning they fill in.[75]

The critical prose is certainly ambiguous, just as the philosophy is. Thus in the dissertation, though Eliot cautions us against confusing feeling (immediate experience) with sensation, he sometimes uses these terms interchangeably.[76] Sensation, we may say, is an aspect of feeling.[77] Further, sensation and perception differ "only in degree," for sensation always involves "some degree of crude perception."[78] And perception, being the perception of an object, involves thought—inexplicit thought.

It is necessary to call attention to these ambiguities if we are to understand the character of the critical prose; and it is the same prose in the uncollected pieces as in the collected essays. It is perhaps worth trying to show this. Here, in "A Sceptical Patrician," is Eliot analyzing the "immaturity" of Henry Adams:

> It is probable that men ripen best through experiences which are at once sensuous and intellectual; certainly many men will admit that their keenest ideas have come to them with the quality of a sense-perception; and that their keenest sensuous experience has been "as if the body thought." There is nothing to indicate that Adams's senses either flowered or fruited: he remains little Paul Dombey asking questions.[79]

The experiences are *at once* sensuous and intellectual; and since we use our senses in thinking, it is as if the body thought. Eliot goes on to compare Adams with Henry James, the difference being "the sensuous contributor to the intelligence."

In "In Memory of Henry James," Meredith and Chesterton are "fertile in ideas," evading "sensation and thought"; but James exemplifies what Eliot calls "thinking with our feelings"[80]—or, as he expresses it elsewhere, "thinking through the senses, or of the senses thinking."[81] The mark of James's superior intelligence is his "escape from Ideas";[82] so, according to Bradley, "we escape from ideas, and from mere universals, by a reference to the real which appears in perception."[83]

In "Reflections on Contemporary Poetry" the subject is the ways by which contemporary verse has tried to escape from "the rhetorical, the abstract, the moralizing." Eliot divides the tendency into its American and English currents. "With the American the effect is more usually an arrest at the object in view; the American poet is fearful of betraying any reaction beyond that revealed in the choice and arrangement; the effect is of an ingenious if sometimes perverse visual imagination in complete detachment from any other faculty." Eliot sees here the influence of the Russian novel, with its trick of letting accidental properties "replace the emotion which gave them their importance"; thus with Dostoevsky "the emotion dissolves in a mass of sensational detail."[84] This is "the preoccupation of the accidental."

The English tendency is "to be preoccupied with the trivial" (not invidiously). The influence is that of Wordsworth, with whom "the emotion is of the object and not of human life." Such emotions must be "either vague (as in Wordsworth) or, if more definite, pleasing." But there is another method, different from both, which is more universal: "It is universally human to attach the strongest emotions to definite tokens." When Donne says:

> When my grave is broke up again . . .
>   And he that digs it, spies
> A bracelet of bright hair about the bone

"the feeling and the material symbol preserve exactly their proper proportions." Donne does not "become absorbed in the hair to the exclusion of the original association which made it significant"; nor does he "endow the hair with ghostly or moralistic meaning." He "sees the thing as it is."[85]

In "Tarr," though it is "a commonplace to compare Mr. Lewis to Dostoevsky," it is the differences that "must be insisted upon." Lewis's interest in his characters is "wholly intellectual," and he interests himself "directly in sensation for its own sake." "The direct contact with the senses, perception of the world of immediate experience with its own scale of values, is like Dostoevsky, but there is always the suggestion of a purely intellectual curiosity in the senses which will disconcert many readers of the Russian novelist"—the absence, that is, of emotion.[86]

In "Reflections on Contemporary Poetry," Jean de Bosschère, in *The Closed Door*, is an "intellectual," not because he goes in for "abstract thought" but because of his "refusal to adulterate his poetic emotions with human emotions"—"he aims directly at emotions of art." But Eliot is uncertain about some of the poems, for he is not always "able to follow the development of [the] images into a logical structure."[87]

In "Beyle and Balzac," Eliot quotes Saintsbury's definition of Balzac's work as the "*union* of Imagination with Observation." But the great artists "do not unite imagination with observation." In a writer like Dostoevsky, imaginative "flights" are "projections,

continuations, of the actual, the observed"; they are "an extension of reality." In the great artist imagination becomes "a fine
and delicate tool for an operation on the sensible world."[88]

In a piece titled "Observations," reviewing an anthology containing the work of Mina Loy and Marianne Moore, Eliot writes:

> [Loy's] "Human Cylinders" is not so good; she needs the support of
> the image, even if only as the point of departure; in this poem she
> becomes abstract, and the word separates from the thing. Miss
> Moore is utterly intellectual, but not abstract; the word never parts
> from the feeling; her ideas, imageless, remain quite personal. Even
> in Laforgue there are unassimilated fragments of metaphysics and,
> on the other hand, of sentiments floating about; I will not assert that
> Miss Moore is as interesting in herself as Laforgue, but the fusion of
> thought and feeling is perhaps more complete.[89]

In regard to Marianne Moore, the point (or so much of it as
we can note here) is that language is a development of feeling as
well as of thought. Thus in the dissertation: "It is not true that
language is simply a development of our ideas; it is a development
of reality as well"—and "the real . . . is felt. 'To find reality we
must betake ourselves to feeling.'" Similarly, in the essay on
Massinger: "But every vital development of language is a development of feeling as well."[90] In Massinger, however, there is "the
decay of the senses," so that his verse "seems to lead us away from
feeling altogether." He dealt "not with emotions so much as with
the social abstractions of emotions," or his feeling is "simple and
overlaid with received ideas."[91] But Marianne Moore felt or
experienced her ideas, so that they remain personal. Thus in the
dissertation, recalling a phrase of Eucken's, *"Es gibt keine
Privatwahrheiten* [There are no private truths]," Eliot says: "But I
should reverse the decision, and say: 'All significant truths are
private truths. As they become public they cease to become
truths; they become facts, or at best, part of the public character;
or at worse, catchwords.'"[92] They become, in this sense, impersonal, so that, as with Massinger, "the defect is precisely a defect
of personality."[93]

Here, to conclude, is a passage from a "London Letter" in
The Dial:

The strongest, like Mr. Joyce, make their feeling into an articulate external world; what might crudely be called a more feminine type, when it is also a very sophisticated type, makes its art by feeling and by contemplating the feeling, rather than the object which has excited it or the object into which the feeling might be made. Of this type of writing the recent book of sketches by Mrs. Woolf, Monday or Tuesday, is the most extreme example. A good deal of the secret of the charm of Mrs. Woolf's shorter pieces consists in the immense disparity between the object and the train of feeling which it has set in motion. Mrs. Woolf gives you the minutest datum, and leads you on to explore, quite consciously, the sequence of images and feelings which float away from it. The result is something which makes Walter Pater appear an unsophisticated rationalist, and the writing is often remarkable. The book is one of the most curious and interesting examples of a process of dissociation which in that direction, it would seem, cannot be exceeded.[94]

7

The Dissociation of Sensibility

Eliot speaks, in "Milton II," of his astonishment at the "success in the world" of his phrase "dissociation of sensibility"—as well as the phrase "objective correlative." It is worth seeing, in view of its "success," what can be done by way of resolving the question of the "dissociation of sensibility."

Its success has, indeed, been astonishing. Thus, for instance, Rosemond Tuve, in *Elizabethan and Metaphysical Imagery*, says of the essay on the Metaphysical Poets that "it has had an influence upon modern criticism of the early seventeenth century which is quite incalculable."[1] The essay has given rise to articles and books both defending and attacking Eliot's theory, the argument often taking the form of "criticism" versus "scholarship"—all of it conducted without reference to Eliot's Bradleyan philosophy.

The question has two aspects, literary and historical; and in "Milton II," speaking of the historical aspect, Eliot says:

> I believe that the general affirmation represented by the phrase "dissociation of sensibility" . . . retains some validity; but I now incline to agree . . . that to lay the burden on the shoulders of Milton and Dryden was a mistake. If such a dissociation did take place, I suspect that the causes are too complex and too profound to justify our accounting for the change in terms of literary criticism. All we can say is, that something like this did happen . . . that we must seek the causes in Europe, not in England alone; and for

what these causes were, we may dig and dig until we get to a depth at which words and concepts fail us.[2]

Commentators, stopping short of that point, have found the cause in Hobbes or in Bacon or more generally in the triumph of the scientific revolution or in that of the Protestant ethos. But this search for causes has been the *ignis fatuus* of a generation of literary history. For the "dissociation of sensibility" is not a historical theory, in the sense of a generalization from historical facts; it is a philosophic theory applied to the history of English poetry— and, as an aesthetic, to literature without distinction of genre or of time and place.

If we seek the causes in England, we may find them in Locke; or if in Europe, in Descartes, or, to dig deeper, in Aristotle (to go no further)—the Aristotle of the representation theory (words are signs of thoughts, and thoughts are signs of things, which are independent of thought).[3] But this division of experience is not a historical event. "Immediate experience . . . is a timeless unity which is not as such present any*where* or to any*one*."[4] Within this unity there is no beginning or end, except as hypothetical limits.

The causes, then, are not to be found in history, and the historical influence of Milton and Dryden is no longer maintained. What remains is the philosophic theory, with its literary application.

The application is sometimes very curious, as in "Donne in Our Time" (1931), where Eliot writes:

> In his whole temper, indeed, Donne is the antithesis of the scholastic, of the mystic and of the philosophical system maker. The encyclopaedic ambitions of the schoolmen were directed always towards unification. . . . In Donne, there is a manifest fissure between thought and sensibility, a chasm which in his poetry he bridged in his own way, which was not the way of medieval poetry. His learning is just information suffused with emotion, or combined with emotion not essentially relevant to it.[5]

Though Eliot now sees in Donne a "fissure" between thought and sensibility, he is still speaking about Donne in the same terms. There is, then, a change of opinion, but no change in theory.

Unification was "a category of medieval thought," and this

unification was "alien to Donne." The unification was "the assumption of an ideal unity in experience," "a unity in existence, a relation of ideal to real, which was not beyond the mind of man to trace in its outlines."[6] In the dissertation, "Within the whole which is experience and is reality there is a distinction of real and ideal . . . : a distinction which turns out to be appearance and not real, inasmuch as the real is largely ideal, and the ideal is also real." For "ultimately the world is completely real or completely ideal, and ideality and reality turn out to be the same."[7] This unity is, to be sure, an ideal limit of experience, but it is not beyond the mind of man to trace in its outlines. And that is all Bradley claimed: to trace it "in its outline"; "to gain an idea of its main features—an idea true so far as it goes, though abstract and incomplete."[8]

Real and ideal (sense and thought) are distinct but inseparable aspects of experience. The relation is that of symbol to symbolized, the sensible world being a sign of the ideal world of meaning, which is nonetheless objective for being ideal. Sensible experience is completed by self-transcendence, and the world of thought is inaccessible apart from sense, which is a condition of that world. The main negative argument of the dissertation is directed against the division of these aspects into "two separate groups of objects" (mental and extramental).[9] This brings us to the parallel of Donne with Descartes, with whom the division is especially marked.

> [Donne's] attitude towards philosophic notions in his poetry may be put by saying that he was more interested in *ideas* themselves as objects than in the *truth* of ideas. In an odd way, he almost anticipates the philosopher of the coming age, Descartes, as in his sixth Meditation:
>
> *Je conçois donc, aisément, que l'imagination se peut faire de cette sorte, s'l est vrai qu'il y ait des corps; et parce que je ne puis rencontrer aucune autre voie pour expliquer comment elle se fait, je conjecture de là probablement qu'il y en a; mais ce n'est que probablement; et quoique j'examine soigneusement toutes choses, je ne trouve pas néanmoins que, de cette idée distincte de la nature corporelle que j'ai en mon imagination, je puisse tirer aucun argument qui conclue avec necessité l'existence de quelque corps.*

I do not mean to suggest that this is a theory to which Donne would immediately have subscribed. But it is a curious parallel: to be interested in philosophies for their own sake, apart from their degree of truth, is not a medieval attitude.[10]

It *is* a curious parallel. To begin with, all that the passage from the *Meditations* indicates is that Descartes brought a sceptical attitude to his inquiries into the physical world, whereas for the Schoolmen, as for Aristotle, the physical world was something given and not questioned. But Descartes questions only to show that we cannot rely for our knowledge of the external world on sense and imagination, but must have recourse to judgment and intellection. Yet Eliot speaks of this rationalistic theory as being interested in *ideas* for their own sake, apart from their degree of truth. For Eliot, the division into mental and external objects is a "clumsy substitute" for degrees of truth and reality;[11] and his meaning is that psychology is interested in *ideas* apart from their reference, whereas logic and metaphysics are interested in their truth or meaning.

Descartes, in the "Sixth Meditation," begins by distinguishing between "imagination and pure intellection [or conception]." For instance, one can "think of a chiliagon" but one "cannot imagine" it. And he goes on to say (this is the sentence directly preceding the words quoted by Eliot): "Thus this method of thinking [imagination] only differs from pure intellection in that the mind, in conceiving, turns somehow toward itself and considers some one of the ideas which it possesses in itself, whereas in imagining it turns toward the body and considers in the latter something conformable to the idea which it has either thought of by itself or perceived through the senses." In the "Third Meditation," speaking of "images of objects," he says: "Now as far as ideas [images] are concerned, if we consider them only in themselves and do not relate them to something else, they cannot, properly speaking, be false; for whether I imagine a sage or a satyr, it is no less true that I imagine the one than the other."[12] Descartes, then, is interested in *ideas* in themselves as objects— as though they had a purely psychological existence.

This is not, Eliot says, a medieval attitude, and he continues:

Donne was, I insist, no sceptic: it is only that he is interested in and amused by ideas in themselves, and interested in the way in which he *feels* an idea; almost as if it were something that he could touch and stroke. To turn the attention to the mind in this way is a kind of creation, because the objects alter by being observed so curiously. To contemplate an idea, because it is present for the moment in my own mind, to observe my emotion color it, and to observe it color my emotions, to play with it, instead of using it as a plain and simple meaning, brings often odd or beautiful objects to light, as a deep sea diver inspects the darting and crawling life of the depths; though it may lend itself, this petting and teasing of one's mental objects, to extremities of torturing of language. . . . But the usual course for Donne is not to pursue the meaning of the idea, but . . . to develop it dialectically, to extract every minim of emotion suspended in it. And as to the poetic justification of this method of dialectic I have no doubts.[13]

There is transformation, by which the poet fabricates something new, something rich and strange; but it is only "a kind of creation." Thus, in the dissertation:

To say that one part of the mind suffers and another part reflects upon the suffering is perhaps to talk in fictions. But we know that those highly-organized beings who are able to objectify their passions, and as passive spectators to contemplate their joys and torments, are also those who suffer and enjoy the most keenly.[14]

The fiction is that of introspection. But the passions here are not mental objects but real objects in the world of objects. And though this is not a medieval attitude, it is an attitude justified by Bradley's aesthetics. Thus Eliot, in the earlier Dante essay:

Without doubt, the effort of the philosopher proper, the man who is trying to deal with ideas in themselves, and the effort of the poet, who may be trying to *realize* ideas, cannot be carried on at the same time. . . . The poet can deal with philosophic ideas, not as matter for argument, but as matter for inspection. . . . But poetry can be penetrated by a philosophic idea, it can deal with this idea when it has reached the point of immediate acceptance, when it has become almost a physical modification.[15]

Though Donne "*feels* an idea, almost as if it were something that he could touch and stroke," he is interested in the idea itself rather than in its reference, and his emotion is, accordingly, irrelevant: unrelated to an "external" object.

In regard to the technique of verse, Donne's affinity is less to the "school of Donne" than to Browning, Laforgue, and Corbière.

> Browning . . . is perhaps *too* objective, without having that large and intricate pattern which objectivity requires: Donne, Corbière, Laforgue begin with their own feelings, and their limitation is that they do not always get much outside or beyond; Shakespeare, one feels, arrives at an objective world by a process from himself, who-ever he was, as the center and starting point; but too often, one thinks with Browning, here is a world with no particular interesting man inside it, no consistent point of view. But the verse method, in all these four men, is similar: either dramatic monologue or drama-tic dialogue; and with Donne and the French poets, the pattern is given by what goes on within the mind, rather than by the exterior events which provoke the mental activity and play of thought and feeling.[16]

There are two contexts, Shakespeare being construed ac-cording to Eliot's philosophy and Donne and the French poets according to popular theory (a common external world and pri-vate inner worlds), a theory repudiated by the philosophy. This pattern of two contexts, positive and negative, underlies much of the critical prose, and it is the pattern of the philosophy.

Eliot's prose is like his verse in this respect: it cannot be paraphrased but only elucidated. But, roughly, Browning does not feel his thought, so that he is *too* objective—impersonal; Donne and the French poets tend to be personal—or, as Eliot says elsewhere of Donne, he is a "personality," concerned with "self-expression"; but Shakespeare is a finite center ("center of feeling" or "center of experience"), and there is a transition from feeling to objectivity, though who Shakespeare was we cannot say, for he varies by self-transcendence.

Though the problems are considerable—sometimes, indeed, they seem intractable—there is nothing problematic about the theoretical basis of the prose. But that is not the accepted view. Let us, then, consider Eliot's relation to Remy de Gourmont, and it will be enough, for our purpose, to examine two treatments of this question: that of F. W. Bateson, in an article with the subtitle

"Dissociation of Sensibility," and that of Glenn S. Burne, in *Remy de Gourmont: His Ideas and Influence in England and America*.

The question is not whether Eliot owes a debt to Gourmont: Eliot has acknowledged the debt, and it is not inconsiderable. He evidently found Gourmont to be a stimulating critic; he borrowed words, phrases, and notions from him; he quoted him in support of his own views. In sum, Gourmont offered (to borrow a phrase of Eliot's) "influences of suggestion."[17] But he did not, as Bateson thinks, provide Eliot with "a *framework* to which his own critical ideas and intuitions . . . were able to attach themselves"; nor did he, as Burne thinks, provide "principles" which Eliot elaborated and applied in his criticism.

Though our subject here is not Gourmont, we must say something about his views if only to show what the problem is. For Gourmont, Symbolism was "the expression of individualism in art";[18] and he sought a justification of individualism in subjective idealism (the world is my representation). Later, though he qualified this position, he seems never to have abandoned it. Philosophy, he came to believe, must be "scientific," which meant for him psychophysiology; and this in his view only led back to (subjective) idealism: so many nervous systems, so many subjective representations of the world, the world itself being unknowable.[19]

The mind is a (material) product of physiology. Everything depends on sensation, starts with it and returns to it (stimulus and response, repeated with modifications). The stages are as follows: "Sensation is transformed into word-images; these into word-ideas; these into word-feelings."[20] That is the framework Gourmont extracted from Hobbes and Locke and from the physiological psychology of his time (*la psychologie positive*) as represented by Taine, Ribot, and others. And the problem of style is "a question of physiology."[21]

An idea is a faded sensation or an effaced image; and when isolated from its sensuous basis it becomes an empty abstraction, attracting and exciting emotion (as in such word-ideas as liberty and justice). This is the abstract (emotive or sentimental) style, in which the sensibility remains "exterior." In the concrete style, the sensibility is incorporated into the writing—and by "sensibility"

Gourmont means, he says, "the general power of feeling."[22] The mark of this style is visual imagery (with some support from the other senses) animated by feeling.

"Sensibility includes reason itself, which is only crystallized sensibility."[23] But thought has no direct contact with life—is not *felt* by the nerve cells. It is valuable only when associated with feeling. In science, thought is dissociated from feeling, all its labor being limited to "the principle of identity";[24] that is, it abstracts from differences, classifies, and notes the relations between things and groups of things—is "sterilized sensibility."[25] Art satisfies the wish to live, and science the wish to know; and these two tendencies deny each other. Gourmont, as a literary critic, was an exponent of "pure" art; and though such art, he held, could not be brought under principles or theories, it is disloyal, he said, to confuse art with rhetoric, or to conceive it as serving the purposes of edification. With Gourmont, "It is undoubtedly a question of doctrines, but what is a doctrine if not the verbal translation of a physiology?"[26]

Now Eliot's idealism has, as he says, a materialistic basis, in substance that of Bosanquet,[27] as stated presumably in *The Principle of Individuality and Value*. Further, with Eliot "structural" psychology "resolves itself into physiology," so that "the mental resolves itself into a curious and intricate mechanism."[28] If, then, Eliot speaks of poets as looking into "the cerebral cortex, the nervous system, and the digestive tracts,"[29] it is because he is "as good a materialist as anybody," though he "would point out what a little way such truths bring us."[30] Bradley, too, in tracing the beginnings of inference, starts with physiology;[31] but Bradley and Eliot do not, like Taine, Ribot, and Gourmont, confuse psychology with physiology;[32] and though, with them, physiology is a condition of knowing, it is not an element in it.

It is not easy in a short space to disentangle Eliot from Gourmont. The trouble is that, though the form of thought is different, the matter is, in certain respects, the same; and if we keep to the purely verbal level, the differences are obscured.

According to Bateson, Eliot took over Gourmont's psychology, and *"dissociation of sensibility"* is a "metaphor" from this psychology. But Eliot soon came to see that the psychology was a ramshackle affair, as is shown by the statement about the fissure in Donne, which reads like "a specific repudiation of the unified sensibility," and by the statement in "Milton II," which, if "not repudiation, neither is it endorsement." In any event, "Gourmont is the *fons et origo* of Mr. Eliot's 'sensuous apprehension of thought'—and so of its modern descendent 'thinking in images.'"[33]

But these locutions are literal transcriptions of philosophic doctrine. It is the same with the statement that Bateson quotes from the essay on Massinger: "With the end of Chapman, Middleton, Webster, Tourneur, Donne we end a period when the intellect was immediately at the tips of the senses." The logical meaning (intellect) *is* at the tips of the senses.

The trouble with Bateson's argument is, as Eric Thompson observes in his reply to Bateson, "a widespread conviction among literary critics . . . that Eliot's criticism exhibits what John Crowe Ransom once called 'theoretical innocence.' " But "Eliot's 'dissociation of sensibility,' " he says, "rests securely on the foundation of Bradley's metaphysics." Nor shall we understand "either the term or the structure [of meaning] by going merely to Remy de Gourmont."[34]

Bateson remained unconvinced. "Mr. Thompson saves the situation . . . only by turning a blind eye on what Eliot actually wrote." "No, the fact must be faced that, however much we dress it up, the Dissociation of Sensibility cannot be made respectable. It's a lovely mouthful, full of sound and fury, but unfortunately it doesn't signify anything."[35]

The merit of Bateson's article is that it directs attention to Eliot's language, but in this case with unhappy results. By *sensibility*, he thinks, Eliot means sensation. "A paradox, therefore, emerges. Sensibility is feeling, i.e. sensation, but it is also *a synthesis of feeling and thinking* (the two elements that are unified in the undissociated sensibility). This is puzzling. If sensibility is sensation, or the faculty of registering sense impressions, how can one of the products of its dissociation be 'thought'? On the other hand, if the unified sensibility is an intellectual as well as a sensuous faculty, how can it be equated with 'feeling'?" For the elucidation of the paradox we must return to Gourmont, for "like Mr. Eliot's, Gourmont's *sensibilité* does and does not include the element of thought. This is because for Gourmont thinking was only a kind of sensation."[36] Again, in his reply to Thompson: "Eliot's feeling ('sensibility') *precedes* thought. It [is] . . . a separate faculty, detached from thought and prior to it."[37] Transposing Eliot's theory to this context, Bateson finds that it does not signify anything.

Eliot's usage is certainly puzzling, but that is a reflection of the philosophy. It was mentioned above that in the dissertation he sometimes uses "feeling" and "sensation" interchangeably, after warning us not to confuse these two terms. Thus: "Subject and object emerge from a state of feeling"; the "transition from sensation to subject-object." Again: "Sensation-in-itself is in the language of Bradley 'feeling' or experience as more original than consciousness; but sensation in itself is not as such capable of being an object of attention (Chapter 1)."[38] The only way in which we can handle feeling intellectually is to turn it into objects; but, though feeling is transcended, it is never analyzed away. "And," Bradley says, "when we seek for a unity which holds together these two aspects of our world, we seem to find given to us nothing but this unity of feeling which is itself transcended."[39]

Bateson rests his case on Eliot's usage—not all but only some of it. And though, as he says, it was not Eliot's habit to use words loosely, Eliot's procedures seem designed to frustrate rather than to facilitate understanding. For instance: "A state, in itself, is nothing whatever"; but the Metaphysical Poets were engaged in trying to find the verbal equivalent for "states of mind and feeling."[40] In the one statement he repudiates popular psychology, and in the other he uses the language of the psychology he repudiates. But is it surprising, given the character of the philosophy, and the limitations of space, that Eliot should resort to popular language? Moreover—and there is irony here—having chosen to preserve his philosophy in cryptogram, he placed himself in a position where he could not reply to charges of inconsistency and self-contradiction; he disavowed any capacity for abstruse thought, thereby doubling the irony.

Bateson, in his reply to Thompson, says that of Bradley's doctrine "there is not . . . the most distant hint."[41] But Eliot does offer hints. For instance, in his preface to Leone Vivante's *English Poetry* (1950): "I ought to call attention to Signor Vivante's speculations on the nature of 'sensation,' and on the isolation of sensation from thought (in which he joins issue with Collingwood)."[42] In "The Idea of a Literary Review": "Pure literature is a chimera of sensation; admit the vestige of an idea and it is already transformed."[43] Elsewhere: "In reading *Hamlet* . . . there is a perfectly clear image of a frosty night, at the beginning; in *Macbeth* there is a clear image of the castle at nightfall where the swallows breed."[44] The image is *of* a frosty night and *of* a castle at nightfall, these being the ideas or (logical) meanings. But the idea is not a faded sensation or an effaced image. Thus, in the dissertation: "And the round square, so far as it is idea (and I do not mean image) is also real."[45]

Bateson writes:

> The word *dissociation* may also derive from Gourmont, with whom it was a favorite, though I have noticed only one example in his writings of the two words in combination. This is the essay called "La Sensibilité de Jules Laforgue" in the first series of the *Promenades Littéraires* (1904). Laforgue's intelligence, Gourmont says in this essay, was closely connected (*liée étroitement*) with his sensibility; he adds that Laforgue died before he had acquired the scepticism which would have enabled him to dissociate his intelligence from his sensibility (*dissocier son intelligence de sa sensibilité*). It is at least possible that this passage may have been at the back of Mr. Eliot's mind when he coined his phrase.[46]

Eliot's "dissociation of sensibility" belongs to one context, and Gourmont's *dissocier son intelligence de sa sensibilité* to another and different one. But there is influence. Thus with Henry Adams, intellectual and sensuous experiences do not go together, and this review is titled "A Sceptical Patrician." "This scepticism is a product, or a cause, or a concomitant, of Unitarianism; it is not destructive, but it is dissolvent."[47] Similarly, the fissure in Donne is related to the scepticism of Descartes. But Donne was not a sceptic in "the modern sense," nor did he know "*doubt* as the modern world has known it." "But he was a sincere churchman not because he has passed through the doubt which his type of mind finds congenial (I say his *type* of mind), but because in theology he has not yet arrived there."[48] Though it is likely that in these utterances there is an influence of suggestion, Eliot's use of the term scepticism, like that of "belief," is independent of Gourmont (as Bateson, I think, would agree).

Burne, alluding to the articles by Bateson and Thompson, says: "But it seems quite probable that more than one source could be involved."[49] But the only "source" he deals with is Gourmont. Eliot, he says, "transferred Gourmont's analysis of the mental processes of the individual to the study of English literary history. That is, the unified sensibility that Gourmont had found in Laforgue, Eliot found in the England of the early seventeenth century."[50]

Still, Burne is not unaware that there are differences between Eliot and Gourmont.

> In his essay on "The Metaphysical Poets" Eliot pursued his early practice of applying Gourmont's words to English writers. He says of Jonson and Chapman, for example, that they "incorporated their erudition into their sensibility: their mode of feeling was directly and freshly altered by their reading and thought. In Chapman especially there is a direct sensuous apprehension of thought, or a recreation of thought into feeling, which is exactly what we find in Donne." At a glance this appears to be pure Gourmont, but in fact it contains certain inversions of thought peculiar to Eliot. Eliot sees his writers as incorporating their erudition into their sensibility. Gourmont would say that their erudition was by an aspect of sensibility—an idea, a thought, *is* a form of sensation. When Eliot speaks of "a direct sensuous apprehension of thought," he is speaking pure Gourmont, but when he speaks of "a recreation of thought into feeling," he is reversing the order of events, as conceived by Gourmont in his three-stage theory of creation. . . . This reverse process is also evident in Eliot's remarks about Laforgue, Corbière, and Baudelaire: "They have the same essential quality of transmuting ideas into sensations . . . Gourmont would say that an idea . . . *is* a sensation.[51]

Burne does well in calling attention to "certain inversions of thought peculiar to Eliot." These are expressions of the doctrine that "feeling becomes object and object becomes feeling,"[52] about which something must now be said.

Subject and object emerge from a state of feeling and are set apart by a distinction, the not-self being opposed to the self. Now there is little, if anything, that belongs exclusively to one side or the other. Thus everything I experience (sensation, emotion, idea) is felt; and, on the other hand, I can think of everything I feel: can make an object of it, or use it to qualify some object; and anything handled in this way becomes a not-self. But we cannot always have before us the objects we think about, altogether and at once. What, then, is to be said about the objects that are not now before us? They have passed, Bradley says, into the back-ground of feeling, from which they are detached, and this means that they have for the time passed into the self. In short, there is "dislocation," the elements on both sides being for the most part "interchangeable." Thus the content of feeling shows mediation, for parts of this content may at some time have been distin-guished into terms and relations, and have been included in the object; but nonetheless this relational content now forms part of my feeling.[53] Bosanquet, dealing with the same point, says that when an object passes into immediacy it carries with it "the marks of thought and the stamp of objective relations," so that "sensa-tion is full of the 'work of thought.' " And he adds: "We cannot separate sensation from thought, and it is not sensation only that can become immediate."[54]

In Eliot's words, "new transpositions of objectivity and feel-ing [are] constantly developing,"[55] or, as in the literary version: ideas are transmuted into sensations, thought is re-created into feeling, feeling is altered by reading and thought, erudition is incorporated into sensibility—all curiously exact renderings of the philosophic doctrine.

Gourmont, it is agreed, was an influence; but to study the influence on the assumption that Eliot was an unphilosophic critic only serves to complicate misunderstanding. For instance, Burne writes that Eliot's "insistence on the identity of thought and sensation" is like Gourmont's, though "he does not give this conception the extreme emphasis that Gourmont did."[56] But this conception is not Eliot's, and to use it as a basis for comparing and contrasting Eliot and Gourmont is gratuitous. Similarly, "The artistic experience is composed of two elements: emotions and feelings. . . . It is evident . . . that Eliot is using the latter word in the sense of 'sensation,' in a manner comparable to Gourmont's."[57] That is a typical illustration of how Eliot "takes up" and "extends" an idea of Gourmont's. But the idea is Brad-ley's and not Gourmont's.

Suppose that Eliot were to write: "I do not believe in any

knowledge which is independent of feeling and sensation. On sensation and feeling I am sure that we depend for the material of our knowledge."[58] To Burne it would be evident that Eliot was here restating Gourmont. Or, to quote Bradley again: "And so, in the end, to know the Universe, we must fall back upon personal experience and sensation."[59] Burne would observe that, though the universe was unknowable for Gourmont, we see here what appears to be a direct borrowing from Gourmont.

Let us consider some instances of what Burne calls "direct reference to the authority of Gourmont." In the essay on Massinger Eliot speaks of great literature as "the transformation of a personality into a personal work of art." And he goes on to quote two passages from *Problème du Style*: "La vie est un dépouillement. Le but de l'activité propre de l'homme est de nettoyer sa personnalité, de la laver de toutes les souillures qu'y déposa l'éducation, de la dégager de toutes les empreintes qu'y laissèrent nos admirations adolescentes"; and again: "Flaubert incorporait toute sa sensibilité à ses oeuvres. . . . Hors de ses livres, où il se transvasait goutte à gouette, jusqu'à la lie, Flaubert est fort peu intéressant."[60]

The idea is Bradley's, and the passages from Gourmont are suggestive analogies. Thus, in the dissertation, " 'My' feeling is certainly in a sense mine. But this is because and in so far as I *am* the feeling."[61] The "I" is the self in the sense of "this-mine": a finite center or unity of feeling. But everything the self feels, including organic sensation and pleasure and pain, may be objectified; and in the process the elements are transformed ("so far as it is taken as a feature in any whole beyond itself, it has to change its character").[62] With poets, the process of objectification is, as Eliot says, "their lifetime's work, long or short." In this way, the poet incorporates his sensibility into his works, transmutes himself, drop by drop. But here the self is not the self of Gourmont; and indeed self-transcendence, or ideality, is alien to Gourmont.

Again, in "The Perfect Critic" Eliot begins with an epigraph from Gourmont: "Eriger en lois ses impressions personnelles, c'est le grand effort d'un homme s'il est sincère."[63]

In the text, the moment you try to put the impression into words you begin "to analyze and construct, to 'eriger en lois.' "

So Swinburne's criticism is "in the direction of analysis and construction, a beginning to 'eriger en lois.'" But the exemplary critic is Aristotle, and the *Poetics* is an example of "intelligence itself swiftly operating the analysis of sensation to the point of principle and definition."[64]

For Bradley, intelligence is the operation of analysis and synthesis in one. And Eliot says, writing about Aristotle: "The form is always ἄτομον (indivisible); thought analyzes and resynthesizes its constituents to give the λόγος τοῦ τί ἦν εἶναι (the reason for a thing being what it is)"—that is, the definition of a thing.[65] Eliot, as was noted earlier, refers to the opening phrases of the *Posterior Analytics*, which read as follows: "All instruction given or received by way of argument proceeds from pre-existent knowledge. This becomes evident upon a survey of all the species of instruction."[66] With Aristotle, demonstration presupposes certain data that are apprehended by intuitive thought—intellectual or conceptual vision. The data are certain "intelligibles": forms, *infimae species*, essential natures. Each of these specific types is an individual unity. But these unities can be unfolded by analysis and synthesis—can be expanded in the form of definitions. And it is in this form that they are used in the discursive reasoning of the man of science.[67]

With Eliot, the preexistent knowledge is immediate experience or feeling (a doctrine which, according to Bradley, is implicit in Aristotle)—or, as we may say, feelings and impressions, that is, the empirical experience of the plain man. Thus everyone experiences the aspect of the world as extended. But the man of science—the Euclidean geometer—expands this common spatial experience into definitions of plane figure and its differentiations. In this way he establishes the objects with which geometry deals and the meaning of these objects—the terms employed in geometry.

Though a species of instruction presupposes the intuitive experience of the objects it deals with, it does not begin with direct, unmediated experience. It is only after the intellect has operated on feelings and impressions that the starting point of a discipline is arrived at. Principles and definitions are not feelings and impressions but intellectual objects. As Bradley says: "We needs must begin our voyage of reasoning by working on something which is felt and not thought. . . . Before reasoning exists, there must come an operation which serves to transform this crude material; and this operation is both analytical and synthetical."[68]

All instruction, then, given or received by way of argument presupposes preexistent knowledge. The point of the instruction (so to speak) is this: Our ordinary experience of space is vague and obscure; but in geometry this vague experience is translated into something definite and precise. Accordingly, if we wish to understand our spatial experience, we must go to geometry, which is the articulation of this experience—the experience rendered explicitly intelligible.

In the language of Eliot's dissertation, the direct experience is a *that* and the geometrical object a *what*. "It continues to be the same *that* but with very different qualities: and the truth in question is found by continually analyzing the given and widening its relations. . . . Whether we may say that this is a new world or not is a matter of practical convenience. But we do *intend* it to be the same, and we feel that it is the reality which we failed at first to grasp. The cruder and vaguer, or more limited, is somehow contained and explained in the wider and more precise."[69]

This brings us to the epigraph which introduces section II of "The Perfect Critic": "L'écrivain de style abstrait est presque toujours un sentimental, du moins un sensitif. L'écrivain artiste n'est presque jamais un sentimental, et très rarement un sensitif."[70]

We may note first what Eliot calls the "confused distinction which exists in most heads between 'abstract' and 'concrete.' "[71] In popular thought, sense and feeling are concrete, and thought is abstract. But, as we have seen, the sensuous experience of space is crude and vague—abstract—whereas in geometry space is determinate and precise—concrete. The paradox is, as Bradley says, that " 'knowledge advances from the abstract [sensuous object] to the concrete' [intellectual object]. . . . In becoming more abstract, we gradually reach a wider realm of ideas; which is thus not sensibly but intellectually concrete. What is abstract for one world is concrete in the other."[72]

There are two ways, Eliot says, in which a word may be "abstract." One way is "verbalism" or "the abstract style in criticism." As for the other, "It may have (the word 'activity,' for example) a meaning which cannot be grasped by appeal to any of the senses; its apprehension may require a deliberate suppression of analogies of visual or muscular experience, which is none the less an effort of imagination. 'Activity' will mean for the trained scientist, if he employ the term, either nothing at all or something still more exact than anything it suggests to us."[73]

According to Bradley, "imagination is not confined to particular images," and "in much imagination we shall find the presence of a discursive element. The idea of a circle, we might say and say falsely, was nothing but an image; but the idea of a chiliagon would show us at once that there is a point where our imagery fails."[74]

Bradley, examining the word activity as employed to mean "force, energy, power," concludes that "activity, under any of the phrases used to carry that idea, is a mass of inconsistency." Its meaning, then, "fails to exhibit itself intelligibly,"[75] so that, as Eliot says, it will mean "nothing at all." For Eliot, the word means "ideal activity" or "ideal construction," or, as Bradley gives it, the "one common process of analysis and synthesis."[76] But this idea is not, Bradley says, "ultimate," or, as Eliot puts it, is not "possible in any sense."[77] This is the word Eliot chose as an example of a meaning which, though "abstract," requires for its grasp an "effort of imagination."

Let us consider one last example of the way in which, according to Burne, Eliot was influenced by Gourmont. Burne, quoting Gourmont to the effect that "esthetic or moral judgments are only generalized sensations," says that Eliot "expands and deepens this concept,"[78] and he goes on to quote (in part) the following passage:

Appreciation in popular psychology is one faculty, and criticism another, an arid cleverness building theoretical scaffolds upon one's own perceptions or those of others. On the contrary, the true generalization is not something superposed upon an accumulation of perceptions; the perceptions do not, in a really appreciative mind, accumulate as a mass, but form themselves as a structure; and criticism is the statement in language of this structure; it is a development of sensibility.[79]

Reasoning, Bradley writes, "has been compared to a scaffolding, which is removed when the edifice of reason has been built."[80] Knowledge, in this metaphor, is like a building, a superstructure resting on a foundation of bricks. The bricks are the facts, and the function of thought is to order and arrange the facts. Since the facts are given independently of thought, and are real because independent, thought makes no difference to the facts. It is simply a scaffolding which, when the edifice has been built, is removed. But the metaphor is inapplicable, for what gives stability to a body of knowledge is not a foundation of independent facts but the coherence of the knowledge. It is stable "not so far as it is a superstructure but so far as in short it is a system."[81]

The facts are the data of sensible perception, the particulars, and inductive generalization goes from the particular to the general. The generalization is superposed upon a collection of particular instances, all of which are alike in having a common property that is arrived at by abstracting from the differences. The instances being repetitions of the same sort of thing, the generalization simply says that what is true of one is true of the others. It leads, accordingly, to nothing new—is an arid cleverness. But in an appreciative mind the perceptions constitute a structure (system), in the sense of a synthesis of differences, which is a new organization. These are two ways of ordering experience, the difference being, as Bosanquet expresses it, between the "true Inductive generalization as consisting in the range of differing data . . . welded into a system . . . as contrasted with the number of recurring cases which may fall under a single abstract statement."[82]

Eliot's logic is neither that of induction nor that of deduction, and the true inductive generalization is not the induction of popular thought. It is the articulation of an identity in and by analysis and construction. Further, the perceptions *form themselves* as a structure; that is, the process is a "self-development"; and that, according to Bradley, is the condition of its validity.[83]

The principles Eliot is transcribing are very general, and they apply, with a difference, to every type of experience. To speak only of poetry and criticism, these are "two directions of sensibility."[84] Thus Swinburne is "one man in his poetry and a different man in his criticism; to this extent and in this respect only, that he is satisfying a different impulse."[85] Every effort to "eriger en lois" proceeds by ideal construction; that is, what generalizes is the operation of analysis and synthesis. Since these are two sides of one process, "the more deeply you analyze a given whole, the wider and larger you make its unity; and the more elements you join in a synthetic construction, so much greater is the detail and more full the differentiation of that totality."[86]

Though the construction of wholes or structures is not arbitrary, there are no rules or formulas for it (and being neither induction nor deduction, it does not figure in orthodox logic).[87] But there is a criterion: in Bradley's words, "coherence and comprehensiveness . . . the two aspects of system";[88] or, as Eliot puts it in his philosophic prose, "completeness and cohesion."[89] In the literary version, "There are two considerations about *order*. One is the amount of material organized, and the degree of difficulty of that material; the other is the completeness of the organization. Rimbaud, for instance, may have the vision of a larger organization than Valéry's: but it is not so achieved."[90] Or, to quote one of various other versions, in reading the plays of Shakespeare we must consider "the degree of unification . . . and the elaborateness of the pattern of unification."[91]

8

The Use of Principles

Communication, according to Eliot, will not explain poetry, nor, it seems, will it explain Eliot's view of prose. Eliot was not unaware of this. "The reader may well, by now, have been asking himself what I have been up to in all these speculations. Have I been toiling to weave a labored web of useless ingenuity? Well, I have been trying to talk, not to myself—as you may have been tempted to think—but to the reader of poetry."[1] The effect is indeed that of a man talking to himself. And in this respect the prose is like the first voice of poetry, the voice of the poet talking to himself—or to nobody.

Again: "I was determined . . . to conceal the origins so well that nobody would identify them until I pointed them out myself. In this at least I have been successful; for no one of my acquaintance (and no dramatic critics) recognized the source of my story. . . . In fact, I have had to go into detailed explanation to convince them."[2] There is the same problem in the origin of the literary theory.

One of the difficulties is the discrepancy in the critical work between the external form and the inner content. The form—reviews, prefaces, essays, lectures—suggests the empirical critic writing *ad hoc*; but the critical pieces are informed by a definite theory, and it is this that binds them together. I do not mean that there is anything systematic about the critical writing: much of it had its origins in books sent for review, and much is no doubt "workshop" criticism. But there is also a consistent point of view, and an internal structure—connections and relations between the various pieces. In one essay, for instance, an impression needs to take its place in a system of impressions, and in an appreciative mind the perceptions form themselves as a structure; in another essay, in the mind of the poet experiences are always forming new wholes. These are different ways of saying the same thing, and what is said applies to both poetry and criticism. This sort of thing occurs throughout the critical work. And though it is not always obvious, to attempt to show it in every instance in which it occurs would leave the reader with a sense of *déjà vu*. And yet our primary concern in this study is with Eliot's style, his procedures in transcribing his philosophy for critical purposes; and we cannot show that without risking a certain amount of repetition.

In the passage about the true generalization—to return for a moment to that—Eliot is contrasting two types of organization: that of the abstract universal and that of the concrete universal. In the true generalization, the deeper the analysis, the wider the range of experiences that is unified. In other words, intension and extension go together: "the increase of one must add to the other." And this, Bradley says, is the antipodes of the doctrine of orthodox logic according to which intension and extension vary inversely: "The less you happen to have of the one, the more you therefore must have of the other," a doctrine which is "either false or frivolous."[3]

As Eliot puts it, in "Experiment in Criticism," the intension and the extension do not fit:

> Now, there is an urgent need for experiment in criticism of a new kind, which will consist largely in a logical and dialectical study of the terms used. . . . We are constantly using terms which have an *in*tension and an *ex*tension which do not quite fit; theoretically they ought to be made to fit; but if they cannot, then some other way must be found of dealing with them so that we may know at every moment what we mean. I will take a very simple example with which I have been dealing myself: the possibility of defining "metaphysical poetry." Here is a term which has a whole history of meanings down to the present time, all of which must be recognized, although it cannot have all of them at once. The term means

on the one hand a certain group of English poets in the seventeenth century. On the other hand it must have an intensive meaning, must stand for a peculiar whole of qualities which is exemplified by the several poets. The ordinary critical method would be to define what "metaphysical poetry" means to you in the abstract, fit as many poets to it as well as you can, and reject the rest. Or else, you take the poets who have been held to be "metaphysical," and find out what they have in common. The odd thing is that by doing the sum, so to speak, in two different ways, you get two different results. . . . Such problems involve, of course, both logic and the theory of knowledge and psychology; there is no one, perhaps, more concerned with them than Mr. I. A. Richards, the author of *Principles of Literary Criticism* and *Practical Criticism*.[4]

There is little to indicate the logical bias of this passage; and the reference to Richards is a characteristic touch.

The question concerns the logical use of a general or class term, its connotation (so called) and denotation. Now for Bradley what in orthodox logic is called a class is an identity in diversity and a diversity in identity. To quote Eliot again on these principles: "Identity, we have learned, is nowhere bare identity, but must be identity in diversity. If we are hit on the head with a club, the club is only 'the same' because it has appeared in two different contexts. There are two different experiences, and the sameness is quite ideal."[5]

Knowledge is knowledge of objects; and, as Eliot says, if anything is to be an object, "it must present identity in difference throughout a span of time."[6] Identity apart from difference is nothing whatever, and difference apart from identity is meaningless (an unrelated disparateness). The identity, since it persists throughout its differences, is a universal, but a universal which is always more or less concrete, according to the degree of its articulation.

These principles apply to every type of object, no matter what. And in what follows we shall consider some of the uses that Eliot makes of these principles.

In "The Music of Poetry" (1942) he begins by speaking of the accepted rules of scansion, remarking that he could never learn from these rules why one line was good and another bad. These rules were established by grammarians for the purpose of studying a dead language; and since a language when living is always in process of change, any "classification of meters" offers only a simplified map of a complicated territory. Or, as he also expresses it, the "analytic study of metric" deals with "abstract forms" which sound extraordinarily different when handled by different poets. In short, "a system of prosody is only a formulation of identities in the rhythms of a succession of poets influenced by each other."[7]

The organization of sound, as we have seen, is the work of the intellect. Further, Eliot speaks, typically, of the "poetic process"; and with him product and process are inseparable, so that organization may be regarded from the side of process or from the side of product. As Bradley says, "It is not in principle alone that analysis and synthesis are essentially one, but in practice also their unity tends to show itself in the product."[8] The sound of a poem is a differentiated identity, single in its complexity, a whole made explicit by distinction and relation.

The analytic method cannot exhibit the character of such an individual whole. Its procedure is to divide the sound into syllables; classify them as long and short; group them into patterns; and formulate rules for their number, kind, and arrangement. Both the syllables and the patterns are treated as mutually exclusive units, the whole consisting of recurring identities. The grammarian, in the same way, analyzes the structural unity of a sentence into nouns, verbs, and modifiers. What is left out in this classification is the organization of the sentence: the aspect of differences in and of an identity. Briefly, the analytic method construes identity as excluding difference. As Russell says, "There is no identity in difference, there is identity and there is difference."[9]

Thus far we have been discussing the sound by itself. But sound and sense are "indissoluble," and either taken by itself is an "abstraction."[10] It should, however, be noted that the sound itself makes sense: sound, that is to say, is symbolic. For example, hearing footsteps in the hall, one may refer them to one's wife, or to some other member of the family, or, failing to recognize them, assume the presence of a stranger. The point is that fresh combinations of sound, in new wholes, produce fresh meanings. These are highly fugitive meanings, indefinite references, connected largely with emotions. They are not paraphrasable, but belong to the region of awareness where (in one sense of Eliot's language) words fail, though meanings still exist.[11]

Of the "music of a word," Eliot says that it is, "so to speak, at the point of intersection: it arises from its relation first to the words immediately preceding and following it, and indefinitely to the rest of its context; and from another relation, that of its immediate meaning in that context to all the other meanings which it has had in other contexts." As a consequence of this last relation, "a word can be made to insinuate the whole history of a language and a civilization," and this is "an allusiveness which is in the nature of words."[12]

It is a commonplace to say that the meaning of a word is determined by, and varies with, its context. But the meaning accruing to a word from its relations in a context cannot be represented by a common predicate of terms in a class. Eliot's "point of intersection" is Bradley's "point of identity": the identity of diverse relations. A word exists only in a context, and the meaning acquired in one context is carried into another context, and with each new context the meaning grows increasingly complex. This development of a word is the extension of its intension. In short, there is enlargement by a synthesis of differences. And if we try to determine the meaning by removing the differences and leaving the identity, we find that when the differences are all gone, the identity is gone too.[13]

Let us consider this logic as expressed in *The Aims of Education* (1950). In the first of these lectures, "Can 'Education' Be Defined?" Eliot introduces an elaborate excursion titled "Notes towards the Definition of Runcibility," or "MacTaggart Refuted"; and he applies the point he is making to the word *education*.

The late John MacTaggart, Eliot says, was a philosopher who enjoyed a considerable reputation in his day. "I have never read any of his works, but I believe that he was an Hegelian; an exponent of a philosophy now out of favor, except in the form of Dialectical Materialism." (MacTaggart is quoted in the footnotes to the dissertation.) Edward Lear, in *The Owl and the Pussycat*, speaks of a "runcible spoon," and in *The Pobble Who Has No Toes* of a "runcible cat." MacTaggart, recognizing that tortoise-shell spoons are sometimes made, and that tortoise-shell cats sometimes occur, affirmed that "tortoise-shell" was the only adjective applicable to both cats and spoons. Eliot notes that MacTaggart overlooked "a runcible hat" in another of Lear's poems, but his objection does not rest on this point. "No, I maintain that Mac-Taggart's method was wrong from the start."[14]

Eliot, showing how, in French and English, the same word may develop two meanings which have no relation to each other except that of derivation from a common root, observes that the transition of a word from one meaning to another may be easy and natural, and that each transition is so imperceptible that the authors, as well as the speakers, responsible for it may be unaware that they are committing any novelty.[15]

This theme, that words "*must* change their meaning, because it is their changes in meaning that keep a language *alive*," and that "every great writer contributes something to the meaning of the key words which he uses,"[16] is frequent in Eliot's writings. It is also a theme of idealist logic. Thus there is "no repetition," Bosanquet writes—"not so much as the recurrent application of a word." Similarly, Nettleship writes, language is "always being made": "the use of language is really a recreating of it, and every one modifies his native language a little, or creates a little new meaning; great authors create a great deal."[17] This keeping language alive by re-creating it is, according to Eliot, the social function of poetry: its general function, as distinguished from the particular functions associated with the kinds of poetry.[18]

"But *runcible* . . . is a pure nonsense word: being such, it has no root. It cannot be defined. But I should deny that there was no relationship between his three uses of the same word. The rightness of the word, in each of these uses, the fact that it satisfies us as applicable to objects so different as a cat, a spoon, and a hat, is something that our sensibility acknowledges: we also feel that in each use there is a different shade of meaning. It is the nonsense shadow of the kind of word with which I am concerned, and so it cannot mean *tortoise-shell*."[19] To keep to the structural aspect, we are aware of an indentification of differences or a differentiation of identity.

As Eliot goes on to say, speaking of his book on culture: "I made . . . some effort to distinguish three senses in which we use the word culture . . . I maintain that it would not do to have three different words . . . because these meanings interpenetrate each other and give significance to each other. . . . And we must remember that . . . there is an implicit unity between all the meanings of a word like 'culture' . . . : this is the unity which we feel is going through the several definitions of the word in current use."[20]

As for education, "words will be constantly used in new contexts," so that "the meaning of a word like 'education' is . . . more than the sum of the meanings given in the dictionary." It is well, then, "to recognize the incompleteness of any definition that we give." In fact, "education does not appear to be definable"; the most that we can do is to show that each of its several purposes, if it is to be called education, "must imply the rest." And although "we cannot define education *simpliciter*, our awareness of the mutual implication of its several purposes gives us a feeling of an identity of the word which is similar to the feeling I have professed to have of identity among the several uses of the word *runcible*. We must continue, however, to speak of 'education' when we mean one of several possible uses of the word; and this felt identity is what makes it impossible for us to substitute, for the sake of clarity, several different words."[21]

When we are aware of difference or diversity, Bradley says, there is always an "implicit sameness," a "felt basis" common to the differences, a "feeling" of identity. And according to Eliot in the dissertation, a "felt identity" is "an identity uniting differences."[22]

It is not our object to pursue the implications of Eliot's statements, but only to show some of the uses he makes of his logical principles.

In "What Is Minor Poetry?" (1944) Eliot begins, characteristically, by saying that he does not propose to offer, either at the beginning or at the end, a definition of minor poetry. What he can do is to take note of the fact that when we speak of a poet as minor, we mean different things at different times; and we can make our minds a little clearer about what these different meanings are, and so avoid confusion and misunderstanding. One association of the term "minor poetry" makes it mean the kind of poems we read only in anthologies. But we must count as minor poets some whose reputation rests upon very long poems, and as major poets, some who wrote only short ones. Long poems are of all sorts, differing in kind and degree of importance, so that it is difficult to distinguish them as major and minor, just as it is difficult to divide short poems into major and minor. But now, the distinction of short and long having led nowhere, we get a statement of principle. Herbert's *The Temple* is not simply a succession of separate lyrics but a whole which is more than the sum of its parts. And even with a poet like Herrick, though his work shows no continuity of conscious purpose, there is still *something* more in the whole than in the sum of its parts. Having begun with the question of what a minor poet is, Eliot has arrived, by a dialectic process, at the criterion of a major poet: the idea of an individual whole. Eliot restates it in the case of *one* long poem as "the proper unity and variety," and in regard to the whole work of a poet as "a unity of underlying pattern," or as "a unifying personality." The important difference is whether the knowledge of the whole work of a poet makes us understand better any one of his poems. That implies a significant unity in his whole work.[23]

> One can't put this increased understanding altogether into words: I could not say just why I think I understand and enjoy *Comus* better for having read *Paradise Lost*, or *Paradise Lost* better for having read *Samson Agonistes*, but I am convinced that this is so. I cannot always say why, through knowing a person in a number of different situations, and observing his behavior in a variety of circumstances, I feel that I understand better his behavior or demeanor on a particular occasion: but we do believe that that person is a unity, however inconsistent his conduct, and that acquaintance with him over a span of time makes him more intelligible.[24]

A person, regarded as an object of knowledge, is, like other such objects, an identity in difference. Thus, for instance, Bradley: "In 'Caesar is sick,' Caesar is not affirmed to be nothing but sick; he is a common bond of many attributes, and is therefore universal."[25] And here, at greater length, is Bosanquet:

> If I say "Caesar crossed the Rubicon," I start with an individual Caesar, whose continued identity extended through a certain space of time and revealed itself in a variety of acts, and I exhibit his identity in one of the acts and moments—its differences—through which it persisted. What I mean by the affirmation is that he, *the*

Caesar who had before conquered Gaul, and who was afterwards murdered on the Ides of March, displayed his character and enacted part of his history by crossing the Rubicon. This is a clear case of exhibiting an identity in difference. But the process has inevitably two aspects. On the one hand, I analyze the individual whole that is called Caesar by specifying one of the differences that may be considered as a part within it; on the other hand, I construct or make synthesis of the individual whole in question, by exhibiting it as a whole that pervades, and absorbs in itself, each or all of its differences. It is only an *individual* whole that is obviously present in *each* as well as in *all* of its differences, as the individual Caesar in the act of crossing the Rubicon.[26]

Bosanquet is here illustrating the doctrine that every judgment is both analytic and synthetic, and this is also the doctrine of identity in difference. Thus "the process of construction is always that of exhibiting a whole in its parts, *i.e.* an identity in its differences; that is to say, it is always both analytic and synthetic."[27]

In "What Is Minor Poetry?" Eliot is dealing with a question of value; and value goes with organization, which is the embodiment of conscious purpose. The general doctrine, briefly stated, is this: The real is the organized; there are degrees of reality; and, as Eliot says, "in any system in which degrees of reality play a part, reality may be defined in terms of value, and value in terms of reality."[28]

We may note here Hugh Kenner's observation that "it is very Bradleyan . . . to argue that 'The whole of Shakespeare's work is *one* poem'; so that 'what is "the whole man" is not simply his greatest or maturest achievement, but the whole pattern formed by the sequence of plays . . . : we must know all of Shakespeare's work in order to know any of it.' "[29] Kenner is quoting from the essay on John Ford, where Eliot is concerned with the classification of Elizabethan and Jacobean dramatists. The standard, which is set by Shakespeare, is that of "a continuous development"; and "the measure in which dramatists and poets approximate to this unity in a lifetime's work is one of the measures of major poetry and drama."[30]

With Shakespeare, Eliot says in "John Ford," the development in each play is "determined increasingly by Shakespeare's state of feeling"; there is an "inner necessity in the feeling: some-thing more profound and more complex than what is ordinarily called 'sincerity.' "[31]

Necessity has to do with "self-development." It is a profound notion, in the etymological sense of the word, for it takes us to the bottom, or what in Eliot's philosophy is called the "ground." It is not the necessity of an external combination of forces, but an inner necessity; and this necessity derives from the character of the whole or subwholes within which the development takes place and upon which it depends (as in geometry it implies and rests upon the character of space). In the dissertation, Eliot ex-presses this in a very general form. Thus in the experience of a red flower, he says, there is an immediate unity, a state of feeling in which "awareness and awared" are one; and this "moment of identity" persists and is essential to the relations which the flower may afterward be discovered to have, relations which "must form a system, must somehow hang together." The development is "organic [rather] than mechanical": it is like "the character of a man, [and] may be said both to be already present at the moment of conception, and on the other hand to develop at every mo-ment into something new and unforeseen. But it will have, from its crudest beginnings, a character to which (though it may belie all our verbal definitions) it will always remain consistent."[32]

Shakespeare's work—like the relations that constitute the flower, or the character of a man as exhibited in the diversity of his experiences—is a self-determined whole.

Eliot is sometimes critical of Bradley while developing a Bradleyan position ("What I have been saying may seem to have no direct bearing upon the metaphysics of Mr. Bradley, but the whole position taken here throughout . . . has been in support of this metaphysic").[33] Thus he objects to certain remarks of Brad-ley's concerning the nature of error, and in support of his argu-ment he quotes a statement of Joachim's from *The Nature of Truth*, taken from the chapter "The Negative Element and Er-ror." Joachim's point in the section of the chapter from which Eliot quotes is that the solution to the problem of error cannot be formulated in the terminology of aesthetics. In art, discords are somehow resolved and made to contribute to the harmony of the whole; but in knowledge an error is not superseded in the growth of truth, and in morality evil is not negated in some wider scheme of good (error and evil, in other words, are not transmuted in the Absolute, as Bradley held). An error always remains an error; or, as Eliot expresses it, the error is not got rid of: is not transcended, transmuted, or dissolved.[34]

It is different in art, as Joachim writes:

> A work of art—e.g. a picture, or still more obviously a musical composition—is, as it were, a miniature significant whole; and the character of its coherence is beauty. A musical masterpiece is essentially a self-fulfilment, which moves through opposition and contrast, and which in that self-contained movement makes and maintains its coherent individuality. The opposition and contrast, as moments in the process, simply enrich the concrete individuality of the whole. . . . In the work of art, none of the contrasting features stand out in glaring hostility. As hostile and as ugly, they *are* not any longer. . . . For *outside* the unity of a work of art there is neither aesthetic beauty nor ugliness. No chord, as such and in itself, is aesthetically discordant or ugly; and no color, in and for itself, can have aesthetic predicates.[35]

And here, in "The Music of Poetry," is Eliot:

> It would be a mistake . . . to assume that all poetry ought to be melodious, or that melody is more than one of the components of the music of words. . . . Dissonance, even cacophony, has its place. . . .
> What matters . . . is the whole poem: and if the whole poem need not be, and often should not be, wholly melodious, it follows that a poem is not made out of "beautiful words." I doubt whether, from the point of view of *sound* alone, any word is more or less beautiful than another. . . . The ugly words are the words not fitted for the company in which they find themselves . . . but I do not believe that any word well-established in its own language is either beautiful or ugly.[36]

This, too, is a commonplace. And the question again arises how the commonplace is to be represented. It is the same question that we have been considering—the logic of organization.

In this philosophy, art is, and is not, like logic. Bradley, speaking of music, says that, though the aesthetic object cannot in one respect be used to illustrate logic, in another respect it can, for it "serves well . . . to illustrate our type of self-contained self-development."[37]

The question is the relation of discord to coherence. Discord—"opposition and contrast," or "dissonance, even cacophony"—represents the negative element, and negation is essential to coherence.

The question concerns the "dialectic process"; and we must distinguish between the Hegelian and the Bradleyan version of the process (Bradley's version being also that of Joachim and Eliot). In the Hegelian version, the self-contradiction of the thesis produces the antithesis, and this discord is resolved in the synthesis, so that there is a reconciliation and balance of opposites. The "heresy" of Bradley's version is that it rejects the notion of negation as self-contradiction.[38] With Bradley, things are not contradictory (or contrary) because they are opposites; the opposites are the internal diversity of an identity, the differences necessary for its articulation. And though these all express the one whole, they are different from one another. And this difference, as Joachim says, is "essential, and is a negative element," for otherwise the whole "would itself have no positive character."[39]

But is this the logic of the passage quoted from "The Music of Poetry"? Everything points to it. Thus Bradley, discussing the "Dialectic Method," says that what is implied is an ideal whole in which every element is united "positively and negatively" with all the rest.[40] And Eliot, in "Tradition and the Individual Talent," commenting on a passage from *The Revenger's Tragedy*, says: "In this passage (as is evident if it is taken in its context) there is a combination of positive and negative emotions: an intensely strong attraction toward beauty and an equally intense fascination by the ugliness which is contrasted with it and which destroys it."[41]

The result is a "*significant* emotion," or, as Joachim calls it, a "significant whole," a whole in which "the constituents cohere in and through their differences." Joachim is expounding the coherence notion of truth, but, as he says, there are "significant wholes" in art as well as in knowledge, and in morality, too.[42]

Eliot is, in principle, doing the same thing that Bradley,

Joachim, and Bosanquet do—using art to illustrate the principles of idealist logic. The poet, too, sometimes tries to realize philosophic ideas; and to bring this out we must rehearse some familiar points.

To think of anything is to make an object of it (though if the object were not there, we could not think of it). An object is a whole of parts or an identity in difference. The identity is continuous throughout its differences; and continuity is, like identity, ideal.[43] So too are the differences, the internal distinctions and relations. An object is then a unity of meaning. But an object is experienced as well as contemplated, has real as well as ideal elements. The real elements are sensations and images. Though these are the real elements, and the logical object is the ideal meaning, actually, owing to the "translocation" of elements, the real is the ideal and the ideal the real. But though real and ideal are inseparable, they are distinguishable; and when for practical convenience they are considered apart, they belong to different orders. Sensations and images, as existences in the order of time and space, are mutually exclusive. Thus the words of a poem (spoken or written), the lines and colors of a painting, the notes of a piece of music are separate and outside one another. They do not themselves realize the unity that is an identity in difference but only symbolize it.

Music, to take it as an example, presents itself as a series of sounds, and the perception of succession requires both identity and diversity;[44] or, what is the same thing, we construct, or reconstruct, the object by analysis and synthesis. In attending to music, we distinguish the elements, however fugitive, and relate them—in a way that is definite but hardly describable—to a whole which is itself in process of construction. Though the physical sounds and the sensations are in time, the perception of the object is not in time. What is there, to use Eliot's language, is the "present of ideal construction, the present of meaning."[45] Though this present endures, it is not a duration in the sense of a present that is opposed to past and future. What is present is not time but the object. And in an ideal object the parts are not separate and externally related, but enter into and modify one another, so that no part is independent of the whole. Nor is there any priority of one part to another, no change and succession of parts, but a development in which the object is continuously modified and transformed. The whole is in all the parts, and it is in the end explicitly what in the beginning it is implicitly, process and product being inseparable.[46]

> *Words move, music moves*
> *Only in time; but that which is only living*
> *Can only die. Words, after speech, reach*
> *Into the silence. Only by the form, the pattern,*
> *Can words or music reach*
> *The stillness, as a Chinese jar still*
> *Moves perpetually in its stillness.*
> *Not the stillness of the violin, while the note lasts,*
> *Not that only, but the co-existence,*
> *Or say that the end precedes the beginning,*
> *And the end and the beginning were always there*
> *Before the beginning and after the end.*
> *And all is always now.*[47]

We touched in an earlier chapter on the question of communication, and now we may consider the principles underlying this question. Bradley, speaking of communication between souls, writes:

> But there is a natural mistake which, perhaps, I should briefly notice. Our inner worlds, I may be told, are divided from each other, but the outer world of experience is common to all; and it is by standing on this basis that we are able to communicate. Such a statement would be incorrect. My external sensations are no less private to myself than are my thoughts or my feelings. In either case my experience falls within my own circle, a circle closed on the outside; and, with all its elements alike, every sphere is opaque to the others which surround it. . . . In brief, regarded as an existence which appears in a soul, the whole world for each is peculiar and private to that soul.[48]

In his discussion of this theme, Bradley employs the principle of existence and content, the real and ideal aspects involved in every experience. The soul, as soul, is defined as "a series of psychical events" regarded merely as occurring in time. But these events (like everything else in time) have an aspect that transcends their existence.[49] Now if we consider these states of mind in abstraction from their reference, they are all private and personal, external sensations, no less than our "inner" thought and feeling.

"But," Bradley goes on (these are the words that Eliot omits from his *Waste Land* note, though they are quoted, in part, in the *Monist* essay on Leibniz and Bradley), "if on the other hand, you are considering identity of content, and, on that basis, are transcending such particular existences, then there is at once, in principle, no difference between the inner and the outer"—no difference, that is, in regard to communication. "No experience can lie open to inspection from the outside; no guarantee of identity is possible. Both our knowledge of sameness, and our way of communication, are indirect and inferential. They must make the circuit, and must use the symbol, of bodily change. . . . The real identity of ideal content, by which all souls live and move, cannot work in common save by the path of external appearance"—that is, sensation and image.[50]

Eliot restates this doctrine in his chapter on solipsism. For instance: We have knowledge of others "only through the mediation of objects" (or, as in the *Monist* essay referred to above: "Other selves . . . are for me ideal objects"). That is one aspect; and the other is that our knowledge of others is "only through physical appearance within our world," or "we have no knowledge of other souls except through their bodies."[51] This means, as Eliot explains in the essay on *Hamlet*, that "the state of mind of Lady Macbeth walking in her sleep has been communicated to you by a skillful accumulation of imagined sensory impressions."[52] We can know the state of mind of Lady Macbeth only by making an object of it, and we apprehend the object by means of sensations and images.

In the *Monist* essay Eliot is concerned with justifying what he finds to be "a likeness between Leibniz and Bradley"; and he adopts, accordingly, what appears to be a neutral attitude toward both writers. But except for his criticism of the Absolute, and his remark that "divine intervention" is as necessary to Bradley's universe as to the universe of Leibniz (a foreshadowing of what was to come), he is, as was said, restating positions he defends in the dissertation. Thus he again quotes the passage of Bosanquet's that he cites in the chapter on solipsism; and he quotes Bradley to the effect that "the world is such that we can make the same intellectual construction. We can, more or less, set up a scheme, in which every one has a place, a system constant and orderly, and in which the relations apprehended by each percipient coincide"[53]—or as Bosanquet, dealing with the same point, says, correspond.[54] Though our sensory experiences are divergent, these experiences refer to the same world of objects; and it is in virtue of this ideal identity of structure that the separate worlds coincide. The basis of human community is thus not sensible but ideal.

To restate the doctrine in a simple form, sensations and images are perishing existences, and we use these fugitive existences to refer to an objective world of meanings, a world which is an ideal construction.[55] We are constantly interpreting our sensations by referring them to objects—past, present, and future. Here—to say a word about the future—is Tiresias in *The Waste Land*:

> I Tiresias . . .
> Perceived the scene, and foretold the rest—
> I too awaited the expected guest.
> . . . .
> (And I Tiresias have foresuffered all
> Enacted on this same divan or bed;
> I who have sat by Thebes below the wall
> And walked among the lowest of the dead.)[56]

Tiresias perceives, foretells, and foresuffers the scene enacted in the apartment of a typist at teatime.

In the dissertation, "Julius Caesar," Eliot says, is not "unreal because he is dead," but "must persist and influence reality."[57] Similarly, in "What Is the Real Julius Caesar?" Bradley writes: "Why should I be forced to believe that the great minds of the past, where they influence me, are unreal, and are themselves simply dead?"[58] Further, speaking of "dead Caesar's knowledge":

A man actually must be there, wherever his knowledge extends, even if that knowledge is of the unseen present or of the past or future. So far as Caesar in his own day foresaw ours, his proper reality was not limited to his own world or time. He was and he is present there, wherever anything that the Universe contains was present to his mind. Caesar of course was not, and he is not, in our own time as we ourselves now are there. The distinction is obvious and to ignore it would be even absurd. On the other hand this separation only holds within limits, and it is perfectly compatible with the real presence of Caesar in his known object. The further result that Caesar's knowledge will affect the being of, and will make a difference to, his object must again be affirmed.[59]

In Eliot's language, "Time present and time past/Are both perhaps present in time future,/And time future contained in time past," and "all time is eternally present."[60] It is not exactly time that is present; but everything that occurs in time, time past and time future, may appear in "the present of ideal construction, the present of meaning." The scene perceived and foretold by Tiresias is "a present reality," and it is "this present future-reality" that Tiresias sees enacted.[61]

Bradley is dealing with the puzzle of how "thoughts and emotions are shared," though we have no direct knowledge of the minds of others.

To consider the question from the other side, we know Caesar by making an object of him, and we know the persons nearest to us, or for that matter ourselves, in the same way. Thus my knowledge of myself, as a being with a past and future, is, like my knowledge of Caesar, largely ideal; and my knowledge of Caesar is, like that of my own past, a present event; is supported, that is, by present sensation and image. And without this support, Caesar, as well as the entire past, would be destroyed. My knowledge of Caesar, at any present moment, is partial and fragmentary; but it is, so far as it goes, knowledge of the real Julius Caesar. Moreover, Caesar makes a difference to the content of my experience (or my world), just as I make a difference to Caesar; for my experience qualifies Caesar, and without it Caesar would not be what he is. But Caesar and I transcend this situation; for I have other objects, and Caesar is an object for other subjects, whose experience of him differs from mine. And if we tried to strip away the diversity of contexts in which Caesar appears, Caesar would disappear from history.[62]

The past (as well as the future) depends upon the present and varies with it. ("That ideal construction in which for us the entire past consists, is based on and is inseparable from present feeling and perception.")[63] Hence, as Eliot says in his introduction to Charlotte Eliot's *Savonarola*, every period of history is "seen differently by every other period," the past being in "perpetual flux." A historical work "tells more . . . about the age in which it is written than about the past," and this is as true of a history written near our time as of one written in some earlier age. Similarly, a work of historical fiction, such as George Eliot's *Romola*, is "much more a document on its own time than on the time portrayed." It is an interpretation, just as our knowledge of the period portrayed in *Romola* "is itself an interpretation and relative."[64]

Again: "The role played by interpretation has often been neglected in the theory of knowledge. . . . Some years ago, in a paper on *The Interpretation of Primitive Ritual*, I made an humble attempt to show that in many cases *no* interpretation of a rite could explain its origin. For the meaning of the series of acts is to the performers themselves an interpretation; the same ritual remaining practically unchanged may assume different meanings for different generations of performers; and the rite may even have originated before 'meaning' meant anything at all."[65]

The paper was written for Josiah Royce's seminar in comparative methodology, 1913–1914. Harry T. Costello, in his record of the seminar, says that Eliot "had been reading Francis Herbert Bradley, and said no single statement was absolutely true"; "no judgment [is] more than more or less true," and "there is no adequate truth short of the whole final truth." "He thought the case of comparative religion especially good to bring this out, for here interpretation has succeeded interpretation, not because the older opinions were refuted, but because the point of view has changed."[66]

Eliot was concerned, Costello reports, with the distinction between "interpretation" and "description," and his year's work "circled around this question of the truth of interpretations."[67] Eliot also presented several notes, one on his use of the term interpretation (Royce and Eliot meant different things by the term, and Eliot wanted to clarify his use of it), another on description and explanation, and another on causality (the last two were assigned topics on which other members of the seminar also presented notes).[68] Though these topics reappear in the dissertation, we cannot go into them here, but we may try to give some indication of the bearing of Eliot's inquiries on his liberal attitude toward literary interpretation.

In the dissertation: "We may mean the character as a presentation to the author's mind; but a figure of fiction may and often does have an existence for us distinct from what is merely our interpretation of what the author 'had in mind.' Frequently we feel more confidence in our own interpretation of the character than in any account of the genesis and meaning which the author may give himself."[69] And in "The Music of Poetry": "The reader's interpretation may differ from the author's and be equally valid—it may even be better."[70]

More generally, Eliot distinguishes between the literal truths of science and the truths of interpretation, the latter being the sort that "the historian, the literary critic, and the metaphysician are engaged with." The "true critic," he says, "is a scrupulous avoider of formulae," for his truths are "lived truths" or "truths of experience," and such truths are "partial and fragmentary."[71] As he states it in "The Music of Poetry," "A poem may appear to mean very different things to different readers, and all of these meanings may be different from what the author thought he meant. . . . The different interpretations all may be partial formulations of one thing."[72]

In his introduction to Wilson Knight's *The Wheel of Fire* (1949) Eliot relates the question of the meaning of "interpretation" in poetry to the question of the interpretation of the universe by metaphysics; and referring to Bradley's *Appearance and Reality* he remarks that "there may be an essential part of error in all interpretation, without which it would not be interpretation at all," and that "in a work of art, as truly as anywhere, reality only exists in and through appearances."[73]

With Bradley, every judgment is "partial and relative"; and "error *is* truth, it is partial truth, that is false only because partial and left incomplete."[74] Since, according to Eliot, every interpretation of a poem is a partial formulation of one thing, there can be no interpretation without error.

The consequence is that "every interpretation, along perhaps with some utterly contradictory interpretation, has to be taken up and reinterpreted by every thinking mind and by every civilization."[75]

9

Imaginary Objects

Within the whole that is reality there are various orders of appearance, and the world of art, of poetry and fiction, is one such order—an imaginary sphere of reality. Bradley's chief text on this theme is his essay "On Floating Ideas and the Imaginary," which may be taken, Bradley says, as a commentary on various aspects of *Appearance and Reality* (he also touches on it in his *Logic*), and Eliot's treatment of the theme, as he remarks, is consistent with Bradley's essay, though it explores some undeveloped consequences of Bradley's position.

Eliot's argument is too complicated to be reproduced here. For one thing, it involves various aspects of doctrine. For another, he discusses, in addition to imaginary objects, the problem of error, objects of hallucination, and unreal objects (such as the present king of France). Finally, in this section of the dissertation, as in the others, the style is condensed, the connecting links are obscure, the vocabulary is ambiguous, and the changes rung on the argument are various. We must, accordingly, limit ourselves to indicating, briefly and roughly, the general character of the theory, and then try to show the use that Eliot makes of it.

We may, to suggest the bearing of the question, begin with a sketch of the ordinary view of things. There is, in this view, a real world with two spheres of fact, inner and outer. The inner, as psychical event, has an existence in time and is, through its connection with the body, continuous with external fact and event.

As for ideas, they refer to sensible fact, inner and outer, and they are, in the logical sense, true or false, or are expressive of facts of mind. Thus it is a fact that Thackeray wrote *Vanity Fair*, but the novel itself is imaginary, because ideal, and the ideal is not the real. Its significance derives from its reference to the real world, which it in some sense represents: in "some sense," for it both resembles and differs from the real world—is, in short, a work of imagination.

Now with Eliot an object is not imaginary because it is ideal (though mathematical truths are not actual facts, we do not call them imaginary). In other words, an object is not imaginary because it is not real. Thus if an imaginary dollar could buy cakes and ale, it would not be a real dollar; and if a real dollar lost its power to buy this cheer, it would not be an imaginary dollar. We are talking about an abstraction from differences, a "mere idea," and a "mere idea" is neither real nor imaginary. To be one or the other, it must be something positive, and it gets its character from a context, from the number and kind of relations that constitute it. The difference, then, is in the relations. And the main point thus far is that an imaginary dollar *is* something, and is, in its degree, as real as an actual dollar.

The imaginary, in general, is defined by exclusion from the real world.[1] This real world is not something found or given; it is an ideal and essentially a practical construction—an interpretation from a narrow and limited point of view.[2] The imaginary and the "real world" are distinctions within reality, and the one is no more "in our head" than is the other. They are differences within a felt whole, a whole in which the elements are related positively and negatively.

The relevant doctrine is that of negation (in effect, the same as that of disjunction). Negation presupposes a positive ground. Thus we do not say of a red color that it is not an elephant, for an elephant does not suggest an alternative to a red color. But when we say that red is not yellow, the yellow is an excluded possibility; that is, we affirm a unity that relates differences that exclude each other. The colors belong to the same subwhole, so that the red, while excluding the yellow, implies it. Similarly, in the wider whole, the imaginary, though excluded by the "real world," is intrinsically related to it. Otherwise it would be devoid of interest and value.[3] In Eliot's version,

> The apprehension of an object known to be imaginary does not differ essentially from the apprehension of any other object, unless we have hocus-pocussed an external reality to which ideas are to "conform." . . . The characters and the situations are all "imaginary," but is there any one act which so apprehends them, cut off and "floating"? In order to be imaginary, they must be contrasted with something which is real. There must, furthermore, be specific points of resemblance and difference: for the type of reality with which the imaginary object is contrasted must be a type to which the latter pretends to belong. Now so far as merely the imaginary object intends such a reality and falls short, it is not an object of any kind real or imaginary, but falls under what I have said previously of "mere idea." If the character in fiction is an imaginary object, it must be by virtue of something more than its being imaginary, i.e. merely intending to be a reality which it is not. It must be, as I said, contrasted with this reality; to be contrasted it must be more than a pure reference; it must have in fact another aspect in which it has a reality of its own distinct from its reference. The fiction is thus more than a fiction: it is a *real* fiction.[4]

If we tried to add to what has already been said, it would only obscure matters. Let us, then, turn to the critical texts. With Swinburne, as we saw, "you find always that the object was not there—only the word." But Eliot says:

> It might seem to be intimated, by what has been said, that the work of Swinburne can be shown to be a sham, just as bad poetry is a sham. It would only be so if you could produce or suggest something that it pretends to be and is not. The world of Swinburne does not depend upon some other world which it simulates; it has the necessary completeness and self-sufficiency for justification and permanence. It is impersonal, and no one else could have made it. The deductions are true to the postulates. It is indestructible.[5]

The same argument occurs in "Ben Jonson." In that essay, it will be recalled, "the important thing is that if fiction can be divided into creative fiction and critical fiction, Jonson's is creative." In the dissertation, we do not, in reading a novel, simply "assume" the characters and the situations; we either accept them as "real" or consider them as "*meanings*, as a criticism of reality from the author's point of view." Actually, "if we did not vacillate between these two extremes (one of which alone would give the 'photographic' novel and the other the arid 'pièce à thèse') a novel would mean very little to us."[6]

"Now a character which is 'lived through,' which is real to us not merely by suggesting 'that sort of person' but by its independent cogency, is to the extent of its success real."[7]

That is the basis of the distinction between Jonson and Flaubert and Molière. The work of the French writers is critical in a sense in which Jonson's is not: it is a "commentary" on the "actual world," a "criticizing [of] the actual"; but with Jonson the "reference to the actual world" is "more tenuous" and "[less] direct." Jonson's work is, accordingly, not defined by the word satire; for though Jonson poses as a satirist, satire like Jonson's is great in the end "not by hitting off its object but by creating it." The satire is "merely the means which leads to the aesthetic result," the creation of "a *unique* world." It is a world in which the characters "conform to the logic of the emotions of their world"; they are "not fancy, because they have a logic of their own; and this logic illuminates the actual world, because it gives a new point of view from which to inspect it."[8]

Eliot's view of satire derives from his theory of imaginary objects—it is a fresh application of the theory sketched in the dissertation, an undeveloped consequence of Bradley's position.

Similarly in "John Dryden," comparing the satire of Dryden with that of Pope, Eliot says of Dryden's verses that "they create the object which they contemplate";[9] and Dryden, he adds, is much nearer to Jonson than to Pope. And in "Wilkie Collins and Dickens," "Dickens's characters are real because there is no one like them; Collins's because they are so painstakingly coherent and lifelike."[10]

But let us return to "Ben Jonson," where the distinction is between "hitting off" an object and "creating it." Eliot cites as an example of Jonson's creating his object the speech of Sylla's ghost in the prologue to *Catiline*. This speech, he says, has nothing to do with "the character of Sulla," nor is it suitable to a "historical Sulla, or to anybody in history," but is a perfect expression for "Sylla's ghost."[11]

In the dissertation, an error of perception is an error because we compare it with a cognate reality, but with a hallucination there is no cognate reality. A specter thus has "a greater degree of substantiality than an error, because of its greater independence."[12] And Eliot passes, by way of this distinction, to a consideration of imaginary objects, which in certain respects do not differ from hallucinatory objects. "Sylla's ghost," in Eliot's account of him, is kin to the specter in the dissertation. He is, it may be said, a philosophic ghost.

Art, it follows from Eliot's theory, is not realistic. That is the argument of "Four Elizabethan Dramatists: A Preface to an Unwritten Book." Thus the weakness of Elizabethan drama is "not its defect of realism, but its attempt at realism; not its conventions, but its lack of conventions." Its great vice was to exceed the limits of art and expand into "the desert of exact likeness to the reality which is perceived by the most commonplace mind." In a play of Aeschylus, "the imitation of life is circumscribed, and the approaches to ordinary speech and withdrawals from ordinary speech are not without relation and effect upon each other." "It is essential that a work of art be self-consistent, that an artist should consciously or unconsciously draw a circle beyond which he does not trespass: . . . actual life is always the material, and . . . an abstraction from actual life is a necessary condition to the creation of the work of art." But in Elizabethan drama there is a "confusion of convention and realism." The fault is "not with the ghost" but with "the confusion between one kind of ghost and another." It is an error that "Shakespeare should have introduced into the same play ghosts belonging to such different categories as the three sisters and the ghost of Banquo." In the Russian school the dancer is "a conventional being, a being which exists only in and for the work of art which is the ballet."[13] Similarly, in "Ben Jonson" "the life of the character is inseparable from the life of the drama." The figures in *Volpone* "are not personifications of passions; separately, they have not even that reality"; they are "constituents," "combinations in a whole."[14] Sylla's ghost, it turns out, is a proper artistic ghost.

The question he is arguing, Eliot says, is not one simply of "personal bias" but requires "an examination of principles."[15] Though Eliot's book remained unwritten, the principles found illustration in what he wrote—and not only in the essays on Elizabethan drama. Thus, in "The Three Voices of Poetry":

> I risk the generalization . . . that dramatic monologue cannot create a character. . . . It is not irrelevant that when the dramatic monologue is not put into the mouth of some character already known to the reader—from history or from fiction—we are likely to ask the question "Who was the original?" About Bishop Blougram people have always been impelled to ask, how far was this intended to be a portrait of Cardinal Manning, or of some other ecclesiastic? The poet, speaking, as Browning does, in his own voice, cannot bring a character to life: he can only mimic a character otherwise known to us. And does not the point of mimicry lie in the recognition of the person mimicked, and in the incompleteness of the illusion? We have to be aware that the mimic and the person mimicked are different people: if we are actually deceived, mimicry becomes impersonation.[16]

Eliot is still finding fresh application for his theory—thirty-seven years after first working it out.

To quote again from the dissertation:

> Finally, I do not see any possibility of saying that the imaginary object either subsists or exists. For when we think of the character in fiction, we go on to think of some aspect in the complex. Becky Sharpe exists in the time-order of *Vanity Fair*, but this time-order does not itself exist. Becky exists as an event in the life of Thackeray, and as an event in the life of every reader in the same way that every real person exists as an event in the life of every other real person with whom he comes in contact. But the object denoted by the word Becky does not exist, for it is simply the identical reference of several points of view.[17]

And in "The Three Voices of Poetry": "It would be only too easy to lose oneself in a maze of speculation about the process by which an imaginary character can become as real for us as people we have known."[18]

Frequently, he says, imaginary objects, under the name of assumptions, are distinguished sharply from objects of belief, both true and erroneous. But this distinction, he feels, is not needed, for assumption may be made to cover every act from acceptance to rejection. And, as we have seen, the apprehension of an imaginary object does not differ essentially from that of any other object.[19]

With Eliot, no view is original or ultimate. But we arbitrarily separate the "real world" from the rest of reality, and everything else we relegate to unreality—as mere feeling, or mere thought, or mere imagination. But these banished worlds are actual constituents of reality.[20] Moreover, though the "real world" provides the material that we use to symbolize the world of imagination, the distinction is only relative, for real and ideal interpenetrate each other, so that the situation is one of "interfusion."[21] Still, the word reality does not take its meaning from existence in the order of time and space. And Becky "is just as real as anything; it is as a real object that [she] is imaginary."[22] But we must leave Becky and imaginary characters and turn to "The Three Voices of Poetry," to which our discussion has brought us.

Though Eliot finds the term lyric unsatisfactory, he notes that "lyric" is defined in part by the Oxford Dictionary as poems "directly expressing the poet's own thoughts and sentiments," and it is the lyric, in this sense, that is relevant to his first voice. And it is in this sense that the German poet Gottfried Benn, in a lecture titled *Probleme der Lyrik*, thinks of "lyric poetry" as "addressed to no one." But where Benn speaks of "lyric poetry," Eliot prefers to say "meditative verse."[23] Further, though for Benn this sort of poem is a totally different kind from that of the poet addressing an audience, for Eliot the three voices are not mutually exclusive (the first and second are found together in nondramatic poetry, and together with the third in dramatic poetry, too).[24]

Eliot writes: "What, asks Herr Benn in this lecture, does the writer of such a poem . . . start with? There is first, he says, an inert embryo or 'creative germ' (*ein dumpfer schöpferischer Keim*) and, on the other hand, the Language, the resources of the words at the poet's command."[25] In Benn's version, *"Erstens ein dumpfer schöpferischer Keim, eine psychische Materie,"*[26] which Eliot thereafter refers to as "psychic material," or "Gottfried Benn and his unknown, dark *psychic material*," or his "rude unknown *psychic material*"[27] (the italics are Eliot's and not Benn's). "When you have the words for it, the 'thing' for which the words had to be found has disappeared, replaced by a poem. What you start from is nothing so definite as an emotion, in any ordinary sense; it is still more certainly not an idea."[28]

Eliot goes on: "I agree with Gottfried Benn, and I would go a little further. . . . [The poet] does not know what he has to say until he has said it; and in the effort to say it he is not concerned with making other people understand anything."[29]

Moreover,

> I don't believe that the relation of a poem to its origins is capable of being more clearly traced. You can read the essays of Paul Valéry, who studied the workings of his own mind in the composition of a poem more perseveringly than any other poet had done. But if, either on the basis of what poets try to tell you, or by biographical research, with or without the tools of the psychologist, you attempt to explain a poem, you will probably be getting further and further away from the poem without arriving at any other destination. The attempt to explain a poem by tracing it back to its origins will distract attention from the poem, to direct it on to something else which, in the form in which it can be apprehended by the critic and his readers, has no relation to the poem and throws no light upon it.[30]

The style—in the sense that we have been speaking of the style—has changed very little There is, as Richard Wollheim has observed, the difficulty of knowing "how literally one is expected to take Eliot's employment . . . of other men's thought." Another difficulty is having to deal with Eliot's irony, in the present instance Benn's "unknown *psychic material*." And to irony must be added ambiguity, for with Eliot "psychic material" is included under feeling in the sense of immediate experience. As Mowbray Allan says, "However much the passage quoted owes to Gottfried Benn, it is an almost perfect application to literary criticism of Bradley's concept of 'immediate experience.' "[31]

It has been part of our aim to bring out the "continuity of conscious purpose" in the critical prose, as well as its internal structure, and though that means returning to familiar doctrine, there is more than one way of understanding the doctrine; and there are aspects of the doctrine that still remain to be noted.

Eliot is reaffirming "this Impersonal theory of poetry," the "laudable aim" of which is "to divert interest from the poet to the poetry." One argument in support of this aim is that poetry does

not lend itself to causal explanation: explanation by reconstructing its antecedent conditions, external and internal. If the history
of a poem is its explanation, the understanding of a poem requires a grasp of "what the poetry is aiming to be"[32]—its
entelechy.

Eliot's concern with this theme is shown in various ways. For
instance, in "Experiment in Criticism" Sainte-Beuve (the type of
historical critic) conceives of literature "as a process of changes in
history, and as a part of the study of history."[33] We attempt to
account for historical change in terms of causation, which gives
some sort of order to the events of the past, and what does not fit
into this order is unaccountable. The real cause is the totality of
relations, and the real effect is as complex as the real cause.[34]
Literature, then, as part of the study of history, has endless connections with everything else in history, and the investigation of
these is a distraction from the understanding and enjoyment of
poetry. Again, in *The Use of Poetry and the Use of Criticism*,
speaking of Abbé Brémond's analogy of poetry and mysticism in
Prayer and Poetry, Eliot says: "Any theory which relates poetry
very closely to a religious or a social scheme of things aims,
probably, to *explain* poetry by discovering its natural laws; but it
is in danger of *binding* poetry by legislation to be observed—and
poetry can recognize no such laws." Nor can poetry be tested or
defined "by reference to its putative antecedents in the mind of
the poet."[35] And in "The Frontiers of Criticism": "Perhaps the
form of criticism in which the danger of excessive reliance upon
causal explanation is greatest is the critical biography, especially
when the biographer supplements his knowledge of external facts
with psychological conjectures about inner experience."[36]

The biographer, as well as the historian and the novelist,
studies the inner experience of individual minds. But this sort of
study is misconceived. Thus, to quote in part from one of Eliot's
many arguments: "We may say that if psychology sets up a sharp
factual line of demarcation between processes and things, and yet
proposes to investigate the former as objects of science, it is
committed to a contradiction. Introspection can give us only
terms, and not processes."[37]

Psychology is supposed to give an account of the facts of
mind, and the facts, for psychology, are psychical events or proc-

esses, states and changes in or of consciousness, the consciousness of individual minds, which are isolated for study. But in the apprehension of an object I am not aware of the psychical process that is said to mediate my apprehension, nor am I aware of it alongside the object apprehended. If there is such a process, it is nothing *for me*. And if, by reflection, I make an object of the process, this object is not the process; it is, like every object of thought, a universal meaning. In the same way, the psychologist who makes an object of my consciousness in not aware of the psychical process that mediates his apprehension of the object. The psychical process, then, is neither *for* me nor *for* the psychologist. The "data" studied by psychology are thus unknown psychic material.[38]

This is the argument Eliot uses in his criticism of Bradley's attempt to treat psychology as a special science—a science dealing with psychical events and the laws of their happening. But this attempt of Bradley's is not essential to his main positions, and Eliot's purpose is to make these positions self-consistent.

With Eliot (and Bradley) there is no separation between experiencing and experienced (process of apprehension and object apprehended); though they are distinct (the object is *for* the subject, and without this internality there could be no object), they are inseparable aspects of a concrete whole. The object is directly known—known, that is, without the interposition of psychological apparatus: ideas or images as mental signs or symbols.[39] The whole process belongs to logic: the meaning apprehended and the sensations and images that refer to the meaning—all this belongs to the study of logic, and on another level to metaphysics. This is the field within which literary criticism moves. And between literary criticism and psychology there is a "radical separation."[40]

As for what the writer of a poem starts with, in *The Use of Poetry*, commenting on Dryden's "invention, or the finding of the thought," Eliot says that he prefers "not to call that which is found by invention by the name of 'idea'"; invention does not mean "finding an 'idea' which is later to be 'clothed and adorned' in a rather literal interpretation of the metaphor." "I believe that Dryden's 'invention' includes the sudden irruption of the germ of a new poem, possibly merely as a state of feeling." That is the "original *donnée*." And he adds: "His 'invention' is surely a finding, a *trouvaille*."[41] The question, as discussed by Bradley, is, in attending to a sensation or feeling that we did not previously notice, was the feeling there or has it been made by our attending?[42] The answer, as Eliot gives it, is that "the attention to the feeling presupposes that there is such an object present, and that the attention has not manufactured the object."[43]

Eliot construes Dryden as he construes Gottfried Benn, in the light of his own theory, including the point that what the poet starts with is not something he makes but something he finds or discovers. This "original *donnée*," whatever else it is, is a state of feeling; and, as Bradley says, "if made an object, it, as such, disappears."[44] That is, the feeling cannot be translated into thought without transformation. Or as Eliot expresses it in the dissertation, there is a starting point which has been expanded and developed, so that the starting point itself is altered, and you cannot say what the starting point was.[45]

Speaking of his "theory of the idea," Eliot says that the "idea is, as idea, Act"; it is "a stage in the process of realization of a world"; the idea "means itself," in the sense of a "pointing toward" its realization; and so far as "the idea is real it is the object."[46] This theory, he says, does not correspond with that of any author with whom he is acquainted, but he believes it to be "substantially in harmony with Mr. Bradley's metaphysics."[47] Brand Blanshard's theory is very much like Eliot's, and throws, it seems to me, retrospective light on it. Thus in "A Theory of the Idea" the idea is a "stage" on the way to its object. The relation is that of "the potential to the actual, or (what is apparently a species of the same) of unrealized to realized purpose." The idea is thus "both identical with its object and different from it." It is identical in the sense "in which anything that truly develops is identical with what it becomes." It is different in the sense "in which any purpose partially realized is different from the same purpose realized wholly."[48] The idea is conceived teleologically, in terms of its end or purpose—its entelechy.

In "The Three Voices of Poetry" Eliot is still speaking of poetry in terms of process—the poem is the "outcome of the process that has taken place."[49] The process is the process of thought, and the idea, as idea, is act or process. But the idea as contrasted with the poem is something which cannot be grasped, for it can only be described in terms of the poem, in which case one has the poem and not the idea. Hence the existence of the idea, in contrast with the poem, is only in the process, eluding our grasp.[50]

The poet, then, "does not know what he has to say until he has said it." Thus Nettleship: "We are apt to suppose that first there is a certain consciousness, and that then we distinguish it. But this is not so: in the act of distinguishing something we are for the first time distinctly conscious of it. The act of distinguishing has also been represented as the act of arresting the flux of consciousness, or as an act of attention; but here again, we must not suppose that first there is x, and then we attend to it: x exists for the first time in the act of attention. If we say then that *naming* is distinguishing or attending . . . we must beware of thinking that we first have the consciousness and then name it." This applies to every form of consciousness. Thus we must not suppose that "we first have the feeling and then express it. It would be truer to say that the expression *is* the completed feeling. . . . What the act of expression does is to fix and distinguish it finally; it then, and then only, becomes *a* determinate feeling."[51] And Bosanquet: "Every emotion exists only as correlative to its expression; . . . we do not first have an emotion and then proceed to express it; but . . . an emotion assumes its character, or becomes what it is, through the mode and degree of its expression; and . . . aesthetic emotion first arises in and is essentially constituted by, expression for expression's sake . . . which has no purpose beyond that of uttering the content of our feeling."[52]

There is another aspect to Eliot's statement that the poet does not know what he has to say until he has said it. Thus in "From Poe to Valéry," discussing *la poésie pure*, he says:

> Here I should like to point out the difference between a theory of poetry propounded by a student of aesthetics, and the same theory as held by a poet. It is one thing when it is simply an account of how the poet writes, without knowing it, and another thing when the poet himself writes consciously according to that theory. In affecting writing, the theory becomes a different thing from what it was merely as an explanation of how the poet writes. And Valéry was a poet who wrote very consciously and deliberately indeed:

perhaps, at his best, not wholly under the guidance of theory; but his theorizing certainly affected the kind of poetry that he wrote. He was the most self-conscious of all poets.

To the extreme of self-consciousness of Valéry must be added another trait: his extreme scepticism. . . . He had ceased to believe in *ends*, and was only interested in *processes*. It often seems as if he had continued to write poetry, simply because he was interested in the introspective observation of himself engaged in writing it. . . . There is a revealing remark in *Variété* V, the last of his books of collected papers: " . . . In my opinion the most authentic philosophy is not in the objects of reflection, so much as in the very act of thought and its manipulation."[53]

It is not only that Valéry was mistaken in his philosophy, he was also mistaken in writing consciously according to his philosophy. For to write poetry under the guidance of any theory is to know what one is going to say before one says it. It is a form of legislation, and poetry can recognize no such legislation. As Eliot says in "Reflections on *Vers Libre*," poets or schools that write according to a theory circumscribe and narrow their poetry. Indeed, according to Bosanquet, it is dangerous even to say that beauty is the aim of art (if it means something other than excellence in art). "It is dangerous . . . if it means to us that we know beforehand what sort or type of thing our beauty is to be. For beauty is above all a creation. . . . And . . . we do not know beforehand what that is to be." The same criticism holds of "art for art's sake" if it means that art is "some limiting conception, some general standard accepted beforehand," for this introduces into the aim of art a "restricting self- consciousness," so that the aim of art is no longer "pure expression"—"pure" in the sense of "expression for expression's sake."[54]

Eliot, still speaking of Valéry and *la poésie pure*, says that "the poet's theories should arise out of his practice rather than his practice out of his theories."[55] That seems to suggest—and has suggested—that Eliot was an antitheoretic critic, the sort of critic who feels that to have a theory of poetry limits and circumscribes the study of poetry. But Eliot is speaking of the writing of poetry, and what he says *is* theory, though obliquely expressed. There is theory, and there is theory of practice. Theory (philosophic aesthetics) does not teach one how to be a poet, any more than it teaches one how to be a literary critic. It teaches, among other things, that poetry has its own end, and is not subservient to other ends, intellectual or moral.

The relation is like that of logic to reasoning. We do not in reasoning think of the principle of contradiction, though our reasoning, if it is to be valid, must not contravene that principle. It is the same with grammar and speech. In speaking and reasoning, it may be said, we take the principles of grammar and logic for granted. As for theory of practice, there is a good deal of that in Eliot's critical writing: theories about meter, rhyme, contemporary speech, urban imagery, the long poem, and much else that arose from his practice of poetry. These theories explain and defend the kind of poetry he wrote or wanted to write; and that is all that a poet who writes his own *art poétique* should hope to do. But such theories are not, and should not be taken as, generalizations about all poetry; and in this sense Eliot has no theory of his own. But theories of practice inevitably give rise to theory in the larger sense, to speculation about the nature of poetry and its place in the economy of mind. And though in Eliot's critical writing these two levels of theory are intermingled or fused, they are, as he indicates in his oblique way, different things.

Of dramatic poetry, Eliot says in "The Three Voices of Poetry" that it starts from "a particular emotional situation, out of which the characters and a plot will emerge."[56] ("We can say, from our point of view, that subject and object emerge from a state of feeling. We can I think say this truly from our point of view.")[57] The state of feeling is "a *that*, merely there"; but it is only as the *that* "becomes a *what*" that "it is even a *that*." Every feeling, in the ordinary sense, has this aspect of immediacy, though it may be at every moment the object of consciousness as well. And Eliot speaks of the "aesthetic expansion" of the object[58]: the feeling which is at the start dim and restricted is completed by expansion and development. The process is in principle the same for all poetry. Thus in "William Blake": "His method of composition . . . is exactly like that of other poets. He has an idea (a feeling, an image), he develops it by accretion or expansion. . . . The idea, of course, simply comes, but upon arrival it is subjected to prolonged manipulation." Blake's poems are those of a man "with a profound interest in human emotions," though "the emotions are presented in an extremely simplified, abstract form."[59]

Poetry has to do with feeling and emotion; and feeling and emotion are, like everything else that is experienced, both felt and thought. But in poetry, and art generally, thought is in the service of feeling, is the means by which feeling and emotion are presented.

Eliot gives various indications of this relation. Thus, in the later Dante essay: "The long oration of Beatrice about the Will . . . is really directed at making us *feel* the reality of the condition of Piccarda. . . . The insistence throughout is upon states of feeling; the reasoning takes only its proper place as a means of realizing these states." And Dante "gives us every aid of images."[60] In the earlier Dante essay, "the allegory is the necessary scaffold" for the "structure of emotions." "It is not essential that the allegory . . . should be understood—only that its presence should be justified. The emotional structure within this scaffold is what must be understood—the structure made possible by the scaffold."[61] Similarly, Lucretius was really trying to find the "poetic equivalent" for a philosophic system, but the philosophy was not rich enough in "variety of feeling" to supply the material for a wholly successful poem. "But I must ask M. Valéry whether the 'aim' of Lucretius' poem was 'to fix or create a notion.'"[62] Again, in "The Possibility of a Poetric Drama," speaking of Goethe: "He embodies a philosophy. A creation of art should not do that: he should *replace* the philosophy. Goethe has not . . . sacrificed . . . his thought to make the drama; the drama is still a means."[63]

In "Shakespeare and the Stoicism of Seneca," Eliot remarks that we say vaguely that some poets think and others do not think. "But what we really mean is not a difference in quality of thought, but a difference in quality of emotion. The poet who 'thinks' is merely the poet who can express the emotional equivalent of thought. But he is not necessarily interested in the thought itself. We talk as if thought was precise and emotion was vague. In reality there is precise emotion and there is vague emotion. To express precise emotion requires as great intellectual power as to express precise thought."[64]

Finally, in "From Poe to Valéry" he says: "All poetry may be

said to start from emotions experienced by human beings in relation to themselves, to each other, to divine beings, and to the
world about them; it is therefore concerned also with thought and
action, which emotion brings about, and out of which emotion
arises."[65] Poetry starts and ends with emotion, thought and action
being the means by which emotion is expressed. "It is only in a
poem of some length that a variety of moods can be expressed; for
a variety of moods requires a number of different themes or
subjects, related either in themselves or in the mind of the poet."
But the subject is not "the purpose of the poem, it [is] simply a
necessary means for the realization of the poem." "It is important
as *means:* the *end* is the poem. The subject exists for the poem,
not the poem for the subject. A poem may employ several subjects, combining them in a particular way; and it may be meaningless to ask 'What is the subject of the poem?' From the union
of several subjects there appears, not another subject, but the
poem."[66]

Again: "The romantic comedy is a skillful concoction of inconsistent emotion, a *revue* of emotion. . . . The debility of
romantic comedy does not depend upon extravagant setting, or
preposterous events, or inconceivable incidents; all these might
be found in a serious tragedy or comedy. It consists in an internal
incoherence of feelings, a concatenation of emotions which sig-
nifies nothing."[67] And speaking of Poe: "The variety and ardor of
his curiosity delight and dazzle; yet in the end the eccentricity
and lack of coherence of his interests tire. There is just that
lacking which gives dignity to the mature man: a consistent view
of life. . . . What is lacking is . . . that maturity of intellect which
comes only with the maturing of the man as a whole, the development and coordination of his various emotions."[68]

The function of thought in art is the development and organization of feeling and emotion. Thus in Bosanquet's version the
emotion is expressed in "the form of an object"; it "has been made
objective in a presentation"; "the emotion simply is the whole
presentation, including both its sensuous and its ideal elements,"
the emotion and the presentation being "precise correlatives."[69]
As for vague and precise emotion: "Even an abstract idea, death,
ruin, fate, triumph, has . . . its correlative element of emotion

. . . ; but so far as the idea is indeterminate, the feeling . . . is also indeterminate, while if the idea is individualized the feeling . . . is . . . individualized along with it." Yet "there is no complete contrast between an abstract idea and the expression of emotion, but only between an abstract idea as an expression of slightly determinate emotion, and an individual idea as an expression of highly determinate emotion."[70] In regard to "representation" in poetry and art, it has no "independent justification"; its "place and value" is as "the instrument of the embodiment of feeling."[71]

Aristotle's theory of tragic emotion serves as an example. "By a typical portrayal of human life in some story that forms an individual whole, the feelings in question are divested of their personal reference, and acquire a content drawn from what is serious and noteworthy in humanity. . . . The aesthetic character lies in the dwelling on and drawing out the feeling, in its fullest reference, by help of a definite presentation which accents its *nature*."[72] Much of his argument, Bosanquet says, could be summed up by saying that "aesthetic emotion is 'impersonal.'" But, since the word is a dangerous one, he would prefer to call it "super-personal." His point is that the impersonality of art does not mean a critical or an intellectual attitude. On the other hand, feeling is not confined to its existence in a person. In becoming aesthetic it "does not become something less but something more";[73] it is "developed," "organized," "transformed."[74]

Bradley, speaking of "poetry as poetry" or "the novel as a novel," says that if we are not moved, we have not understood. But the interest is "impersonal." "Even where the poetry is lyrical, the emotion is felt to be idealized, raised above the being of the mere moment, and so made impersonal."[75] Indeed, "everywhere in literature, enjoyed as literature," the "ideas and feelings" are attached to "an object or world of objects"; it is that object which "our ideas and feelings color." The "ideas and emotions therefore qualify and are appropriated by this other world." "Detached from our life they go on to realize themselves in that world which we only contemplate. And in this detachment lies the freedom which is bestowed on us by every form of genuine art."[76]

Let us return briefly to imaginary objects. Eliot, after expounding the notion of a *real* fiction, says:

We thus analyze the intended object of fiction into its reference and its reality. The reality in its turn is not a simple object but an intended object, for it includes everything from the antecedents of the character in the author's mind, to the symbols which express the character on paper. . . .

. . . When we speak of the character as a fiction we mean a relation between an object real from one point of view and certain entities (ultimately physical) which are real from another point of view. The imaginary object, it will follow, is a highly complex ideal construction. It exists as such only from a third point of view which includes the two just mentioned; but these two also are in the closest dependence upon one another. For the real relations of the intended object (the mental and physical conditions which attended the genesis and realization of that character of fiction) would not be such as they are without the intention to realize a fiction.[77]

An imaginary object is a complex of real and ideal elements and relations: of ideality and its psychophysiological foundation (the mental and physical conditions). The ideal side consists of the object (logical meaning) and the idea (act or process), which is the realization of the object (or, what is the same thing, its idealization). The real elements include the word, which denotes the object; the sensation and image, which refer to the object; and the feeling and emotion. The feeling is *of* the object, qualifies it, and in this sense, apparently, is an integral part of the meaning of the object.[78] The feeling is, like the symbols which express it, continuous with the object; and, like the symbols, it determines, and is determined by, the object. But the real elements are not themselves objects; for stripped of their reference, which is an activity, they are not those elements. They vary with the context. And apart from a context they are indeterminate, unreal abstractions.

The object could not exist without "the '*Mitmensch*' (fellow man):"[79] it implies an external as well as an internal point of view. The outside view is that of another person; but it may be that of the poet himself, the poet as reader.[80] But the poet as reader is not the same self as the poet as writer, or rather he is the same but different. A point of view need not be regarded as identical with one human consciousness; and within one such consciousness there is a movement from one point of view to another, or the self may occupy several points of view at the same time.[81] Still, one may put oneself at the individual or the social point of view, as one pleases; but these are not deducible one from the other, and they are equally valid.[82]

10

A Logic of the Imagination

The problem we set out to define is roughly this: we cannot, as a rule, find a meaning for Eliot's language in the context of popular thought; and what is more, owing to the style of the critical prose and the character of the philosophy, it is not easy to find a meaning in the context of the philosophy—or at least to state it in an intelligible way.

To take an example, here is Eliot in "Ben Jonson":

> The ways in which the passions and desires of the creator may be satisfied in the work of art are complex and devious. In a painter they may take the form of a predilection for certain colors, tones, or lightings; in a writer the original impulse may be even more strangely transmuted. Now, we may say . . . that Falstaff or a score of Shakespeare's characters have a "third dimension" that Jonson's have not. This will mean, not that Shakespeare's spring from the feelings or imagination and Jonson's from the intellect or invention; they have equally an emotional source; but that Shakespeare's represent a more complicated tissue of feelings and desires, as well as a more supple, a more susceptible temperament. Falstaff is not only the roast Manning-tree ox with the pudding in his belly; he also "grows old," and, finally, his nose is as sharp as a pen. He was perhaps the *satisfaction* of more, and of more complicated feelings.[1]

Art, Bosanquet says, is "the satisfaction of feeling," the satisfaction of "a complete embodiment of feeling," a satisfaction found in "the character and detail of the object."[2]

There is in all experience an impulse or striving (nisus, conation) toward organization, and value is coexistent with organization. Art is one form of this impulse to a whole. This is a teleological notion, and Eliot's *satisfaction* is an aspect of the teleology of mind.[3]

Eliot is here transcribing philosophic doctrine, but the doctrine throws little light on Eliot's use of it. This is like "tying knots in the east wind." In general, the complications are such that there is a limit to what can be done with the critical prose, or done at any one time. But—this is the other side of the problem—little or nothing can be done apart from the philosophy.

Here is Eliot again:

> But when Coleridge released the truth that Shakespeare already in *Venus and Adonis* and *Lucrece* gave proof of a "most profound, energetic and *philosophic* mind" he was perfectly right, if we use these adjectives rightly, but he supplied a dangerous stimulant to the more adventurous. "Philosophic" is of course not the right word, but it cannot simply be erased: you must find another word to put in its place, and the word has not yet been found. The sense of the profundity of Shakespeare's "thought," or of his thinking-in-images, has so oppressed some critics that they have been forced to explain themselves by unintelligibles.[4]

According to F. W. Bateson, "the concept of 'thinking in images'" is "essentially a metaphor." Since statements by poets, philosophers, and scientists involve the use of words, "it is natural . . . to applaud the 'beauty' of philosophical argument, or the 'logic' of a poem's structure. But such flowers of speech must not be taken too seriously. . . . The fact is, surely, that propositional thinking is *different* from poetic thinking, and it only causes confusion to use the same word for both processes. In so far as there *is* thinking in images in poetry, it is not 'thinking' in the ordinary sense."[5]

In the same vein, Frank Kermode, commenting on Eliot's dictum that "there is a logic of the imagination as well as a logic of concepts," writes: "(We, I hope, understand what this means, and can see how sharply such a belief separates the modern from the 'Metaphysical' poet.) It is hard to resist Winters' argument that here 'the word *logic* is used figuratively,' that it indicates nothing but 'qualitative progression,' 'graduated progression of feeling.' Yet for all that the argument is false. It indicates no *progression* of any sort. Time and space are exorcised; the emblem of this 'logic' is the Dancer. This misunderstanding . . . shows that the difference between these two critics is extremely wide."[6]

Kermode assumes, as does Winters, that Eliot is here using the word logic in a figurative sense. And that is a natural assumption; for if thought and imagination are two separate faculties, it is only by an analogy that one speaks of a logic of the imagination.

In popular theory, sense and imagination are concrete, and thought is abstract. But in Eliot's philosophy thought is concrete as well as abstract—what Eliot calls "sensuous thought." Thus Joachim, speaking of sense perception, says that it involves a "discursive or mediate process." It is "inexplicit" thought, "a thinking immersed in and inseparable from sensation," an experience in which "the mind thinks sensuously." Inexplicit thought is continuous with, and akin to, thought free and explicit. It is "intellectual" activity, implicit judgment and inference.[7]

As for imagination, Bradley says: "Thought is abstract, we may be assured, while imagination is concrete." But with Bradley imagination may be abstract as well as concrete; that is, it may employ ideas while using little or no imagery. "In short, to set up imagination and thought as two separate faculties, and to speak of one using the other or again being applied to its service, is from first to last erroneous and indefensible." What makes the difference is "the special nature of the end and the special nature of the control."[8]

We tend, in popular thought, to think of the mind as consisting of sensations, feelings, perceptions, memories, imaginations, and thoughts. But thought is not a separate faculty: it is present in all the experiences of the mind—in, say, perception, memory, and imagination, as well as in inference. Though these experiences are differentiated in various ways, they are alike in being intellectual (ideal) constructions. Moreover, though memory is not inference proper, there is inference in memory. Similarly, in fancy or the mere imagination the images may follow a strict logical sequence, but at some point there is a breach of logical continuity, so that the mere imagination fails to be inference. But the mere imagination, when controlled logically, is itself inference—thinking in the narrow and strict sense. As for the aesthetic imagination, though its end is not intellectual (theoretic), it may or may not be logical.[9] Thus far Bradley.

Here is Bosanquet:

> There is a tendency to think of imagination as a sort of separate faculty, creative of images, a tendency which puts a premium on the arbitrary and fantastic in beauty, rather than the logical and penetrative. But this . . . is simply a blunder. The imagination is precisely the mind at work, pursuing and exploring the possibilities suggested by the connection of its experience. It may operate . . . in the service of logical inquiry, and of exact science itself. . . . [The only difference is that when imagination is operating not in the service of theoretical truth but in that of aesthetic feeling, its guiding purpose is the satisfaction of feeling.] And its method need not be logical, though it often is so, and . . . is so in the best imaginative work. By saying it need not be logical, I mean that in following out a suggestion it need not adhere to the main thread of connection. It may start afresh on any incidental feature that presents itself.[10]

Eliot, discussing "the connection of content" in memory and imagination, says:

> It is not true that the ideas of a great poet are in any sense arbitrary: certainly in the sense in which imagination is capricious, the ideas of a lunatic or an imbecile are more "imaginative" than those of a poet. In really great imaginative work the connections are felt to be bound by as logical necessity as any connections to be found anywhere.[11]

Though it is no part of our task to expound idealist logic, we cannot get along without certain distinctions. Thus intellectual is a wider term than logical.[12] All thought is intellectual (ideal), including imaginative thought, and imaginative thought may or may not be logical. Further, thought is inexplicit (sensuous, concrete) as well as explicit (abstract). Inexplicit thought is sometimes called intuitive understanding, that is, implicit judgment and inference.[13]

As for the term logic, it has a wider and a narrower meaning with idealists. Idealist logic is concerned with wholes or structures; and a work of art is a type of logical whole,[14] or quasi-logical whole—it is everywhere a question of degree. Thus when Eliot says that "in the mind of the poet these experiences are always forming new wholes," he is stating the central doctrine of idealist logic ("the impulse toward unity and coherence,"[15] to quote Bosanquet again). The structure of a work of art and the structure of a syllogistic argument (as construed by idealist logic) are both informed by the same logical spirit—what Eliot in the dissertation calls "logical activity." Similarly, poetry is, in its degree, as coherent and rational as a geometrical demonstration, the difference being that in poetry it is the whole man that thinks. It is the same with poetry and philosophy. Poetry is not, of course, philosophy, any more than it is geometry; but if, as people who read poetry for its ideas seem to think, poetry is a kind of philosophy, it can only be an inferior kind. But it is not that thought is one thing for the poet and another for the philosopher; it is rather that thought operates at different levels of itself, is directed to different ends, and satisfies different desires.

These matters are indicated in Eliot's critical prose—in a word, a phrase, an argument, an attitude. And this is our first interest, not the philosophic logic but the use that Eliot makes of it—his style, as we have called it. In this chapter we shall examine the style as shown in texts that deal with logic and imagination.

The style conceals more than it reveals, and what it reveals is open to misconstruction. Thus Rosemond Tuve asks: "Would Donne, or any Metaphysical poet, have understood T. S. Eliot's attribution to him of a 'direct sensuous apprehension of thought,' or have recognized himself in that intellectual poet who 'feels his thought as immediately as the odor of a rose'?"[16]

The question concerns the function of images. In the poetics of the Renaissance, images are significant of "a coherent meaning rationally imposed by the author and rationally apprehensible by the reader." But with Eliot the function of images is to communicate a state of mind, "without, for example, further indication by the author of an intended meaning." Moreover, "If they 'feel their thought as immediately as the odor of a rose,' transmuting their ideas into sensations, their images will not support or illustrate or elucidate, but somehow rather be, thoughts."[17] This

use of images is alogical, whereas Renaissance poetics is characterized by the logic of images.

Though that is not an unreasonable interpretation of Eliot's
language, the position it ascribes to Eliot can hardly be correct.
Thus, for example, in *John Dryden: The Poet, the Dramatist, the
Critic* (1932), quoting the passage in which Dryden speaks of
invention, fancy, and elocution as the three stages of imagination, Eliot writes:

> It will be observed that it does not occur to Dryden to distinguish to
> the point of isolation the reasoning from the imaginative faculty; it
> would not have occurred to him that there was or should be any-
> thing *irrational* in poetic imagination. . . . The distinction between
> thought and image, and the distinction between the thought and
> the clothing of it in elocution, are foreign to modern theory of
> poetry; but I think that these distinctions are safer than many that
> more recent wirters have made; and the part played by inspiration
> (or free association) and the part of conscious labor are justly kept
> in place.[18]

Eliot commends Dryden for his distinction between thought
and image, for not isolating thought from imagination, and
for not thinking that there is anything *irrational* in poetic
imagination.

The key to "modern theory of poetry" is given in parentheses—not, as we have seen, an uncommon practice with Eliot.
The allusion is to theory based on the psychology of association,
in which the image is the idea. Bradley begins his *Principles of
Logic* by criticizing this image theory. "The image, or psychological idea, is for logic nothing but a sensible reality. It is on a level
with the mere sensations of the senses. For both are facts and
neither is a meaning."[19] Again, in regard to the distinction between thought and the clothing of it in elocution, Bradley says:
"The universal, and even our awareness of it, come . . . long
before language is developed. . . . On the other hand, I agree
that it is only through language that the universal becomes
known as such."[20] And Eliot: "The idea, though largely depen-
dent for its existence upon the forms of its expression, must yet
not be confused with these forms."[21]

The psychology of the Renaissance, Tuve observes, derives

from the *De Anima*. Now with Aristotle a thought is not an image, though we cannot think without images, which support and assist thought (as in the use the geometer makes of particular triangles). The power of imagining is, with Aristotle, a function of the sensitive faculty, of the soul *qua* sentient.[22] Accordingly, thought and imagination are two separate faculties, imagination being (as Bradley puts it) in the service of thought.[23] Still, Eliot and Bradley are, in their idealistic way, Aristotlelians. Thus Eliot: "For Aristotle . . . the true nature of mind is found in the activity which it exercises. Attempt to analyze the mind, as a thing, and it is nothing. It is an operation. Aristotle's psychology therefore starts with psycho-physics, and ascends to speculative reason. It is only then that we perceive what mind is, and in retrospect find that it was present in the simplest sensation."[24] This view of the mind, implicit in Aristotle, is worked out in detail by Bradley in his *Principles of Logic*,[25] and it is the view of Eliot in his dissertation.

Eliot does not "pretend that Dryden as a critic is often profound."[26] Indeed, the only passage of any theoretical interest he quotes is that in which Dryden speaks of imagination as including invention, fancy, and elocution. It is a passage whose meaning is quite uncertain. It is interesting to see the use that Eliot makes of this passage, as well as passages of other critics—interesting as showing the idiosyncratic character of the critical prose.

In *The Use of Poetry and the Use of Criticism* he quotes Dryden's passage twice, both times in conjunction with Coleridge's distinction of fancy and imagination. On the first occasion, the question is "whether what we have here is two radically opposed theories of Poetic Imagination, or whether the two may be reconciled." On the second occasion, "I am not sure," he says, "that Coleridge has made as satisfactory an analysis as that of Dryden."[27]

In his examination of Dryden's passage he writes:

It ["invention"] corresponds to the inception of any piece of imaginative writing. It is not casting about for a subject, upon which, when found, the "imagination" is to be exercised; for we must remark that "invention" is the first moment in a process only the *whole* of which Dryden calls "imagination." . . ."Invention" in the sense used here by Dryden does not seem to me to be properly covered by the *New English Dictionary*, which quotes this very passage in support of the following definition: "The devising of a subject, idea, or method of treatment, by exercise of the intellect or imagination." The words "intellect or imagination" strike me as a burking of the question: if there is a clear distinction between invention by exercise of intellect and invention by exercise of imagination, then two definitions are called for; and if there is no difference between intellectual and imaginative invention there can hardly be much difference between imagination and intellect. But Dryden is talking expressly about imagination, not about intellect. . . . Fancy is an activity of the imagination rather than of the intellect, but is necessarily in part an intellectual activity, inasmuch as it is a "moulding of the thought as judgment represents it proper." Dryden does not, I believe, necessarily imply that the "third happiness" of poetic imagination, "elocution," is a third *act*; I mean, that the act of finding the proper words . . . begins only after the operation of fancy is complete. In fancy the finding of the words seems to me already to have begun; that is, fancy is partly verbal. . . .

We are liable, I think, to underrate Dryden's critical analyses, by assuming that they only apply to the kind of poetry that he writes himself; and thus we may overlook his meaning, as of the word "invention." Even if Dryden's poetry seems to us of . . . a peculiarly unpoetic type, we need not conclude that his mind operated quite differently from those of poets at other periods.[28]

This prose is like a tangled ball of yarn, and to disentangle it one has to pull on one strand and then on another. Dryden is talking expressly about imagination, not about intellect. Elsewhere, *Agamemnon* and *Macbeth* are "as much works of the 'intellect' as the writings of Aristotle."[29] These works are ideal constructions, and in that sense they are intellectual. But the end of imaginative writing is not truth but beauty; and truth and beauty are different values. Thus of Keats's "statement of equivalence" Eliot says that it "means nothing" to him; it is "meaningless."[30]

As for the rest, the question that Tuve asks about Donne might also be asked about Dryden. But it is common practice with philosophers to attach new meanings to old terms. And as Eliot says in the dissertation: "We are forced to the assumption that truth is one, and to the assumption that reality is one. But dissension rises when we ask: what one? Our system has pretended to be about the world of those who do not accept it as much as about the world of those who do."[31] Dryden's *art poétique* is, as Eliot construes it, theory in the larger sense.

Eliot next takes up Addison's account of fancy and imagination, of which he says:

> It would seem . . . that Addison had never read, certainly never pondered, Dryden's remarks upon the subject. . . . For Dryden "imagination" was the whole process of poetic creation in which fancy was one element. Addison starts out to "fix and determine" the notion of the two words; I cannot find any fixing or determining of the word "fancy" . . . ; he is . . . occupied . . . solely with the visual imagination according to Mr. Locke. That is a debt which he hastens to acknowledge: he pays a handsome testimonial to the scientific truths which Locke has established. Alas, philosophy is not science, nor is literary criticism; and it is an elementary error to think that we have discovered as objective laws what we have merely imposed by private legislation.[32]

Addison refers the reader to the doctrine of primary and secondary qualities, as explained by Locke, according to which the visible impressions apprehended by the imagination are "only Ideas in the Mind,"[33] and have no existence in external objects (a doctrine criticized by Bradley in the first chapter of *Appearance and Reality*.) Locke was also an exponent of the association of ideas (the phrase is his). Addison's papers on "the Pleasures of the Imagination" deal with the psychology of what is pleasing or displeasing to the mind; and they take the empirical facts of taste (accidents of association) for objective laws. Hence Addison's "whole discussion of the nature of imagination," though "a very interesting attempt at a general aesthetics," is "fruitless for the purposes of literary criticism."[34]

Eliot writes of Wordsworth:

> In the matter of mimesis he is more deeply Aristotelian than some who have aimed at following Aristotle more closely. He says of the poet:
>
> *To these qualities he has added . . . an ability of conjuring up in himself passions, which are indeed far from being the same as those produced by real events, yet . . . do more nearly resemble the passions produced by real events, than anything which, from the*

motions of their own minds merely, other men are accustomed to feel in themselves.

Here is the new version of Imitation, and I think it is the best so far:

Aristotle, I have been told, has said, that Poetry is the most philosophic of all writing; it is so: its object is truth, not individual and local, but general, and operative.[35]

For Eliot, poetry is not philosophy, any more than it was for Aristotle. It is the objectification of passions, the transmutation of the individual and local into the universal and impersonal.

In the "Note" on Herbert Read's discussion of Wordsworth, Eliot says:

[Read] considers that the poetic process of a mind like Dryden's and that of a mind like Wordsworth's are essentially diverse. . . . Now I cannot see why Dryden's and Wordsworth's minds should have worked any more differently from each other than those of any other two poets. I do not believe that any two poets' minds work quite in the same way, so far as we can know enough about the matter for "working" to mean anything at all; . . . but there must also be something in common in the poetic process of all poets' minds. Mr. Read quotes, in support of his contention, a passage from the *Annus Mirabilis* which I have not given:

The Composition of all poems is or ought to be of wit; and wit in the Poet, or wit writing (if you will give me leave to use a School distinction), is no other than the faculty of imagination in the Writer; . . . which searches over all the Memory for the Species or Ideas of those things which it designs to represent. Wit written is that which is well defined, the happy result of Thought, or product of Imagination.

I should have thought this merely a happy description in the language available at Dryden's time, and at a less profound level of insight than that of Coleridge or Wordsworth at their best, of the same sort of process that the latter were attempting to describe in language nearer to our own. But Mr. Read says No, what Dryden is talking about is something different: it is *wit written*, not poetry. Mr. Read seems to me to have fallen into the error which I mentioned in the text, of thinking that Dryden is only talking of his own kind of poetic composition. . . .[36]

That is as far as Eliot's use of Dryden goes. We come now to Coleridge.

In "Experiment in Criticism": "One thing that Coleridge did effect for literary criticism is this. He brought out clearly the relation of literary criticism to that branch of philosophy which has flourished amazingly under the name of esthetics; and . . . he puts the criticism of literature in its place as merely one department of the theoretic study of the Fine Arts in general. His fine discrimination of Fancy and Imagination cannot be held as permanent, for terms and relations change; but it remains one of the important texts for all who would consider the nature of poetic imagination."[37] In *The Use of Poetry*, Eliot says that Coleridge's distinction is "too simple," and the arguments Coleridge bases on it ("Milton has a highly imaginative, Cowley a very fanciful mind") are "specious."[38]

With Coleridge, imagination "dissolves, diffuses, dissipates, in order to recreate; or where this process is rendered impossible . . . it struggles to idealize and to unify." Fancy, on the other hand, "has no other counters to play with, but fixities and definites." It is "a mode of memory emancipated from the order of time and space"; and "equally with the ordinary memory the Fancy must receive all its materials ready made from the law of association."[39]

Though, Eliot says, he has read some Hegel and Fichte, as well as Hartley (who turns up at any moment with Coleridge), his mind is too heavy and concrete for any flight of abstruse reasoning, so that it may be he fails wholly to appreciate this distinction. If, as he suggested, the difference between imagination and fancy amounts in practice to no more than the difference between good and bad poetry, have we done more than take a turn round Robin Hood's barn? Still, it seems unwise of Coleridge to talk of memory in connection with fancy and omit it altogether from the account of imagination, for memory plays a very large part in imagination. An image, a phrase, a word might lie about in the mind for years, and "re-appear transformed in some verse-context charged with great imaginative pressure."[40] What Coleridge's distinction gives one is not distinct imagination and distinct fancy but only "degrees of imaginative success."[41] And one has to forget all about Coleridge's fancy to learn anything from him about imagination, as with Addison—but from Coleridge there is a good deal to learn.

Coleridge's distinction is a distinction of value, but he conceives it as a difference of kind rather than degree. And he draws on two incompatible views of mind: his own idealist version[42] and Hartley's mechanistic version. But there is no need of two operations, one dissolving in order to re-create and the other separating and combining static units. What counts is the "imaginative pressure" (the intensity of the artistic process, the pressure, so to speak, under which the fusion takes place), and this gives one "degrees of imaginative success."

To quote again from *The Use of Poetry:*

> The faith in mystical inspiration is responsible for the exaggerated repute of *Kubla Khan*. The imagery of that fragment, certainly, whatever its origins in Coleridge's reading, sank to the depths of Coleridge's feeling, was saturated, transformed there—"those are pearls that were his eyes"—and brought up into daylight again. But it is not *used:* the poem has not been written. A single verse is not poetry unless it is a one-verse poem; and even the finest line draws its life from its context. Organization is necessary as well as "inspiration." The re-creation of word and image . . . happens almost incessantly with Shakespeare. Again and again, in his use of a word, he will give a new meaning or extract a latent one; again and again the right imagery, saturated while it lay in the depths of Shakespeare's memory, will rise like Anadyomene from the sea. In Shakespeare's poetry this reborn image or word will have its rational use and justification; in much good poetry the organization will not reach to so rational a level.[43]

If, Bradley says, "by mere imagination we mean our mental flow so far as that is subject to no control whatever, and is so not 'used' at all, this certainly is not imagination in the higher sense of the word."[44]

Transformation and organization—those are the key notions of Eliot's theory. What gives the imagery its intensity, he goes on to say, is its "saturation—I will not say with 'associations,' for I do not want to revert to Hartley—but with feelings too obscure for the authors even to know quite what they were." And "memories may have symbolic value, but of what we cannot tell, for they come to represent the depths of feeling into which we cannot peer."[45]

A word or an image enters innumerable contexts, so that it

becomes "saturated" with the meanings acquired from its many contexts, and its "intensity" is owing to its "saturation."

In the dissertation, there is no "priority of image over emotion, or vice versa," for "feeling and image react upon each other inextricably, and the two aspects are so closely related, that you cannot say that the relation is casual." Further, "It is a bad metaphor to speak of the change from percept to memory-image as a decay. There is an alteration . . . in content. There are two essentially different points of view."[46]

An image is not simply a faded sensation or a weakened copy of a perception. Its alteration of content is a consequence of the various contexts into which it has entered, so that its life is largely independent of the perception in which it originated. So with the feelings that attach to images: they, too, in becoming "saturated" have undergone alteration, so that though they may have symbolic value, of what we cannot tell.

Eliot, of course, resorts to figurative language, but his metaphors must not be pressed, for they are not always compatible with one another or with his philosophy. Thus: "The poet's mind is in fact a receptacle for seizing and storing up numberless feelings, phrases, images, which remain there until all the particles which can unite to form a new compound are present together."[47] Similarly, the imagery "sank to the depths of Coleridge's feeling, was saturated, transformed there" or "the right imagery saturated while it lay in the depths of Shakespeare's memory, will rise like Anadyomene from the sea."

For Eliot, the mind is not a receptacle or a storehouse; it is an activity or operation. Images do not lie about in the mind waiting to be used, for there are no images that are purely subjective. Every image has, or has had, an object, so that from the very first images belong as much to the objective world as to the subjective. (Subjectivity is not a stratum, but an aspect, of experience.)[48] It is through its "association" with objects that an image acquires its significance, and its "saturation" is a consequence of its "associations."[49]

The "association," as we have seen, is part of a logical process (thus Bradley speaks of "the intellectual identification of the image with the object" as "this logical process").[50] Eliot, in his discussion of the poems of Jean de Bosschére, is not always able, he says, to follow "the development of [the] images into a logical structure."[51] In the later Dante essay, speaking of the *Inferno*, "we get," he says, "a succession of . . . images, of images which are coherent, in that each reinforces the last."[52] Similarly, in the *Anabasis* of St.-Jean Perse, "the sequence of images coincides and concentrates into an intense impression of barbaric civilization," and the "reasonableness" of the images lies in the "total effect" they produce. "Its sequences, its logic of imagery, are those of poetry and not of prose."[53] The difference is in the concentration, the telescoping, of the images—the imaginative pressure.

It is easy to overlook Eliot's meaning. After all, the principle of unity and coherence is a rhetorical commonplace, and an artistic one as well. If a literary work, like a freshman composition, is to be intelligible, it must not be inconsistent. Further, its parts must be, or be taken as, related to one another and adjusted to the aim of the whole; or the parts must have, or be taken as having, some particular order and arrangement, so that the work is one thing rather than another. The literary critic, accordingly, endeavors to show the internal coherence of the work, and in so doing accounts for the feeling of satisfaction he finds in the work. But with Eliot coherence is not merely a rhetorical principle; it is a logical doctrine. Thus Bosanquet, in the preface to *Implication and Linear Inference*: "Still following Mr. Bradley . . . I have laid even more stress than before on the principle of coherence, and have insisted on 'implication' as a term free from reference to reasoning in its traditional shapes."[54] Idealist logic is a logic of coherence, that is, of the idea of system (coherence, comprehensiveness, and noncontradiction).

Eliot says, speaking of the *Anabasis*:

> Such selection of a sequence of images and ideas has nothing chaotic about it. There is a logic of the imagination as well as a logic of concepts. People who do not appreciate poetry find it difficult to distinguish between order and chaos in the arrangement of images. . . . And if, as I suggest, such an arrangement of imagery requires just as much "fundamental brain-work" as the arrangement of an argument, it is to be expected that the reader of a poem should take at least as much trouble as a barrister reading an important decision on a complicated case.[55]

The hint is "fundamental brain-work" (the phrase is Rossetti's).

If, Bosanquet writes, we fail to see that "not the invention of novelty, but the logic which lays bare the heart and structure of things . . . is the true secret of art," it is "not because we are too rational, but because we are not rational enough." And he continues:

> The "fundamental brainwork" is lacking to us; as is a special capacity for the infinitely delicate logic of expression, by which the passionate thought . . . is embodied in a million ramifications of detail, constituting a tissue of precise determination in which alone the thought in question with its passion could find utterance—could become itself. If we say that the process is not rational, because it is largely unconscious, we are committing a serious confusion. The process itself is an intense and exquisitely adjusted and organized consciousness to a great extent obviously and plainly logical. . . . In short, then, all logical activity is a world of content reshaping itself . . . in [the] presence of new suggestions; a syllogism is in principle nothing less, and a Parthenon or "Paradise Lost" is in principle nothing more.[56]

Bosanquet is discussing the notion that, as it may be put, the geometer thinks whereas the poet feels, or feels and imagines; in other words, that the geometric result, being arrived at by deduction, is rational, whereas the artistic achievement, being unpredictable, is irrational and unaccountable, something that can only be attributed to genius and inspiration—a view that makes a division in the life of the mind, taking thought and sensibility to be exclusive, and on the side of sensibility finding a diversity without identity. Thus it is a common notion (he has Bergson especially in mind) that "the creative imagination of the artist is a faculty of originaltiy *de novo*."[57] In life and organic process there is continuity; but the creative imagination is a present without a past, a conclusion without data or premises. In this view, art, cut off from life and logic, is "a pure incarnation of the new."[58] Now, Bosanquet says, though there is an obvious contrast between a work of art and an abstract argument, it does not follow that "the creative nature of an artistic achievement rests on a fundamentally different principle from that involved in all advance and completion effected by the spirit of logic, which lies in the continuity of the universal."[59] And "when we say 'continuity,' we say 'logic.'"[60]

This brings us to the introduction (1928) to *Ezra Pound: Selected Poems*, where Eliot writes:

> I should say first that Pound's versification is objectionable to those who object to it as "modern," because they have not sufficient education (in verse) to understand development. Poets may be divided into those who develop technique, those who imitate technique, and those who invent technique. When I say "invent," I should use inverted commas, for invention would be irreproachable if it were possible. "Invention" is wrong only because it is impossible. I mean that the difference between the "development" and the "sport" is, in poetry, a capital one. There are two kinds of "sports" in poetry, in the florticultural sense. One is the imitation of development, and the other is the imitation of some Idea of originality. The former is commonplace, a waste product of civilization. The latter is contrary to life. The poem which is absolutely original is absolutely bad; it is, in the bad sense, "subjective" with no relation to the world to which it appeals.
>
> Originality, in other words, is by no means a simple idea in the criticism of poetry. True originality is merely development; and if it is right development it may appear in the end so *inevitable* that we almost come to the point of view of denying all "original" virtue to the poet. He simply did the next thing. I do not deny that *true* and *spurious* originality may hit the public with the same shock; indeed spurious originality ("spurious" when we use the word "originality" properly, that is to say, within the limitations of life, and when we use the word absolutely and therefore improperly, "genuine") may give the greater shock.
>
> Now Pound's originality is genuine in that his versification is a *logical* development of the verse of his English predecessors. Whitman's originality is both genuine and spurious. It is genuine in so far as it is a *logical* development of certain English prose; Whitman was a great prose writer. It is spurious in so far as Whitman wrote in a way that asserted that his great prose was a new form of verse. . . . The word "revolutionary" has no meaning, for this reason: we confound under the same name those who are revolutionary because they develop logically, and those who are "revolutionary" because they innovate illogically. It is *very* difficult at any moment, to discriminate between the two.[61]

The theme is tradition, the historical sense, the relation of the present to the past, here illustrated by Pound's versification. The past being gone, it exists only in our knowledge of it; and the logical form of all knowledge (a flower, a self, a society, art, or anything else we choose to make an object, such as Pound's versification) is that of identity in difference. Logic is the development of a single subject, an identity or a universal, which is realized in its differences. If the development is to be logical (objective and necessary), the subject or universal must be present throughout, and it is continuously altered and transformed, without prejudice to its identity. Now an argument is, like a work of art, an individual whole. Thus a syllogism is an organized whole or structure. It is a coherence of differences in and of an identity. The premises, or differences, are in the process modified and altered, so that the result is a new whole (a reshaping of the elements that entered into it).[62] Truth is thus individual. Since there are no rules to prescribe beforehand what the development is to be, it is difficult to discriminate between an illogical innovation and a logical development. It is only from the point of view of a later stage that an earlier stage can be judged to have been right or wrong. Thus if, as Eliot says, it turns out to have been the right one, it will appear to be *inevitable*. Truth (this is the principle) is not a copy of an external reality which serves as its criterion; truth is its own criterion, and the only test of truth is the fuller truth.[63]

Eliot renders the exact sense and nuance of the logical doctrine: mediation through universals, and development through stages, each of which is incomplete, a partial realization of the varieties of versification (that being the subject here). It is not a question of better or worse but of its being "modern," right for its time (in the same way that Newtonian physics can be seen in retrospect to have been right for its time, though the introduction of the new led to a reorganization of the system of physics as it was at that stage of development, with an alteration of the relations and values of its elements).

In "A Note on Ezra Pound" (1918): "What we commonly find among contemporary poets is a mentality which has remained in the age of Wordsworth or in the age of Tennyson, with a technique which is actually inferior to that of either of these. . . . But while the mind of man has altered, verse has stood still."

But Pound, though "superficially he may seem so much the archaeologist," is always "modern."[64] In "Ezra Pound" (1946), the critical activity of Pound has "a particular relation to poetry in a particular age"; a criticism like Pound's is "advocacy of a certain kind of poetry; it is an assertion that poetry written in the immediate future must, if it is to be good poetry, observe certain methods and take certain directions. The important question is, whether the critic is right in his judgment of the situation: if so, his criticism will be permanent, as Dryden's and Wordsworth's are."[65] And Eliot finds "nothing to abate" in his introduction of 1928 to Pound's *Selected Poems*.

We shall return to this theme. But first we must take note of Eliot's remarks in the introduction of 1928 on the nature of translation:

> As for *Cathay*, it must be pointed out that Pound is the inventor of Chinese poetry for our time. I suspect that every age has had, and will have, the same illusion concerning translations, an illusion which is not altogether an illusion either. When a foreign poet is successfully done into the idiom of our own language and our own time, we believe that he has been "translated"; we believe that through this translation we really at last get the original. The Elizabethans must have thought they *got* Homer through Chapman, Plutarch through North. Not being Elizabethans, we have not that illusion; we see that Chapman is more Chapman than Homer, and North more North than Plutarch, both localized three hundred years ago. We perceive also that modern scholarly translations, Loeb or other, do not give us what the Tudors gave. If a modern Chapman, or North or Florio appeared, we should believe that he was the real translator: we should, in other words, do him the compliment of believing that his translation was translucence. For contemporaries, no doubt the Tudor translations were translucencies; for us they are "significant specimens of Tudor prose." The same fate impends upon Pound. His translations seem to be—and that is the test of excellence—translucencies: we *think* we are closer to the Chinese than when we read, for instance, Legge. I doubt this: I predict that in three hundred years Pound's *Cathay* will be a "Windsor Translation" as Chapman and North are now

"Tudor Translations": it will be called (and justly) a "magnificent specimen of XXth Century poetry" rather than a "translation." Each generation must translate for itself.

This is as much as to say that Chinese poetry, as we know it today, is something invented by Ezra Pound. It is not to say that there is a Chinese poetry-in-itself, waiting for some ideal translator who shall be only translator; but Pound has enriched modern English poetry as Fitzgerald enriched it. . . . People of today who like Chinese poetry are really no more liking Chinese poetry than the people who like Willow pottery and Chinesische-Turms in Munich and Kew like Chinese Art. It is probable that the Chinese . . . influenced Pound . . . ; on the other hand, it is certain that Pound has influenced the Chinese and the Provencals and the Italians and the Saxons—not the matter *an sich*, which is unknowable, but the matter as we know it.[66]

That is, like the argument on logical development, a clear example of the way in which Eliot elaborates for critical purposes some doctrine or aspect of doctrine. The trouble is that a full explanation of the doctrine would require a restatement of Bradley's *Appearance and Reality*, the aim of which is to reunite what Kant set apart. The Thing in itself or Things in themselves are, according to Bradley, abstractions from experience, and quite nonsensical.[67] Knowledge is knowledge of reality, but the reality is not something copied by knowledge. In the appendix of his treatise on history Bradley has a fable concerning a historical figure whom artists in successive generations have painted, some from life and other from copies. And though it is agreed that the reality must be a copy of the original, there is disagreement about the original—the historical person as he really was. And wishing to have a copy of the original, they corrected, remolded, and altered the earlier pictures. The problem is that the new picture is to be a copy of the original, but the original is known only through the pictures. There is only one answer: the artist must construct his picture through his experience of the present, which is the only reality he knows. "You wish to see the real; but I know no reality save that which I see and study now for myself. You ask for truth; I know no truth but the accordance of the drawing with this my world. . . . It comes to this—I have no reality but one, you must have that or nothing. It may be things were different in the past; I cannot help that, I did not live then. If you object to a past brought into harmony with the present, you can have nothing from me at all." "And I must tell you that really there is no copying. Every man has his style, and cannot help having it. I have mine."[68]

Eliot, for his part, classifies Kant as a "dualistic realist," and a good deal of the argument in the dissertation is directed against "realistic assumptions." For instance, he says of Meinong: "This seems to me essentially the position of the critical philosophy: the thing is known through its appearances, but as soon as the distinction is made appearance and thing fall apart, and appearance replaces thing as a point of attention." Again: "The distinction between inferior [real] and superior [ideal] objects, on the whole, strikes me as thoroughly critical. To treat things, not as moments of objectivity, but as ultimate lumps which can be grasped after all relations have been stripped away, seems to be the attempt of both Meinong and Kant." And in a footnote: "'For a thing to exist it must possess identity. . . . And, further, this identity is ideal. . . .' *Appearance*, p. 61." And as we have already seen, "There is no one club, no one world, without a diversity of points of view for it to be one to." This means, among other things, that "the identity of one man's world and another's does not consist, as we readily are led to believe, in one world . . . which is, apart from being known, exactly what it is when we know it."[69]

The arguments concerning logical development and the nature of translation complement each other: on the one hand, the past varies with the present; and on the other hand, the present is the past transformed. There is, in other words, a "continuous reality," for "all identity is ideal . . . 'in this sense that it involves the self-transcendence of that which is identical' (*Appearance*, p. 526)." What is continuous is "ideality," which is "a universality of function . . . recognized through a diversity of situation."[70]

The two arguments we have been considering are elaborated in a way that is unusual with Eliot. The style is normally condensed, concentrated, and suggestive, in the way that Eliot thinks poetry should be written. In effect, the prose does what poetry is supposed to do—replace the philosophy.

In *After Strange Gods* (1934) Eliot reformulates his idea of tradition; but though he is not dealing with tradition as a purely literary matter, he does "not repudiate" what he wrote in "Tradition and the Individual Talent." Thus one danger is "to associate tradition with the immovable; to think of it as something hostile to all change"; but "the word itself implies a movement." A superficial apprehension of the term might suggest "the assumption that . . . the possible forms of expression have all been discovered and developed; the assumption that novelty of form and of substance was always to be deprecated." What is objectionable is novelty that is deliberately sought, whereas originality is the result of an "inner necessity." Nor is Gerard Hopkins an orthodox and traditional poet. "His innovations certainly were good, but . . . they operate only within a narrow range, and are easily imitated though not adaptable for many purposes; furthermore, they sometimes strike me as lacking inevitability—that is to say, they sometimes come near to being purely *verbal*, in that a whole poem will give us *more* of the same thing, an accumulation, rather than a real development of thought or feeling" (recurrence, repeated effects, not expansion and alteration).[71]

In "American Literature and the American Language" (1953) Eliot again brings up the limitations of the novelties introduced by Whitman and Hopkins. Though, he says, the term "American literature" has for him a clear and distinct meaning, this meaning is not wholly definable, nor is it desirable to try to define it. Like other terms, "American literature" has altered and developed its meaning in the course of time. It means something different for us today from what it could have meant a hundred years ago; it has a much fuller meaning now than it could have had then; and it is only in retrospect that the Americanness of the writers of a century ago is fully visible. As landmarks for the indication of American literature Eliot chooses Poe, Whitman, and Twain; but he is not asserting that from a study of these three writers one could arrive at a formula of Americanism in literature. "What their common American characteristics may be, is something I should consider it folly to attempt to define; and in seeking for their common qualities, one might easily overlook the essence of each." (Common qualities are arrived at by abstraction from differences.) What distinguishes Twain, at least in *Huckleberry Finn*, is that he discovered "a new way of writing, valid not only for [himself] but for others"; he is thus one of those

rare writers "who have brought their language up to date."
Huckleberry Finn exhibits "the strong local flavor combined with
unconscious universality." That accounts for the continued
appreciation of Twain by foreign readers. "The foreigner may at
first be attracted by the differences: an author is found interesting
because he is so unlike anything in the foreigner's own literature.
But a vogue due to novel differences will soon fade out; it will not
survive unless the foreign reader recognizes, perhaps unconsciously, identity as well as difference."

Having got so far, Eliot takes up the necessity of change and
development if we are to have contemporary living literatures.
There occurs from time to time a revolution, a reaction against a
way of writing that is found to be out of date. The new kind of
writing (he is talking of the movement of which he was a part) was
not "destructive but re-creative." "It is not that we have repudiated the past . . . but that we have enlarged our conception
of the past; and that in the light of what is new we see the past in a
new pattern." And he compares such a "transformation" to what
takes place when a new discovery is made in the fields of science.
It is difficult to arrive at a satisfactory definition of what constitutes an American "tradition" in poetry, because "the moment
you produce your definition, and the neater the definition is, the
more surely some poet will turn up who doesn't fit into it at all,
but who is nevertheless definitely . . . American." (If the extension is increased, so is the meaning.) "And the tradition itself, as I
have said long ago, is altered by every new writer of genius."[72]

The poet who does the next thing, the original poet, Eliot
said in the essay he alludes to, must possess erudition. And in "A
Note on Ezra Pound," speaking of Pound's "cultivation of the
historical sense," of "the poet's relation to poets of the past," he
says that "this perception of relation involves an organized view
of the course of European poetry from Homer."[73]

Relations, and the terms related, imply and depend upon a
whole of which they are the expression (and implication, the
interdependence of parts, holds only within wholes, the types of
implication varying with the nature of the wholes). Space and
number are types of wholes, and poetry is another type. Resemblance and difference lead to the abstract universal and the
idea of a class, whereas identity and difference lead to the idea of

"organic wholes" or systems. The whole or universal is a generic subject which persists as an identity through differences; and since the extension is virtually unlimited, there can be no adequate definition of the subject.[74]

The logical character of a generic subject is difficult and obscure. We may note, to begin with, its relation to the tools of the critic. Thus in "Studies in Contemporary Criticism" (1918): "The work of the critic is almost wholly comprehended in the 'complementary activities' of comparison and analysis. The one activity implies the other; and together they provide the only way of asserting standards and of isolating a writer's peculiar merits."[75]

Analysis is the differentiation of a unity, and comparison rests on a unity of differences. Thus Bradley says of the operations of comparison and distinction that "both exhibit a double aspect of unity and diversity." These processes bring out identity against a background of difference or difference against a background of identity; and they both depend on, and take place within, an "ideal whole" (Eliot's "ideal order").[76]

Eliot does, of course, use the tools of comparison and analysis. Moreover, the critic "must not coerce, and he must not make judgments of worse and better. He must simply elucidate: the reader will form the correct judgment for himself."[77] But, it is said, Eliot *does* make judgments of better and worse. No doubt he does. But his point is that the true critic is "a scrupulous avoider of formulae; he refrains from statements which pretend to be literally true; he finds fact nowhere and approximation always."[78]

To take an example: Twain, in respect to bringing language up to date, is placed with Dryden and Swift, and put above Hawthorne, though no finer a stylist, and in obvious ways a less profound explorer of the human soul.[79] Now the question is, Are these relations true or false? And, further, is there empirical evidence that can be brought in support of them? Though we cannot enter into the details of this question—it is too large for that—we may try to show what the problem is.

We explain something by referring it to something else, of which it is the consequence or the antecedent. But the generic subject is taken here as a self-related whole, an identity which determines its own differences; and it is so taken because it is a unity that has an interest for its own sake or in itself. But cannot the critic support his judgments by analyzing the particular works of the writers in question? The trouble is that this is the same problem. That is to say, an individual work is, for critical purposes, taken as a self-contained whole. The critic does not, in dealing with it, copy or represent anything. Even an intuitive understanding of the work involves inexplicit analysis and construction, and this is interpretation. And as Eliot says in "The Function of Criticism," "it is difficult to confirm the 'interpretation' by external evidence."[80] Similarly, in the dissertation there is, "strictly speaking, no imaginary objective"[81]—that is, no sphere of "matter of fact" in which judgments must be either right or wrong. The object the critic is looking at is a point of attention, a *that*, and this is the reality; the interpretation is a *what*, and this is the appearance.

Now Eliot says "there may be an identity uniting differences of quality. It is obvious that it is this felt identity between appearance and reality that will constitute explanation, and that the identity is a fragile and insecure thing."[82] And again, "an interpretation is essentially unverifiable."[83] Accordingly, all that the critic can do is to exhibit the principle at work in his judgments, that is, the identity uniting differences; and he can support his judgments by citing parallel cases, arguing, that is, by analogy. The parallel cases illuminate each other, and bring out the identity while preserving the differences or bring out the differences while showing the identity. But the analogical reasoning is subordinate to the grasp of identity, for otherwise it could not be known which cases were parallel. This is a form of the hermeneutic circle. In the end, the appeal is to the teleology of imaginative thought, the impulse to construct wholes that satisfy feeling.[84]

A literary (or other) work of art has an aesthetic side (feeling) and a discursive side, and on its discursive side it does not differ from any other complex object (set of terms and relations). Thus organization is necessary in poetry as well as in prose, though in poetry it is not always "rational"—that is, explicit. Further, the discursive analysis of a literary work is a means and not an end, a means to fuller aesthetic appreciation.[85] But our concern here is with the discursive or logical side. And on this side, Bradley says, an aesthetic object may offer itself as "mediated . . . by internal necessity," and it may be seen "to be mediated ideally, to contain inference and judgment."[86]

Eliot does not offer many examples, and those he does are in his customary oblique style. Thus Hardy, he says in *After Strange Gods*, tends to introduce personal emotion, emotion irrelevant to the situation. But in *The Mayor of Casterbridge* "he comes the nearest to producing an air of inevitability, and of making the crises seem the consequences of the character of Henchard."[87] In the essay on *Hamlet:* "The words of Macbeth on learning of his wife's death strike us as if, given the sequence of events, these words were automatically released by the last event in the series. The artistic 'inevitability' lies in this complete adequacy of the external to the emotion; and this is precisely what is deficient in *Hamlet.*"[88] Macbeth, preparing for battle, is told: "The queen, my Lord, is dead." And he says: "She should have died hereafter;/ There would have been a time for such a word." He had acted for his wife's sake; and now that she is dead, he no longer has a motive for the battle; and this releases the speech about tomorrow, and tomorrow, and tomorrow. This seems to be the sort of thing Eliot means when he speaks of the organization of Shakespeare's poetry being "rational."

There is more here than Aristotle's necessary or probable sequence of events. Still, as Bosanquet says: "As Aristotle told us in his *Aesthetic*, no object is a whole which is not logically coherent. This is one of the truths which is always admitted, and never applied."[89] But Eliot's logic is not the traditional Aristotelian logic. Thus in *After Strange Gods*, still speaking of Hardy: "But it is by no means self-evident that human beings are most real when most violently excited; violent physical passions do not in themselves differentiate men from each other . . . ; and the passion has significance only in relation to the character and behavior of the man at other moments of his life and in other contexts."[90] That is, of course, the principle of identity and difference stated once again.

So much for the novel and drama. As for verse, Eliot writes in "The Metaphysical Poets":

In *A Valediction*, [Donne develops] the comparison of two lovers to a pair of compasses. But elsewhere we find, instead of the mere explication of the content of a comparison, a development by rapid association of thought. . . .

> On a round ball
> A workman that hath copies by, can lay
> An Europe, Afrique, and an Asia,
> And quickly make that, which was nothing, All,
>> So doth each teare,
>> Which thee doth weare,
> A globe, yea, world by that impression grow,
> Till thy tears mixt with mine do overflow
> This world, by waters sent from thee, my heaven dissolved so.

Here we find at least two connections which are not implicit in the first figure, but are forced upon it by the poet: from the geographer's globe to the tear, and the tear to the deluge.[91]

The poet, as we have seen, has an idea (feeling, image), and "he develops it by accretion or expansion." Here the development is by accretion.

Though that is all Eliot says here, these two methods sum up a good deal of Bradley's logical doctrine. The general pattern is as follows: there is a starting point (data, premises or premise), an intellectual (ideal) process, and a modification of the starting point. Development by expansion is predominantly analytic: it constructs a whole by distinguishing and recombining what was implicit in the starting point. Development by accretion is predominantly synthetic: it extends the given by adding elements external to it, and both the given and the added elements reappear as constituents of the completed whole. If there is no solution of continuity, the process is in principle logical; and if there is a break in the continuity, the process, though intellectual, is not logical.[92]

Here, in "A Note on Ezra Pound," is Eliot commenting on "Pound's recent unfinished epic, three cantos of which appear in the American edition of 'Lustra'":

> In appearance, it is a rag-bag of Mr. Pound's reading in various languages, from which one fragment after another is dragged to light, and illuminated by the beauty of his phrase.
>
> Home to sweet rest, and to the waves deep laughter
> sends one back to Catullus. Or a sharp reminiscence of travel:

> *It juts into the sky, Gordon that is,*
> *Like a thin spire. Blue night pulled down about it*
> *Like tent-flaps or sails close-hauled. When I was there,*
> *La Noche de San Juan, a score of players*
> *Were walking about the streets in masquerade,*
> *Pike-staves and paper helmets . . .*

but apparently no continuity. And yet the thing has, after one has read it once or twice, a positive coherence; it is an objective and reticent autobiography.[93]

It is the continuity that gives it coherence and makes it objective. Here—this is our last instance—is Eliot in the introduction of 1928:

A Girl

> *The tree has entered my hands,*
> *The sap has ascended my arms,*
> *The tree has grown into my breast—*
> *Downward,*
> *The branches grow out of me, like arms.*
>
> *Tree you are,*
> *Moss you are,*
> *You are violets with wind above them.*
> *A child—so high—you are,*
> *And all this is folly to the world.*

There, you see, the "feeling" is original in the best sense, but the phrasing is not quite "completed"; for the last line is one which I or half a dozen other men might have written. Yet it is not "wrong," and I certainly could not improve upon it.[94]

The development is arrested, and the conclusion is not got from the starting point but is added from the outside. If the phrasing is not "wrong," neither is it "right." In art this is a question of aesthetic necessity—of inevitability.[95]

An idea *is* (not *has*) an object,[96] and here the idea is not fully realized. Whenever we think, we start with an incomplete idea and seek, relatively, to complete it. And we never know, when we have an idea, what it means until it has been unfolded. An idea is not a fixed meaning but is capable of expansion and contraction, so that we are constantly saying more or less than what we mean.[97] To say that we start with an incomplete idea means that the starting point of thought—its premise—is always a whole that exhibits itself as two or more elements of a unity, or two or more differences of an identity; and the effort of thought is to complete a partially realized whole. In short, the object of thought is (in a double sense) the object of thought—or the idea means itself.

Eliot's inverted commas indicate a certain reservation about talking of art in logical terms. For though beauty, Bradley says, is an object, an aesthetic object is not in the logical sense true; it is "true" if "truth" is taken widely, in the sense of that which is an individual reality, something that is at once real and ideal, self-contained and self-existent.[98]

There is space only to deal very briefly with these dark sayings. But first a word about truth. A judgment is the predication of an idea of reality; and though the idea has an existential side, it is separated from its existence and referred to some other *that*. An idea so used is purely ideal, and cannot be said to exist. And truth consists of such ideas.

In a work of art, on the other hand, there is a union of existence and idea (*that* and *what*).[99] An aesthetic judgment is a sensible perception, and such perception involves inexplicit or intuitive thought, thought immersed in and inseparable from sense and feeling. That is the aesthetic attitude (the end of the enjoyment of poetry, the pure contemplation, as Eliot says in "The Perfect Critic"). But when, Bradley says, we begin to reflect and analyze, the whole has so far been broken up, and so far, as aesthetic, it has ceased to be itself. Or, as he also puts it, if we ask of a poem, Is this true? we have, for better or worse, left behind the poetry.[100] So Bosanquet: "Mr. Matthew Arnold's phrase 'criticism of life,' applied to poetry explains what is meant by saying that art contains reason. That the reason must be in the form of feeling this term 'criticism' appears to ignore."[101] By the "form of feeling" is meant the feeling of a whole implicitly distinguished and related, the felt meaning below the level of explicit thought.

Anything may be considered in and for itself or in relation to something else. That is the basis of Eliot's distinction between criticism and scholarship. The scholar is concerned with fact and truth, whereas the critic is concerned with aesthetic value and beauty. Thus Eliot, in "Poetry and Propaganda" (1930), criticizing Whitehead for summoning Shelley and Wordsworth "to *prove* something," asks: "Can poetry be cited to *prove* anything? and to what extent can it even be cited to *illustrate* anything?" The reply is that poetry "cannot prove that anything is *true*."[102]

Logically, a work of art may be regarded as a supposition, or a hypothetical judgment, a form of thought that deals not with fact but with possibility. In a work of fiction, to take that as an example, the author starts with certain characters in a certain situation and investigates what follows, given these premises. But though the whole be coherent and rational, it is not true; for a supposition makes no assertion about actual fact. On the other hand, if what it asserts did not refer to actual fact, it would be meaningless. It is related to actual fact both positively and negatively. This, in another form, is the argument about imaginary objects.[103]

Here, to sum up, is Eliot in the essay on *Hamlet:* "*Qua* work of art, the work of art cannot be interpreted; there is nothing to interpret; we can only criticize it according to standards, in comparison to other works of art; and for 'interpretation' the chief task is the presentation of relevant historical facts which the reader is not assumed to know." Again: "It is not merely the 'guilt of a mother' that cannot be handled as Shakespeare handled the suspicion of Othello, the infatuation of Antony, or the pride of Coriolanus. The subject might conceivably have expanded into a tragedy like these, intelligible, self-complete, in the sunlight."[104]

Eliot states his position quite plainly. But his characteristic statements are marked by indirection. Thus in "From Poe to Valéry":

> In the course of an introduction which is primarily a sketch of the man Poe and his biography, Baudelaire lets fall one remark indicative of an aesthetic that brings us to Valéry:
>
> > He believed [*says Baudelaire*], *true poet that he was, that the goal of poetry is of the same nature as its principle, and that it should have nothing in view but itself.*
>
> "A poem does not say something—it *is* something": that doctrine has been held in more recent times.[105]

The last statement, though it is given as a quotation, is not Baudelaire but Eliot. And the allusion, for Eliot, is to I. A.

Richards ("as Mr. Richards says, 'it is never what a poem *says* that matters, but what it *is*' ").[106]

As for what a poem says, Richards is quoted in *The Use of Poetry* to the following effect:

> Coleridge, when he remarked that a "willing suspension of disbe-lief" accompanied much poetry, was noting an important fact, but not quite in the happiest terms, for we are neither aware of a disbe-lief nor voluntarily suspending it in these cases. It is better to say that the question of belief or disbelief, in the intellectual sense, never arises when we are reading well. If unfortunately it does arise, either through the poet's fault or our own, we have for the moment ceased to be reading and have become astronomers, or theologians, or moralists, persons engaged in quite a different type of activity.[107]

Now this, as it happens, is Eliot's position; and as he says, it "comes very aptly to our help." But Eliot's understanding of the matter is quite different from Richards's—different in virtually every point, including the nature of belief. Nor is Eliot's theory that of the French Symbolists, unless Bradley and Bosanquet are to be accounted Symbolists.

With Eliot, the idea realized in the object means itself. A poem is thus, as Bradley says, a "self-contained unity," in which the "tendency of the content to pass beyond the limits of the thing is not always forced on your notice."[108] It is a relative whole which for critical purposes is taken as absolute: a relative absolute—in the end, like everything else, a mere appearance, but an appearance with a high degree of reality. In the aesthetic attitude, to use Bradley's words, the content of a poem does not stand "for something other than its own intent and meaning";[109] or as Bosanquet gives it: "In its essence, as a thing of beauty, . . . it is self-contained and a true whole, possessing its significance in itself, and not driving our thought beyond it to a detached mean-ing and explanation."[110] In brief, a poem does not represent or symbolize something other than itself; it is what is symbolized.

This view of a poem is part of a metaphysical argument. Eliot says: "For a metaphysics to be accepted, good-will is essential. Two men must *intend* the same object, and *both* men must admit that the object intended is the same." And "if I do not recognize the identity, then it is not."[111] The same condition attaches to literary criticism.

Is Eliot's critical attitude, as we have tried to show, a reflection of his philosophic logic? According to the dissertation, "every perception involves some degree of recognition and the operation of a universal."[112] It is a question of recognizing an identity in difference. And here we find ourselves turning in a double circle.

Notes

Introduction

1. "Rational knowledge is opposed to *historical* knowledge. The former is knowledge from principles . . . ; the latter is knowledge from data. . . . Knowledge, however, may have originated from reason, and yet be historical; as for example, when a mere littérateur learns the product of the reason of others, then his knowledge of such rational products is merely historical" (*Kant's Introduction to Logic*, trans. Thomas Kingsmill Abbott [New York: Philosophical Library, 1963], p. 12). Eliot speaks of his dissertation as "a critical examination of first principles," and the dissertation is evidence that the literary critic was not a "mere littérateur" (*Knowledge and Experience in the Philosophy of F. H. Bradley* [London: Faber & Faber, 1964], p. 102).

2. Cf. Eric Thompson: "But anyone who wants to think through Eliot's criticism must see it in conjunction with a philosophy." "We have to know something of the epistemological system, the terms of which control the terms of Eliot's literary criticism" (*T. S. Eliot: The Metaphysical Perspective* [Carbondale: Southern Illinois University Press, 1963], pp. 56, 52). And Anne C. Bolgan: "Eliot's major critical concepts, in every case, are but the literary equivalents of his philosophical doctrines and . . . there is no way of coming to terms conceptually with the former except through the latter." "Any commentary . . . that proceeds in ignorance of the depth and pervasiveness of Bradley's influence, or that prefers to discount it, seems to me doomed from the start either to irrelevance or to ineptitude" ("The Philosophy of F. H. Bradley and the Mind and Art of T. S. Eliot: An Introduction," in *English Literature and British Philosophy: A Collection of Essays*, ed. S. P. Rosenbaum [Chicago: University of Chicago Press, 1971], pp. 262, 257).

3. See "Experiment in Criticism," in *Literary Opinion in America*, ed. Morton D. Zabel (3d ed. rev., 2 vols.; New York: Harper & Row, 1937), 2:613–14, and *The Use of Poetry and the Use of Criticism: Studies in the*

Relation of Criticism to Poetry in England (London: Faber & Faber, 1964), p. 125.

It is not that Kermode has not written a "sensible" introduction. Thus, though he takes his lead from "To Criticize the Critic," he does not wholly accept Eliot's demarcation of his work into essays of generalization and appreciations of individual authors (p. 12); he also notes that Eliot's mind continued to engage "the old problems in new and shifting forms," so that the "early essays . . . are seen to be continuous with the later thought" (p. 21). He even goes so far as to say that there may be something in the critical work that is "perhaps theoretical" (p. 14), but the "theory" has its origins in "Eliot's own creative reading of past poetry" (p. 13), for example, Eliot's statement, which Kermode alludes to twice, that the experience of a poem is "never repeated integrally; and yet . . . would become destitute of significance if it did not survive in a larger whole of experience" (p. 14). With Eliot, nothing has its significance by itself, for outside of a whole of experience it is nothing whatever, and in becoming an element in a larger whole it undergoes alteration. Eliot here has given, in a particular application, the central doctrine of his philosophy.

4. Thompson, *The Metaphysical Perspective*, p. vii.

5. Wollheim, *F. H. Bradley* (Harmondsworth: Penguin Books, 1959), p. ii.

6. Bolgan, "The Philosophy of F. H. Bradley and the Mind and Art of T. S. Eliot," p. 257.

7. "A Prediction in Regard to Three English Authors," *Vanity Fair* 21 (1924): 29.

8. "Now, I am a follower of Bradley, though I was a pupil of [Thomas Hill] Green and still value his work very highly. . . . Since the appearance of Ethical Studies in 1876 I have recognized him as my master; and there is never, I think, any more than a verbal difference of emphasis between us." And again: "For me to argue . . . with you, when you have Bradley's books at hand (and though difficult in places, he is the most brilliant of English writers on philosophy) would be really making you study, in my bad writing, and in inferior form, what you have in your possession in the best possible form, and when you read what I write, you will be apt to say, 'But this is only Bradley again,' *and so it is*" (Bosanquet to Lello Vivante, 27 March 1920, in *Bernard Bosanquet and His Friends: Letters Illustrating the Sources and the Development of His Philosophical Opinions*, ed. J. H. Muirhead [London: George Allen & Unwin, 1935], pp. 262–63). "And he is wonderfully generous to me; gives me credit whenever he can; he is really a remarkably unselfish man" (Bosanquet to R. F. A. Hoernlé, 1 February 1914, in ibid., p. 153). "I regret that Dr. Bosanquet's *Implication and Linear Inference* came too late to be used. But I cannot end this Preface without some expression of my gratitude to Dr. Bosanquet for all that, since 1883, I have owed to him, and without some acknowledgment of how deeply this reissue is in debt to his invaluable works on Logic" (*Principles of Logic* [2d ed. rev., 2 vols.; Oxford: Oxford University Press, 1922], p. viii).

There are numerous references to Bosanquet in the second edition of Bradley's logical work, in the "Additional Notes" and the footnotes to the Terminal Essays, and frequent references in the second edition of *Appearance and Reality* and in *Essays on Truth and Reality*. Bradley speaks in these references of the view or views they hold in common, each in his own way, and of Bosanquet's *Logic* as in many points a great advance on his own work. J. H. Muirhead discusses Bradley and Bosanquet under the rubric "Dioscuri" (*The Platonic Tradition in Anglo-Saxon Philosophy: Studies in the History of Idealism in England and America* [New York: Macmillan, 1931], pp. 255–56), Brand Blanshard says of Bosanquet's *Logic* that "a certain want of literary skill . . . for many has drawn a veil over its soundness of conception and workmanship" (*The Nature of Thought* [2 vols.; London: George Allen & Unwin, 1939], 2:35).

9. See Muirhead, *Bosanquet and His Friends*, pp. 23–26; Harold H. Joachim, *Logical Studies* (Oxford: Oxford University Press, 1948), pp. 4n, 5, 263, 211–12, and *The Nature of Truth* (Oxford: Clarendon Press, 1906), pp. 119–21, 139, 177–79.

10. The point concerns "floating ideas." Bradley began by holding, as he later put it, that "ideas may be recognized as merely imaginary, and, taken in this character, they float suspended above the real world"; but "from the first and throughout, Prof. Bosanquet has consistently advocated the true doctrine" (*Essays on Truth and Reality* [Oxford: Clarendon Press, 1914], pp. 29, 29n). For Bosanquet's criticism of Bradley's earlier view see *Knowledge and Reality* (1885; New York: Kraus Reprint Co., 1968), pp. 140–55. On p. 149n there is a reference to *Principles of Logic* (p. 411); the passage referred to is in the second edition on p. 446.

11. "Royce's two series of the World and the Individual are full of the ideas about will and personality. . . . You don't mention Bradley's *Appearance and Reality*, which is still to me the gospel among all modern philosophical books" (Bosanquet to Hilda D. Oakeley, 28 December 1902, in Muirhead, *Bosanquet and His Friends*, p. 97). Muirhead observes that "the reference in it to the gospel according to Bradley and its criticism of 'Personalism' are not likely to escape the reader's notice" (ibid., p. 96). For Royce and "Personalism" see Muirhead, *The Platonic Tradition*, pp. 204–11, 214–18, 351, 366, 367, 368, 375–76, 379, 386–98, 410–12, 432–40; G. Watts Cunningham, *The Idealistic Argument in Recent British and American Philosophy* (1933; Freeport, N.Y.: Books for Libraries Press, 1967), pp. 256–57, 287–91, 337–38, 340–45. Royce tends to give precedence to will (morality and religion). For Bradley's criticism of the supremacy of will see *Appearance and Reality: A Metaphysical Essay* (2d ed.; Oxford: Clarendon Press, 1897), pp. 427–29, and for the "personal idealist" see *Essays on Truth and Reality*, pp. 89–90. Eliot, criticizing Samuel Alexander, says: "I see no reason for making will more original than thought. . . . It is as possible to state will in intellectual terms, and to say (what I do not believe to be any truer) that will is the self-realization of an idea" (*Knowledge and Experience*, p. 69). For the criticism of this last

view—Bradley's psychological definition of will—see ibid., pp. 76–81, where Eliot criticizes Bradley's psychology of will from the point of view of Bradley's metaphysics. "I would not wish to make truth the function of the will" (Eliot to Bonamy Dobrée, in *T. S. Eliot: The Man and His Work*, ed. Allen Tate [New York: Delacorte, 1966], p. 75). For Bradley on Royce's view of mathematics see *Essays on Truth and Reality*, pp. 276–88, and cf. Eliot on "immediate experience" and "the mathematician engaged upon a problem" (*Knowledge and Experience*, p. 16).

12. In his review of *Mens Creatrix* by William Temple, Eliot writes: "Mr. Temple wishes to demonstrate that philosophy, art, morality, education and politics all aim at a completion which they never of themselves reach, and that they find this completion in Christianity." "Mr. Temple has not exactly shown us that all roads of speculation lead to the Anglican Communion. . . . He does not demonstrate that any form of philosphy leads to Christianity; he takes a particular type, absolute idealism, and shows that the idealistic absolute is a failure unless it can be identified with a personal Deity. Influenced by Mr. Bradley, he yet rejects his Absolute as unmoral and unmeaning." "There is much that is suggestive, and even cogent, in the course of the argument. But to agree with the author we must not only concede that 'Intellect and Imagination, Science and Art, would reach their culmination in the apprehension and contemplation of the supreme principle of the universe adequately embodied and incarnate,' but that this culmination is found in Christianity. And might it not be maintained that religion, however poor our lives would be without it, is only one form of satisfaction among others, rather than the culminating satisfaction of all satisfactions?" (*International Journal of Ethics* 27 [1917]: 542–43). That is Bradley. In his review of *Religion and Philosophy* by R. G. Collingwood he says of philosophy: "Its freedom of interpretation is limited only by its obligation to exclude nothing. Religion, on the other hand, or at least the Christian religion, depends upon one important fact. Philosophy may show, if it can, the meaning of the statement that Jesus was the son of God. But Christianity—orthodox Christianity—must base itself upon a unique fact: that Jesus was born of a virgin: a proposition which is either true or false, its terms having a fixed meaning." And he adds that "the philosophical interpretation of the Incarnation, of the Atonement and of Miracle, are extremely well handled" (ibid., p. 543). For Bradley on the Incarnation see *Ethical Studies* [2d ed. rev.; Oxford: Clarendon Press, 1927], pp. 323–26, 330, 344, and for Bosanquet see Muirhead, *Bosanquet and His Friends*, pp. 239–47; for Bradley on philosophy and religion see *Essays on Truth and Reality*, pp. 446–47. For Eliot (this is the point), there are two distinct interpretations of the Incarnation: philosophic and religious.

13. "The doctrine of degrees in reality and truth is the fundamental answer to our problem" (*Appearance and Reality*, p. 431).

1
A Problem of Order

1. Blackmur, "In the Hope of Straightening Things Out," in *T. S. Eliot: A Collection of Critical Essays*, ed. Hugh Kenner (Englewood Cliffs, N.J.: Prentice-Hall, 1962), pp. 138–39.

2. "T. S. Eliot: From 'Ash Wednesday' to 'Murder in the Cathedral,'" in *The Double Agent* (New York: Arrow, 1935), pp. 203–4.

3. *Selected Essays* (new ed.; New York: Harcourt, Brace & World, 1950), pp. 229–30. Cf. H. H. Joachim, *Aristotle: The Nichomachean Ethics*, ed. D. A. Rees (Oxford: Clarendon Press, 1951), pp. 173, 209, 233.

4. *Selected Essays*, p. 388.

5. Ibid., p. 385.

6. *The Use of Poetry and the Use of Criticism: Studies in the Relation of Criticism to Poetry in England* (London: Faber & Faber, 1964), p. 112.

7. *Selected Essays*, p. 391.

8. Ibid., p. 432.

9. Ibid., p. 385.

10. Ibid.

11. *The Use of Poetry*, p. 118.

12. *Selected Essays*, pp. 389, 391.

13. *The Use of Poetry*, p. 113.

14. "The Criticism of T. S. Eliot," *Sewanee Review* 64 (1956): 432.

15. *Selected Essays*, pp. 435, 383, 436, 434.

16. Ibid., pp. 433–34.

17. Ibid., p. 400.

18. Ibid., p. 399.

19. *The Use of Poetry*, p. 122.

20. *Selected Essays*, p. 382. See Arnold on his "want of talent for abstract reasoning" and his "want of philosophy and philosophical principles." But this want did not trouble Arnold, for his notion was that literary culture ("letters and history") offered a better means of "seeing things as they really are" than philosophy. Thus, addressing himself to "plain unphilosophical people" who have been won "by the modern spirit to habits of intellectual seriousness," he says that "at the mention of that name *metaphysics* lo, essence, existence, substance, finite and infinite, cause and succession, something and nothing, begin to weave their eternal dance before us" (*God and the Bible* [New York: Macmillan, 1893], pp. 59, 54, 50).

21. *Ethical Studies* (2d ed. rev.; Oxford: Clarendon Press, 1927), pp. 315–16.

22. *Selected Essays*, p. 382; *The Use of Poetry*, p. 122.

23. *Selected Essays*, p. 390.

24. *Ethical Studies*, pp. 337-38.

25. *Selected Essays*, p. 403.

26. *Appearance and Reality: A Metaphysical Essay* (2d ed.; Oxford: Clarendon Press, 1897), p. 399.

27. *The Sacred Wood: Essays on Poetry and Criticism* (London: Methuen, 1928), p. 9.

28. *Selected Essays*, p. 404.

29. *Appearance and Reality*, pp. 401, 402, 403.

30. "A Prediction in Regard to Three English Authors," *Vanity Fair* 21 (1924): 29.

31. "The Development of Leibniz's Monadism," in *Knowledge and Experience in the Philosophy of F. H. Bradley* (London: Faber & Faber, 1964), app. 1, pp. 190, 195.

32. See H. H. Joachim, *Logical Studies* (Oxford: Clarendon Press, 1948), p. 21; *Aristotle: The Nichomachean Ethics*, pp. 5-7, 201, 291-97.

33. *The Use of Poetry*, p. 105.

34. *Selected Essays*, p. 333.

35. *Knowledge and Experience*, app. 1, pp. 189, 185.

36. Arnold's "conduct" in nine-tenths of life is "a coarse and popular method, which divides into parts instead of distinguishing aspects" (*Ethical Studies*, p. 215).

37. Ibid., p. 2.

38. Joachim, *Logical Studies*, pp. 211-12.

39. *Collected Essays* (2 vols., 1935; Freeport, N.Y.: Books for Libraries Press, 1968), 2:372.

40. Ibid., 1:205n.

41. *Knowledge and Experience*, pp. 34, 77, 80, 82, 81. Cf. Joachim, *Logical Studies*, pp. 206-12, and A. E. Taylor, *Elements of Metaphysics* (1903; London: Methuen, 1961), bk. 4, chap. 1.

42. *Knowledge and Experience*, pp. 18, 71, 88, 136-38.

43. *The Sacred Wood*, pp. 9-10.

44. *Selected Essays*, p. 305.

45. *Knowledge and Experience*, p. 34.

46. "A Prediction," p. 29.

47. *Principles of Logic* (2d ed. rev., 2 vols.; Oxford: Oxford University Press, 1922), 2:713, 722, 728; *Essays on Truth and Reality* (Oxford: Clarendon Press, 1914), pp. 89-91, 220-21.

48. *Essays on Truth and Reality*, pp. 87, 86, 123-24, 267, 430-32; see also Taylor, *Elements of Metaphysics*, bk. 3, chap. 6.

49. *Principles of Logic*, 1:268-71, 2:619-21.

50. *The Use of Poetry*, p. 143. Cf. *Ethical Studies*, p. 193; Bernard Bosanquet, *Three Lectures on Aesthetic* (1915; Indianapolis: Bobbs-Merrill, 1963), p. 5.

51. *The Use of Poetry*, pp. 20, 21.

52. *Selected Essays*, pp. 304-5.

53. *The Sacred Wood*, p. 10.

54. *Knowledge and Experience*, app. 1, p. 177; ibid., p. 163.

55. *The Sacred Wood*, p. 11.

56. *Knowledge and Experience*, app. 1, p. 184n.

57. *Posterior Analytics*, 2. 19. 100a15–17, in *The Student's Oxford Aristotle*, trans. under editorship of W. D. Ross, vol. 1.

58. See Joachim, *Nichomachean Ethics*, pp. 29–30; Bradley, *Principles of Logic*, 1:104–6, and *Appearance and Reality*, p. 328.

59. *The Sacred Wood*, pp. 16, 13. For "degrees of intelligence" see Joachim, *Logical Studies*, pp. 49–51.

60. *Metaphysics*, Γ. 2. 1004a30, in *The Student's Oxford Aristotle*, vol. 4.

61. *Selected Essays*, pp. 386, 387.

62. *Metaphysics*, E. 4. 1027b25.

63. *Collected Essays*, 1:227.

64. *God and the Bible*, p. 64

65. *Metaphysics*, Γ. 1. 1003a20–25.

66. Cf. *Knowledge and Experience*, pp. 86, 73.

67. *Posterior Analytics*, 1. II. 77a25.

68. *The Presuppositions of Critical History*, ed. (with intro. and commentary) Lionel Rubinoff (Chicago: Quadrangle, 1968), p. 82; *Collected Essays*, 1:6.

69. *Posterior Analytics*, 1. II. 76b35.

70. *Metaphysics*, M. 3. 1078a20. For this whole topic see Joachim, *Nicomachean Ethics*, pp. 1–18, 196–97; *Aristotle: On Coming-to-Be and Passing Away* (Oxford: Clarendon Press, 1922), pp. xiii–xxvi; *Logical Studies*, pp. 35–36; *The Nature of Truth* (Oxford: Clarendon Press, 1906), p. 139.

71. *Essays on Truth and Reality*, p. 266.

72. *Principles of Logic*, 2:604.

73. Ibid., pp. 496–97.

74. *Ethical Studies*, p. 321.

75. *Appearance and Reality*, p. 442; *Principles of Logic*, 2:612–17.

76. *Principles of Logic*, p. 605; *Essays on Truth and Reality*, p. 266.

77. *The Use of Poetry*, pp. 113–14.

78. *Appearance and Reality*, pp. 429, 130–36, 399–400, 410–11, 405.

79. *Knowledge and Experience*, pp. 162, 35, 60–61.

80. *Selected Essays*, p. 12.

81. *Ethical Studies*, p. 22.

82. *Essays on Truth and Reality*, pp. 202–3, 241.

83. *Selected Essays*, pp. 12–13, 19–20, 22.

84. *Knowledge and Experience*, p. 60.

85. The problem, in Bradley's language, of "the various orders of appearance" (*Appearance and Reality*, p. 330).

86. *Knowledge and Experience*, p. 60.

87. *Selected Essays*, pp. 20, 21.

88. Ibid., p. 402.

89. *Knowledge and Experience*, p. 82.

90. *The Use of Poetry*, p. 18.

91. "The Education of Taste," *Athenaeum*, no. 4652 (1919), p. 520.

92. *The Sacred Wood*, p. 14.

93. Ibid., p. viii.

94. *Essays on Truth and Reality*, p. 10.

95. *Appearance and Reality*, pp. 414–15.

96. *The Sacred Wood*, pp. ix–x.

97. *Appearance and Reality*, p. 392.

98. *Knowledge and Experience*, p. 153.

99. *Selected Essays*, p. 36; for art as amusement see *Essays on Truth and Reality*, p. 346.

100. "Poetry and Propaganda," in *Literary Opinion in America*, ed. Morton D. Zabel (3d ed. rev., 2 vols.; New York: Harper & Row, 1937), 1:106.

101. *Selected Essays*, pp. 392–93.

102. *Ethical Studies*, p. 320.

103. *Notes towards the Definition of Culture* (London: Faber & Faber, 1948), p. 68.

104. *Essays on Truth and Reality*, p. 172; *Knowledge and Experience*, p. 28.

105. *Knowledge and Experience*, p. 16.

106. *Appearance and Reality*, p. 413.

107. *Notes*, p. 33; *Essays on Truth and Reality*, p. 176.

108. *Knowledge and Experience*, p. 27; *Notes*, pp. 27–28.

109. *Ethical Studies*, p. 321.

110. *Appearance and Reality*, pp. 404, 415, 429, 135, 136; *Essays on Truth and Reality*, pp. 10–15.

111. *Selected Essays*, p. 343; *The Sacred Wood*, p. viii. For "the 'greatness' of literature" cf. Samuel Alexander, "Beauty and Greatness in Art," *Proceedings of the Aristotelian Society*, n.s., vol. 30 (1929–30), largely reproduced in *Beauty and Other Forms of Value* (London: Macmillan, 1933), chap. 8, "Beauty and Greatness."

112. *Selected Essays*, pp. 346–47, 348, 349.

113. "The Education of Taste," p. 521.

114. *Selected Essays*, p. 212.

115. *The Use of Poetry*, pp. 18, 19, 36.

116. *Knowledge and Experience*, p. 82.

117. "The Function of a Literary Review," *Criterion* 1 (1923): 421.

2

A Question of Language

1. Bradbrook, in *T. S. Eliot: A Study of His Writings by Several Hands*, ed. B. Rajan (New York: Haskell House, 1964), p. 119.

2. Kenner, *The Invisible Poet: T. S. Eliot* (New York: Ivan Obolensky,

1959), p. 94; idem ed., *T.S. Eliot: A Collection of Critical Essays* (Englewood Cliffs, N.J.: Prentice-Hall, 1962), p. 12.

3. Wheelwright, in *T. S. Eliot*, ed. Rajan, p. 96.

4. Blackmur, "In the Hope of Straightening Things Out," in *T. S. Eliot*, ed. Kenner, p. 142.

5. Richards, *Coleridge on Imagination* (3d ed.; London: Routledge & Kegan Paul, 1962), pp. 3–5. What interests Richards in Coleridge is not so much the philosopher as the psychologist (pp. 10,11).

6. Ransom, in *Literary Opinion in America*, ed. Morton D. Zabel (3d ed. rev., 2 vols.; New York: Harper & Row, 1937), 2:640, 641, 642.

7. Wellek, in *Sewanee Review* 64 (1956): 410.

8. Blackmur, "In the Hope of Straightening Things Out," pp. 144–46.

9. *Selected Essays* (new ed.; New York: Harcourt, Brace & World, 1950), pp. 11, 200.

10. Leavis, "T. S. Eliot as Critic," in *Anna Karenina and Other Essays* (New York: Pantheon, 1952), p. 180.

11. Frye, *T. S. Eliot* (Edinburgh: Oliver & Boyd, 1963), p. 34.

12. Kermode, "A Babylonish Dialect," in *T. S. Eliot: The Man and His Work*, ed. Allan Tate (New York: Delacorte, 1966), p. 234.

13. Wellek, "The Criticism of T. S. Eliot," p. 406.

14. *Knowledge and Experience in the Philosophy of F. H. Bradley* (London: Faber & Faber, 1964), p. 115.

15. Ibid., pp. 16, 22.

16. Ibid., pp. 26, 24.

17. *The Sacred Wood: Essays on Poetry and Criticism* (London: Methuen, 1928), p. x.

18. Ibid., pp. 64–65.

19. "Kipling Redivivus," *Athenaeum*, no. 4645 (1919), p. 298.

20. *The Sacred Wood*, p. 170.

21. Ibid., p. 167.

22. *Principles of Logic* (2d ed. rev., 2 vols.; London: Oxford University Press, 1922), 2:443, 449n, 33.

23. *The Sacred Wood*, pp. 10, 12–13.

24. Ibid., pp. 14–15.

25. H. H. Joachim, *Aristotle: The Nicomachean Ethics*, ed. D. A. Rees (Oxford: Clarendon Press, 1951), p. 287.

26. *Selected Essays*, pp. 7, 11. See Joachim, *Nicomachean Ethics*, p. 290.

27. *Knowledge and Experience*, app. 1, p. 184. "When we understand necessity, as Spinoza knew, we are free because we assent" (*The Sacred Wood*, p. 11). The allusion is to God as a "free cause" (see Joachim, *The Nature of Truth* [Oxford: Clarendon Press, 1906], p. 151, and Bernard Bosanquet, *The Principle of Individuality and Value* [1912; London: Macmillan, 1927], p. 66).

28. *Ethical Studies* (2d ed. rev.; Oxford: Clarendon Press, 1927), pp. 320–21.

29. For Aristotle on intellectual vision see Joachim, *Nicomachean Ethics*, pp. 287–97, and for Spinoza, idem, *A Study of the Ethics of Spinoza* (1901; New York: Russell & Russell, 1964), pp. 181, 305.

30. *The Sacred Wood*, p. 170.

31. *Knowledge and Experience*, pp. 165, 139.

32. *The Sacred Wood*, pp. 170–71.

33. *Principles of Logic*, 2:626–27.

34. *The Sacred Wood*, p. 9.

35. *Knowledge and Experience*, pp. 105–8.

36. Ibid., p. 94.

37. *Essays on Truth and Reality* (Oxford: Clarendon Press, 1914), p. 269. All people, according to William James, believe that they "feel themselves thinking" (*The Principles of Psychology* [2 vols., 1890; New York: Dover Publications, 1950], 1:185); but James is talking about mental states and introspection, and for Eliot there are no such things. In the dissertation, Eliot distinguishes Bradley's view of experience from that of James. For Bradley's criticism of James see *Essays on Truth and Reality*, pp. 149–58.

38. *The Sacred Wood*, p. 9.

39. *Selected Essays*, pp. 308–9.

40. *Knowledge and Experience*, pp. 19–20.

41. Ibid., p. 25.

42. *The Sacred Wood*, p. 7.

43. *Knowledge and Experience*, p. 80.

44. *Ethical Studies*, p. 260n.

45. Ibid., p. 267.

46. *The Sacred Wood*, pp. 2–3.

47. *The Presuppositions of Critical History*, ed. Lionel Rubinoff (Chicago: Quadrangle, 1968), pp. 84–85; F. H. Bradley, *Collected Essays* (2 vols., 1935; Freeport, N.Y.: Books for Libraries Press, 1968), 1:11, 9.

48. Rubinoff, pp. 90, 89; *Collected Essays*, 1:11, 14.

49. *The Sacred Wood*, p. 5. The general point, it may be said, is that feelings and impressions are not logical premises, and nothing valid follows from them. Cf. Joachim, *Immediate Experience and Mediation: An Inaugural Lecture Delivered before the University of Oxford, 20 November 1919* (Oxford: Clarendon Press, 1919), pp. 9–10.

50. *Knowledge and Experience*, pp. 18, 20, 23, 26.

51. *The Sacred Wood*, p. 15.

52. *Knowledge and Experience*, p. 33.

53. *Kant's Introduction to Logic*, trans. Thomas Kingsmill Abbott (New York: Philosophical Library, 1963), pp. 26–27.

54. *Knowledge and Experience*, p. 18.

55. Cf. A. E. Taylor, *Elements of Metaphysics* (1903; London: Methuen, 1961), pp. 32–33.

56. *Knowledge and Experience*, p. 27.

57. *On Poetry and Poets* (London: Faber & Faber, 1957), p. 115.

58. *To Criticize the Critic and Other Writings* (London: Faber & Faber, 1965), p. 20.

59. *Knowledge and Experience*, p. 18.

60. *The Use of Poetry and the Use of Criticism: Studies in the Relation of Criticism to Poetry in England* (London: Faber & Faber, 1964), p. 16.

61. Cf. Kenner: " 'Sensibility' is Eliot's term for . . . 'immediate experience' " (*The Invisible Poet*, p. 53).

62. Thought is relational, and "within experience we always find relations" (*Knowledge and Experience*, p. 27). Cf. Joachim, *Logical Studies* (Oxford: Clarendon Press, 1948), pp. 278–80, 108–9.

63. *Knowledge and Experience*, p. 160.

64. *Selected Essays*, p. 124.

65. *The Use of Poetry*, p. 143. If we accept that, we shall have to say that he has a theory about theory.

66. *Essays on Truth and Reality*, p. 283.

67. *Selected Essays*, pp. 394–95.

68. Matthiessen, *The Achievement of T. S. Eliot: An Essay on the Nature of Poetry* (2d ed. rev.; New York: Oxford University Press, 1947), pp. 148–49.

69. *Selected Essays*, p. 285.

70. *Knowledge and Experience*, p. 133.

71. Ibid., p. 104.

72. Ibid., p. 129.

73. Praz, "T. S. Eliot as a Critic," in *T. S. Eliot*, ed. Tate, pp. 263–64.

74. *Knowledge and Experience*, p. 33.

75. Praz, "T. S. Eliot as a Critic," pp. 266, 274, 277.

76. Warren, "Eliot's Literary Criticism," in *T. S. Eliot*, ed. Tate, pp. 291, 279.

77. Kermode, "A Babylonish Dialect," p. 236.

78. *Romantic Image* (London: Routledge & Kegan Paul, 1957), pp. 141–45.

79. *Selected Essays*, p. 247; ibid., p. 115; *The Sacred Wood*, p. 65.

80. *Romantic Image*, p. 143.

81. *Knowledge and Experience*, p. 75.

82. Krieger, "The Critical Legacy of Matthew Arnold; Or, the Strange Brotherhood of T. S. Eliot, I. A. Richards, and Northrop Frye," *Southern Review* 5 (1969): 458; Stanford, "Classicism and the Modern Poet," ibid., pp. 477, 484.

83. "T. S. Eliot as a Critic," p. 179.

84. Ibid., pp. 179, 181, 183.

85. *The Sacred Wood*, pp. 65, 68.

3
Eliot and Bradley: A Brief Review

1. Howarth, *Notes on Some Figures behind T. S. Eliot* (London: Chatto & Windus, 1965), p. 207.

2. Frye, *T. S. Eliot* (Edinburgh: Oliver & Boyd, 1963), pp. 43–45.

3. Margolis, *T. S. Eliot's Intellectual Development, 1922–1939* (Chicago: University of Chicago Press, 1972), p. 14n.

4. Ibid., pp. ix, xv, 110.

5. Smidt, *Poetry and Belief in the Work of T. S. Eliot* (London: Routledge & Kegan Paul, 1961), pp. 34, 36, 36–37, 35.

6. Ibid., p. 61.

7. Ibid., pp. xii, 162, 42, 40, 42, 40, 45, 43.

8. Smith, *T. S. Eliot's Poetry and Plays: A Study in Sources and Meaning* (2d ed.; Chicago: University of Chicago Press, 1974), pp. 4–5. For philosophic glosses and readings Smith goes to Bergson (see, e.g., pp. 24–25).

9. Smidt, *Poetry and Belief*, pp. 158, 15, 137, 160, 124, 211.

10. *Knowledge and Experience in the Philosophy of F. H. Bradley* (London: Faber & Faber, 1964), app. 1, p. 207. In Eliot's footnote, p. 613 should be p. 413.

11. Ibid., pp. 146–47.

12. Ibid., p. 205.

13. *Essays on Truth and Reality* (Oxford: Clarendon Press, 1914), p. 420.

14. Ibid., pp. 248–49.

15. *Knowledge and Experience*, p. 207.

16. Smidt, *Poetry and Belief*, p. 125.

17. *Appearance and Reality: A Metaphysical Essay* (2d ed.; Oxford: Clarendon Press, 1897), pp. 304, 307.

18. Cf. Richard Wollheim, "Eliot and F. H. Bradley: An Account," in *Eliot in Perspective: A Symposium*, ed. Graham Martin (London: Macmillan, 1970), pp. 185–86; Anne C. Bolgan, *What the Thunder Really Said: A Retrospective Essay on the Making of the Waste Land* (Montreal: McGill-Queen's University Press, 1973), app. 2, pp. 179–81.

19. *Essays on Truth and Reality*, p. 246.

20. Ibid., p. 428.

21. *Selected Essays* (new ed.; New York: Harcourt, Brace & World, 1950), p. 404.

22. Whiteside, "T. S. Eliot's Dissertation," *ELH* 34 (1967): 400–401, 424.

23. Ibid., pp. 410, 408n.

24. Ibid., pp. 410–11.

25. Ibid., pp. 402, 404, 405.

26. Ibid., pp. 418–19.

27. Ibid., pp. 420–21.

28. *Knowledge and Experience*, p. 153. For Bradley the Absolute is "the necessary conclusion from what certainly is given" (*Essays on Truth and Reality*, p. 249). But for Eliot, "The Absolute responds only to an imaginary demand of thought. . . . Pretending to be something which makes finite centers cohere, it turns out to be merely the assertion that they do." Again, Bradley's Absolute "dissolves at a touch into its constituents" (*Knowledge and Experience*, app. 2, pp. 202, 200). For a more detailed criticism of the Absolute, see R. F. A. Hoernlè, "Pragmatism v. Absolutism (1)," *Mind* 14 (1902): 297–334; for a general account of the issues, see J. H. Muirhead, *The Platonic Tradition in Anglo-American Philosophy: Studies in the History of Idealism in England and America* (New York: Macmillan, 1931), pp. 204–18, 432–40; for an idealist criticism of the Absolute, see G. Watts Cunningham, *The Idealist Argument in Recent British and American Philosophy* (1933; Freeport, N.Y.: Books for Libraries Press, 1967), pp. 340–45, 382–407, 523–40, and H. H. Joachim, *Logical Studies* (Oxford: Clarendon Press, 1948), pp. 276–92; for a discussion of this criticism, see Garrett L. Vander Veer, *Bradley's Metaphysics and the Self* (New Haven: Yale University Press, 1970), chap. 5, "The Idealist Criticism of the Theory of Relations"; see also Sushil Kumar Saxena, *Studies in the Metaphysics of Bradley* (London: George Allen & Unwin, 1967).

29. *Knowledge and Experience*, p. 151.

30. "Eeldrop and Apoplex, 1," *Little Review* 4 (1917): 10.

31. *Knowledge and Experience*, p. 19.

32. *Essays on Truth and Reality*, p. 177.

33. *The Sacred Wood: Essays on Poetry and Criticism* (London: Methuen, 1928), p. 9.

34. Smidt, *Poetry and Belief*, pp. 136–38.

35. Kenner, *The Invisible Poet: T. S. Eliot* (New York: Ivan Obolensky, 1959), pp. 46, 45.

36. *Knowledge and Experience*, p. 31.

37. "A Prediction in Regard to Three English Authors," *Vanity Fair* 21 (1924): 29, 98.

38. *Knowledge and Experience*, p. 56.

39. *Criterion* 9 (1924): 2.

40. *Selected Essays*, p. 399.

41. Smidt, *Poetry and Belief*, p. 124.

42. Kenner, *The Invisible Poet*, p. 47.

43. *Appearance and Reality*, pp. 498, 380; *Essays on Truth and Reality*, p. 17.

44. *Appearance and Reality*, pp. 1–2.

45. Ibid., pp. 119, 130–31, 140–42, 453, 461; *Essays on Truth and Reality*, pp. 241, 118.

46. Ibid., pp. 445, 118n.

47. "And . . . *if* the intellect is satisfied, the question is settled. For we may feel as we please about the intellectual conclusion, but we cannot, on such external grounds, protest that it is false" (*Appearance and Reality*, p. 136). "But a metaphysical doctrine pretends to be *'true'* simply, and none of our pragmatic tests will apply. . . . A metaphysic may be accepted or rejected without our assuming that from the practical point of view it is either true or false" (*Knowledge and Experience*, p. 169). "Bradley's position here is . . . opposed to William James' brand of pragmatism. To say that 'truth works' . . . is to confuse the theoretical and practical in man's activity. Bradley agrees that ideas are true because they 'work,' but the working of ideas, which is their truth, lies not at all in their ability to satisfy us emotionally or to provide a framework within which we can lead a more comfortable, satisfying life. Ideas can do all this and more and still be quite false" (Vander Veer, *Bradley's Metaphysics and the Self*, p. 139).

48. Bollier, "T. S. Eliot and F. H. Bradley: A Question of Influence," *Tulane Studies in English* 12 (1962): 88, 97–102.

49. Ibid., pp. 109, 110.

50. *Essays on Truth and Reality*, pp. 342, 330.

51. *Appearance and Reality*, p. 486.

52. Bollier, "T. S. Eliot and F. H. Bradley," p. 109.

53. Cunningham, "Continuity and Coherence in Eliot's Religious Thought," in *Eliot in Perspective*, p. 218.

54. *Knowledge and Experience*, pp. 147–48.

55. Cunningham, "Continuity and Coherence," p. 222.

56. *Notes towards the Definition of Culture* (London: Faber & Faber, 1948), p. 28; see also p. 33.

57. Miller, "T. S. Eliot," in *Poets of Reality: Six Twentieth-Century Writers* (Cambridge, Mass.: Harvard University Press, 1965), chap. 4. Miller's account is written in such a way that it was found impractical to give page references.

58. On Miller's "grossly misleading statements" see Bolgan, *What the Thunder Really Said*, p. 138. For "subjectivism" see Bradley, *Essays on Truth and Reality*, pp. 349–50.

59. "It is not true that we deny the existence of an external world, for anyone who pursues this path of inquiry will come to the conclusion that this question is ultimately meaningless. But demanding at the start what it is that we know for most certain (and this method deserves the name of empiricism as much as anything) we find that we are certain of everything,—relatively, and of nothing,—positively, and that no knowledge will survive analysis. The virtue of metaphysical analysis is in showing the destructibility of everything, since analysis gives us something equally real, and for some purposes more real, than that which is analyzed" (*Knowledge and Experience*, p. 157).

60. "We must be careful not to identify feeling with either *my* feeling, or a collective feeling, or an impersonal current of feeling" (ibid., p. 10).

61. *The Use of Poetry and the Use of Criticism: Studies in the Relation of Criticism to Poetry in England* (London: Faber & Faber, 1964), p. 10.

62. Ibid., p. 155.

63. Wollheim, "Eliot, Bradley and Immediate Experience," *New Statesman* 67 (13 March 1964): 401.

64. Ibid., p. 402.

65. "The Aims of Education," in *To Criticize the Critic and Other Writings* (London: Faber & Faber, 1965), p. 74.

66. "From Poe to Valéry," ibid., p. 34.

67. *Notes towards the Definition of Culture*, pp. 41, 120.

68. Wollheim, "Eliot, Bradley and Immediate Experience," p. 402.

69. Revised and enlarged in "Eliot and F. H. Bradley," in *On Art and the Mind* (Cambridge, Mass.: Harvard University Press, 1974).

70. Wollheim, "Eliot and F. H. Bradley: An Account," pp. 184, 186–89.

71. Ibid., p. 170.

72. Ibid., pp. 186, 189.

73. *Knowledge and Experience*, p. 74.

74. *The Sacred Wood*, p. 170.

75. Allan, *T. S. Eliot's Impersonal Theory of Poetry* (Lewisburg, Pa.: Bucknell University Press, 1974), pp. 10, 17.

76. Ibid., p. 43.

77. Ibid., pp. 139, 140.

78. Ibid., pp. 131, 133.

79. Ibid., p. 77.

80. Ibid., p. 129.

81. Ibid., p. 131.

82. Ibid., pp. 25, 78, 79.

83. *Knowledge and Experience*, p. 34.

84. Allan, pp. 172–74.

85. *Times Literary Supplement*, 1 August 1975, p. 866.

4
The Invisible Critic

1. Kenner, *The Invisible Poet: T. S. Eliot* (New York: Ivan Obolensky, 1959), pp. 109, 43, 115.

2. *T. S. Eliot: A Collection of Critical Essays*, ed. Kenner (Englewood Cliffs, N.J.: Prentice-Hall, 1962), p. 12.

3. *The Invisible Poet*, p. 47.

4. Ibid., pp. 45–47. "Bradley has an attractive mind, though he has perhaps nothing to tell us. He is an experience, like the taste of nectarines or the style of Henry James; to rethink him is to recall with labor a landscape once seen in a dream; he is like a vivid dream in that, as Eliot

said, he modifies the sensibility" (p. 63). "Though he has no message to
deliver, he fills the mind, yet each time we want to see with what he fills it,
we must reread the book" (p. 66). "He arrives at no conclusions, at no
incitements to action" (p. 68). If Kenner is not wrong, neither is he right.
Or, to borrow some verses of Eliot's, as quoted by Kenner:

> There was nothing exactly precisely wrong,
> It wasn't too mild and it wasn't too strong,
> There was nothing you'd want to subtract,
> Only something or other that it lacked.

5. Ibid., p. 57.

6. Ibid., pp. 52–53, 101–2, 104.

7. Ibid., p. 102.

8. *Selected Essays* (new ed.; New York: Harcourt, Brace & World,
1950), p. 166; ibid., p. 125.

9. *The Sacred Wood: Essays on Poetry and Criticism* (London:
Methuen, 1928), pp. 64–65; *Selected Essays*, pp. 124–25.

10. *Selected Essays*, p. 277, 290.

11. *The Invisible Poet*, pp. 55, 57, 116.

12. Ibid., pp. 117–18.

13. *Essays on Truth and Reality* (Oxford: Clarendon Press, 1914),
p. 425.

14. *The Presuppositions of Critical History*, ed. Lionel Rubinoff
(Chicago: Quadrangle, 1968), p. 96; F. H. Bradley, *Collected Essays* (2
vols., 1935; Freeport, N.Y.: Books for Libraries Press, 1968), 1:20.

15. *The Invisible Poet*, p. 116.

16. *Essays on Truth and Reality*, p. 342; *Knowledge and Experience in
the Philosophy of F. H. Bradley* (London: Faber & Faber, 1964), p. 136.

17. Frye, *T. S. Eliot* (Edinburgh: Oliver & Boyd, 1963), p. 48.

18. See H. H. Joachim, *Logical Studies* (Oxford: Clarendon Press,
1948), pp. 50n, 58; idem, *Descartes's Rules for the Direction of the Mind*,
ed. Errol E. Harris (London: George Allen & Unwin, 1957), pp. 118–19.

19. *The Invisible Poet*, p. 95.

20. *The Sacred Wood*, p. viii.

21. Ibid., p. 7.

22. Thompson, *T. S. Eliot: The Metaphysical Perspective*
(Carbondale: Southern Illinois University Press, 1963), p. 52.

23. *The Invisible Poet*, p. 101.

24. *Knowledge and Experience*, pp. 124, 124n.

25. *Selected Essays*, p. 131.

26. *The Invisible Poet*, p. 54. "Swinburne," *Athenaeum*, no. 4681
(1920), p. 73, reprinted as "Swinburne as Poet" in *Selected Essays*, p. 285.

27. *The Invisible Poet*, pp. 103–4. "Kipling Redivivus," *Athenaeum*,
no. 4645 (1919), pp. 297–98.

28. *Knowledge and Experience*, p. 21.

29. Ibid., p. 150.

30. Ibid., p. 114.

31. Ibid., pp. 121–22.

32. Ibid., p. 20.

33. *The Use of Poetry and the Use of Criticism: Studies in the Relation of Criticism to Poetry in England* (London: Faber & Faber, 1964), p. 30.

34. *On Poetry and Poets* (London: Faber & Faber, 1957), p. 26.

35. Ibid., p. 238.

36. *Knowledge and Experience*, pp. 148–49.

37. *The Invisible Poet*, pp. 104, 104n.

38. "Kipling Redivivus," p. 298.

39. *Knowledge and Experience*, p. 166.

40. *Essays on Truth and Reality*, p. 31.

41. *Knowledge and Experience*, p. 120. Though this is said of objects of hallucination, it applies to objects of all kinds, including aesthetic objects, as is evident from the context.

42. "A Prediction in Regard to Three English Authors," *Vanity Fair* 21 (1924): 29.

43. "Henry James: 1. In Memory," in *The Shock of Recognition*, ed. Edmund Wilson (New York: Farrar, Straus & Giroux, 1955), pp. 856–57, reprinted from *Little Review* 4 (1918): 44–47.

44. Cf. Bernard Bosanquet, "On the Philosophical Distinction between 'Knowledge' and 'Opinion,' " in *Science and Philosophy and Other Essays* (1927; Freeport, N.Y.: Books for Libraries Press, 1967), p. 53.

45. *The Sacred Wood*, pp. 67, 68.

46. *The Invisible Poet*, p. 114; "A Romantic Patrician," *Athenaeum*, no. 4644 (1919), pp. 265–67, reprinted as "A Romantic Aristocrat," *The Sacred Wood*, pp. 24–32.

47. *Knowledge and Experience*, p. 154.

48. *Essays on Truth and Reality*, pp. 326, 415; *Appearance and Reality: A Metaphysical Essay* (2d ed.; Oxford: Clarendon Press, 1897), p. 228. "Not only is all beauty an object," Bradley writes, "but it is even taken as that which is self-existent" (*Essays on Truth and Reality*, p. 341n). And Eliot: "The poem has its own existence, apart from us; it was there before us and will endure after us" (*The Use of Poetry*, p. 34). "'A voyage among masterpieces' is, I believe, the phrase that Anatole France used to describe his own criticism, implying that it was merely an account of his own feelings—yet the phrase itself admits that the masterpieces were there as masterpieces, before the voyage began" ("Poetry and Propaganda," in *Literary Opinion in America*, ed. Morton D. Zabel [3d ed. rev., 2 vols.; New York: Harper & Row, 1937], 1:102).

49. *Selected Essays*, p. 15.

50. *Knowledge and Experience*, pp. 138, 139.

51. Ibid., p. 126.

52. Cf. Joachim, *Logical Studies*, pp. 182, 241, 261.

53. *The Invisible Poet*, p. 50.

54. "Literature, Science, and Dogma," *The Dial* 82 (1927): 307.

55. Ibid., pp. 306–7.

56. *The Use of Poetry*, p. 123.

57. *Knowledge and Experience*, pp. 40, 76; see also p. 80.

58. *Criterion* 4 (1926): 753.

59. Ibid., pp. 754–55.

60. Ibid., p. 755.

61. *Essays on Truth and Reality*, p. 247; *Appearance and Reality*, p. 466. "And of course the fact of one's existence, *in some sense*, is quite beyond doubt. But as to the sense in which this existence is so certain, there the case is far otherwise. . . . We are all sure that we exist, but in what sense and what character—as to that we are most of us in helpless uncertainty and blind confusion. For . . . we never know what we mean when we talk of it. But the meaning and the sense is surely for metaphysics the vital point. . . . Anything the meaning of which is inconsistent and unintelligible is appearance, and not reality" (ibid., pp. 64–65). "Naturally the self is a fact, to some extent and in some sense; and this, of course, is not the issue. The question is whether the self in any of its meanings can, as such, be real" (ibid., p. 88). "In whatever way the self is taken, it will prove to be appearance. . . . And . . . the self is in any case unintelligible" (ibid., p. 103).

62. *Knowledge and Experience*, p. 105.

63. Ibid., pp. 98, 146.

64. *Essays on Truth and Reality*, p. 246.

65. *Criterion* 4 (1926): 755.

66. Ibid., p. 756.

67. Ibid., p. 753. "When I first met Eliot, I was from an intellectual point of view both ignorant and *naïf*. I had not had the advantage of his orderly education and philosophical training" (Sir Herbert Read, "T. S. E.—A Memoir," in *T. S. Eliot: The Man and His Work*, ed. Allen Tate [New York: Delacorte, 1966], p. 18). "My own faith was judged certainly not antagonistic to his own. But what was my own faith? It was to be defined, tentatively, in the volume of essays which Eliot asked me to prepare for the first list of the reorganized firm of Faber and Gwyer (later Faber and Faber), which he had joined as an editorial director. This book, *Reason and Romanticism*, was published in 1926, and though the Reason of it owes something to Hulme and even more to Eliot, the Romanticism was my own" (ibid., pp. 21–22). "He had been, as is well known, a serious student of philosophy, but he did not parade his knowledge of the subject. He would occasionally refer to Bradley, and more often, in an anecdote fashion, to his Oxford tutor in philosophy, Harold Joachim" (ibid., p. 28).

68. *Knowledge and Experience*, p. 86.

69. *Appearance and Reality*, p. 65. See also Bosanquet, *Logic* (2d ed., 2 vols., 1911; New York: Kraus Reprint Co., 1968), 2:271, 271n.

70. *The Nature of Truth* (Oxford: Clarendon Press, 1906), p. 169.

71. *Criterion* 4 (1926): 756.

72. *Knowledge and Experience*, p. 48.

73. See Joachim, "Psychical Process," *Mind*, n.s., 18 (1909): 67–69: *Logical Studies*, pp. 219–29.

74. *Knowledge and Experience*, p. 62; see also pp. 78, 130.

75. *Criterion* 4 (1926): 756–57.

76. "Mr. Middleton Murry's Synthesis," *Criterion* 6 (1927): 345.

77. *Knowledge and Experience*, pp. 85–86. See also A. E. Taylor, *Elements of Metaphysics* (1903; London: Methuen, 1961), bk. 4, chap. 1, pp. 303–10.

78. Bosanquet, *Implication and Linear Inference* (1920; New York: Kraus Reprint Co., 1968), pp. 15, 78–81, 141, 143n; Joachim, *Logical Studies*, pp. 245, 246, 248n.

79. *Knowledge and Experience*, p. 94.

80. *Principles of Logic* (2d ed. rev., 2 vols.; Oxford: Oxford University Press, 1922), 2:515.

81. *Logical Studies*, p. 24.

82. *Knowledge and Experience*, p. 84; *Appearance and Reality*, p. 220.

83. See Joachim, *Logical Studies*, pp. 24–27, 152–71.

84. *Appearance and Reality*, pp. 159, 157, 156.

85. "Murry's Synthesis," p. 341.

86. Ibid., p. 342.

87. *Knowledge and Experience*, pp. 155, 31, 17.

88. *Essays on Truth and Reality*, pp. 190, 190n, 227n, 238–39, 269; *Appearance and Reality*, pp. 140–41.

89. *Selected Essays*, p. 115.

90. *Appearance and Reality*, pp. 92–94; see *Knowledge and Experience*, p. 46.

91. *The Nature of Truth*, pp. 55–58. See also Garrett L. Vander Leer, *Bradley's Metaphysics and the Self* (New Haven: Yale University Press, 1970), pp. 109–10.

92. "Murry's Synthesis," p. 343.

93. Ibid.

94. Ibid., pp. 343–44.

95. *The Use of Poetry*, p. 99.

96. We shall return to the question of intuition and artistic perception in a later chapter.

97. *Homage to John Dryden: Three Essays on Poetry of the Seventeenth Century* (London: Hogarth Press, 1924), pref., p. 9.

5

The Mind of the Poet

1. *Selected Essays* (new ed.; New York: Harcourt, Brace & World, 1950), p. 11.

2. "Mr. Webb's objections to the theories of Lévy-Bruhl and

Durkheim . . . may be summed up in two classes: one religious, the other philosophical. . . . These two classes of objections should be kept quite distinct." "The growth of the scientific spirit has been unfavorable to mysticism, and . . . mysticism has had an obscurantist effect in science. The contrast between the part played by the 'mystical mentality' in the daily life of the savage and in that of the civilized man is a sound one. Lévy-Bruhl maintains that a sharp differentiation of function is necessary, without abandoning either of two essential attitudes of the human mind. This is the 'empiricism' to which Mr. Webb objects. His objection is, at bottom, the objection of the theologian—neither mystic nor scientist. It is the struggle between the theologian and the mystic, rather than that between the believer in religion and the scientist, which is here represented" (review of *Group Theories of Religion and the Religion of the Individual* by Clement C. J. Webb, in *International Journal of Ethics* 27 [1916]: 115–16). "It is difficult," Bradley writes, "for morality, and it is still more difficult for religion, to recognize its own limits with regard to art or philosophy. [And] . . . to invade the region of philosophy is contrary to the interest of a sound morality or religion. Any such invasion is likely to lead to a disastrous conflict with our nature" (*Essays on Truth and Reality* [Oxford: Clarendon Press, 1914], p. 11). "And, so far as philosophy is religious, to that extent . . . it has passed into religion, and has ceased, as such, any longer to be philosophy" (*Appearance and Reality: A Metaphysical Essay* [2d ed.; Oxford: Clarendon Press, 1897], p. 402). "Every special science must be left at liberty to follow its own methods. . . . But where, quite beyond the scope of any special science, assertions are made, the metaphysician may protest" (ibid., p. 439). If we ignore or confuse Eliot's distinctions, we shall be in a muddle about his work, the poetry as well as the prose. The distinctions, as I have tried to indicate, derive from Aristotle's *Posterior Analytics* and *Metaphysics*. As for the statement we started with—this essay proposes to halt at "the frontier of metaphysics or mysticism"—it owes something to the quotation from Aristotle on mind which directly precedes it (see H. H. Joachim, *Aristotle: The Nicomachean Ethics*, ed. D. A. Rees [Oxford: Clarendon Press, 1951], pp. 288–91).

3. *Mysticism and Logic and Other Essays* (London: George Allen & Unwin, 1917), p. 8. Russell's "A Free Man's Worship" is a version of popular mysticism.

4. *The Sacred Wood: Essays in Poetry and Criticism* (London: Methuen, 1928), p. 12.

5. "Experiment in Criticism," in *Literary Opinion in America*, ed. Morton D. Zabel (3d ed. rev., 2 vols.; New York: Harper, 1951), 2:609–10.

6. *Knowledge and Experience in the Philosophy of F. H. Bradley* (London: Faber & Faber, 1964), pp. 10–11.

7. "It is possible—in fact, not hard—to disagree with Eliot's comparison of his style to Bradley's: just as it is possible to disagree with the other comparison Eliot makes in the same essay, of Bradley's style to

Arnold's. Indeed, the passages he cites serve his case none too well" (Richard Wollheim, "Eliot and F. H. Bradley," in *On Art and the Mind* [Cambridge, Mass.: Harvard University Press, 1974], p. 221). "It is worth observing that there are at least two versions of this preface, one of which was set up in proof before it was also decided to reprint the *Monist* articles, the other being the published version. The change in tone between the two versions indicates a growing seriousness with which Eliot was prepared to take his philosophical writings" (ibid., p. 220n).

8. *Appearance and Reality*, pp. 86–87, 143–144, 197–212, 224, 229; *Ethical Studies* (2d ed. rev.; Oxford: Clarendon Press, 1927), p. 84 passim.

9. *Essays on Truth and Reality*, p. 337.

10. *Knowledge and Experience*, p. 19. "This theory of partial truth, the fluidity of object and subject in their definition by context and relationship, indicates a pervasive characteristic of Eliot's processes of thought, the fairly consistent and deliberate evasion of precise definition. . . . Eliot's writing is often at the most crucial points simultaneously dense, allusive, elliptical, the meaning suggested only in the organization of a particular context. This stylistic feature sits closely with his philosophical preoccupations and suggests that many alleged inconsistencies and contradictions in his critical theories might be re-examined for their substantial coherence. . . . In fact the continuity with the work on Bradley . . ." (Adrian Cunningham, "Continuity and Coherence in Eliot's Religious Thought," in *Eliot in Perspective: A Symposium*, ed. Graham Martin [London: Macmillan, 1970], p. 215.

11. *Selected Essays*, p. 10.

12. Ibid., pp. 6–7.

13. Ibid., p. 7.

14. *Essays on Truth and Reality*, p. 310; *Appearance and Reality*, p. 418.

15. *Selected Essays*, p. 231.

16. Ibid., p. 17.

17. Ibid., pp. 7–8.

18. *Knowledge and Experience*, p. 76.

19. This is a standard topic of idealists. See H. H. Joachim, *Logical Studies* (Oxford: Clarendon Press, 1948), pp. 85–88; Bernard Bosanquet, *The Principle of Individuality and Value* (1912; London: Macmillan, 1927), pp. 72, 218–20, 281–90; A. E. Taylor, *Elements of Metaphysics* (1903; London: Methuen, 1961), bk. 4, chap. 3; R. L. Nettleship, *Philosophical Lectures and Remains*, ed. A. C. Bradley and G. R. Benson (2 vols.; London: Macmillan, 1897), 1:2–6, 34–35, 38, 160–64, 203–9.

20. *Selected Essays*, pp. 8, 247.

21. "Association and Thought," in *Collected Essays*, 2 vols. (1935; Freeport, N.Y.: Books for Libraries Press, 1968), 1:212.

22. *Selected Essays*, p. 8.

23. "Association and Thought," p. 211.

24. *Selected Essays*, p. 8.

25. "Association and Thought," pp. 213, 236.

26. *Principles of Logic* (2d ed. rev., 2 vols.; Oxford: Oxford University Press, 1922), 1:342.

27. *Essays on Truth and Reality*, p. 189.

28. Ibid., p. 174.

29. "Association and Thought," pp. 212–13.

30. *Principles of Logic*, 1:301.

31. "Association and Thought," p. 213.

32. *Principles of Logic*, 1:301.

33. "Association and Thought," pp. 229, 231.

34. *Principles of Logic*, 2:470, 471.

35. *Appearance and Reality*, pp. 518–19.

36. *Principles of Logic*, 1:347 n. 16.

37. *Selected Essays*, p. 8.

38. *Essays on Truth and Reality*, pp. 166–69.

39. *Selected Essays*, pp. 8, 10.

40. *Knowledge and Experience*, p. 27.

41. *Selected Essays*, p. 10.

42. *Appearance and Reality*, p. 462.

43. *Selected Essays*, pp. 190, 188.

44. Ibid., p. 171.

45. Ibid., p. 10.

46. *Knowledge and Experience*, pp. 49–51.

47. *Selected Essays*, p. 11.

48. *The Use of Poetry and the Use of Criticism: Studies in the Relation of Criticism to Poetry in England* (London: Faber & Faber, 1964), p. 115.

49. *Principles of Logic*, 1:306.

50. Ibid., p. 44.

51. *Ethical Studies*, p. 149.

52. "Association and Thought," p. 208.

53. "The Problems of the Shakespeare Sonnets," *Nation and Athenaeum* 40 (1927): 666; "Written in a foreign tongue" (Bradley, *The Presuppositions of Critical History*, ed. Lionel Rubinoff [Chicago: Quadrangle, 1968], p. 100; *Collected Essays*, 1:25).

54. *Essays on Truth and Reality*, pp. 354, 362.

55. See Joachim, *Logical Studies*, pp. 87, 95, 120–21.

56. *The Use of Poetry*, p. 79.

57. *Principles of Logic*, 1:307.

58. Ibid., pp. 308–9; see also p. 443.

59. *The Use of Poetry*, p. 138.

60. *Selected Essays*, p. 11.

61. Ibid., p. 117.

62. Ibid., p. 31.

63. Sartre, *The Transcendence of the Ego: An Existentialist Theory of Consciousness*, trans. Forrest Williams and Robert Kirkpatrick (New York: Farrar, Straus & Giroux, 1957), pp. 94–95. On Sartre see Garrett L.

Vander Veer, *Bradley's Metaphysics and the Self* (New Haven: Yale University Press, 1970), pp. 222–26.

64. *Knowledge and Experience*, p. 26.

65. Ibid., p. 27.

66. *Essays on Truth and Reality*, p. 119; see also *Appearance and Reality*, pp. 417–18.

67. *Essays on Truth and Reality*, p. 119n.

68. "A Commentary," *Criterion* 12 (1932): 76–77.

69. *Selected Essays*, p. 9.

70. *Knowledge and Experience*, p. 153.

71. *Essays on Truth and Reality*, p. 119n.

72. *Knowledge and Experience*, p. 79.

73. Ibid., p. 83.

74. *Essays on Truth and Reality*, p. 218. See also p. 243.

75. For the term personal see William James, *The Principles of Psychology* (2 vols.; New York: Dover, 1950), 1:225–27; for "subjective" see Joachim, *Logical Studies*, pp. 151–52.

76. *On Poetry and Poets* (London: Faber & Faber, 1957), p. 112.

77. *Knowledge and Experience*, app. 1, pp. 194–95.

78. *Ethical Studies*, p. 34.

79. Joachim, *Logical Studies*, pp. 94, 98.

80. *Knowledge and Experience*, p. 139.

81. *Appearance and Reality*, p. 427.

82. Joachim, *Logical Studies*, pp. 17–18; *The Nature of Truth* (Oxford: Clarendon Press, 1906), pp. 75–77.

83. *Selected Essays*, p. 8. See also *The Use of Poetry*, p. 130.

84. *The Presuppositions of Critical History*, p. 127n; *Collected Essays*, 1:52.

85. Rubinoff, p. 94; *Collected Essays*, p. 18.

86. Rubinoff, p. 144; *Collected Essays*, p. 67.

87. *Ethical Studies*, pp. 184, 202, 324n.

88. *Selected Essays*, p. 6.

89. Rubinoff, p. 116; *Collected Essays*, p. 40.

90. Rubinoff, pp. 119–20; *Collected Essays*, p. 44.

91. Rubinoff, p. 115; *Collected Essays*, pp. 39–40.

92. *Ethical Studies*, p. 66n.

93. *Savonarola: A Dramatic Poem*, by Charlotte Eliot (London: R. Cobden-Sanderson, 1926), p. viii n. Similarly, Eliot says of Lévy-Bruhl that "he exaggerates the difference between the mind of the savage and the mind of the civilized man" (a review of *Group Theories of Religion*, *IJE* 27 [1916]: 116). See also *The Use of Poetry*, p. 148n.

94. *Knowledge and Experience*, p. 17.

95. *Principles of Logic*, 2:506.

96. *Appearance and Reality*, p. 424.

97. *Principles of Logic*, 1:309.

98. *Ethical Studies*, p. 191n; *Appearance and Reality*, p. 417. "For you

cannot even say it changes except in reference to something which does not change; the idea of change is impossible without the idea of permanence" (Eliot to Bonamy Dobrée, in *T. S. Eliot: The Man and His Work*, ed. Allen Tate [New York: Delacorte, 1966], p. 75).

99. *Selected Essays*, pp. 4, 11.

100. Ibid., p. 4.

101. *Principles of Logic*, 1:309.

102. *Essays on Truth and Reality*, pp. 338–39.

103. *The Nature of Truth*, pp. 163, 65.

104. *The Use of Poetry*, pp. 27, 141, 142.

105. *Selected Essays*, p. 5.

106. *The Use of Poetry*, pp. 18–19.

107. *Appearance and Reality*, p. 417; *The Nature of Truth*, pp. 68n. 167.

108. Ibid., pp. 100, 94.

109. Bosanquet, *Individuality and Value*, pp. 118–19.

110. *Knowledge and Experience*, p. 144.

111. *Selected Essays*, p. 4.

112. *Appearance and Reality*, p. 290; *Principles of Logic*, 2:633, 697; Bosanquet, *Logic* (2d ed., 2 vols., 1911; New York: Kraus Reprint Co., 1968), 1:257–62; A. E. Taylor, *Elements of Metaphysics*, pp. 164–68, 175.

113. *Selected Essays*, p. 5.

114. *Knowledge and Experience*, p. 144. "By examining differences and identities" (*The Use of Poetry*, p. 28). Eliot's "ideal order" is a system, and a system is an identity that determines and is determined by its differences; and every judgment expresses identity in difference or difference in identity. We shall have occasion to return to this doctrine in later chapters.

115. *Selected Essays*, pp. 3–4.

116. *Ethical Studies*, pp. 83, 164, 166, 163.

117. *Essays on Truth and Reality*, pp. 434–35.

118. *Ethical Studies*, p. 180.

119. Ibid., p. 69.

120. Ibid., pp. 187–88, 162–63.

121. *Selected Essays*, pp. 12–13.

122. Ibid., p. 13.

123. *Ethical Studies*, p. 138.

124. "Literature and the Modern World," *American Prefaces* 1 (1935): 20.

125. *Ethical Studies*, p. 80.

126. Ibid., pp. 222–23.

127. "A Commentary," *Criterion* 11 (1932): 470–71.

128. *Ethical Studies*, p. 84.

129. Ibid., p. 309.

130. *Knowledge and Experience*, p. 158.

131. "A Brief Introduction to the Method of Paul Valéry," *Le Serpent*,

by Paul Valéry, trans. Mark Wardle (London: R. Cobden-Sanderson, 1924), p. 14.

132. "Poetry and Propaganda," in *Literary Opinion in America*, 1:102–3.

133. Ibid., p. 106.

134. *Appearance and Reality*, p. 485. See Vander Leer, "Bradley's Metaphysical Method and Common Sense," in *Bradley's Metaphysics and the Self*, pp. 92–102.

135. "There is a philosophic borderline, which you must not transgress too far or too often, if you wish to preserve your standing as a critic, and are not prepared to present yourself as a philosopher, metaphysician, sociologist, or psychologist instead" (*The Use of Poetry*, p. 64). "The Principles of Literary Criticism is a milestone, though not an altogether satisfactory one. Mr. Richards had difficult things to say, and he had not wholly mastered the art of saying them; it is probable that what he has said there with much difficulty, he will be able to say much better. The present little book marks a distinct advance in Mr. Richards' power of expression and arrangement. It is very readable." ("Literature, Science, and Dogma," *The Dial* 82 [1927]: 305).

6
Taste and Theory

1. *To Criticize the Critic and Other Writings* (London: Faber & Faber, 1965), p. 20.

2. *Selected Essays* (new ed.; New York: Harcourt, Brace & World, 1950), pp. 394–95.

3. *To Criticize the Critic*, p. 17.

4. "Experiment in Criticism," in *Literary Opinion in America*, ed. Morton Z. Zabel (3d ed. rev., 2 vols.; New York: Harper, 1937), 2:616.

5. *The Use of Poetry and the Use of Criticism: Studies in the Relation of Criticism to Poetry in England* (London: Faber & Faber, 1964), p. 128.

6. *Knowledge and Experience in the Philosophy of F. H. Bradley* (London: Faber & Faber, 1964), p. 103.

7. *To Criticize the Critic*, pp. 18, 20, 19, 25.

8. *Knowledge and Experience*, pp. 18, 163.

9. *Selected Essays*, p. 292.

10. *Appearance and Reality: A Metaphysical Essay* (2d ed.; Oxford: Clarendon Press, 1897), p. 434; see also pp. 231, 236, 259.

11. *Selected Essays*, p. 292.

12. *Essays on Truth and Reality* (Oxford: Clarendon Press, 1914), p. 452.

13. *Selected Essays*, p. 291.

14. *On Poetry and Poets* (London: Faber & Faber, 1957), p. 205.

15. *Selected Essays*, pp. 223–24.

16. Ibid., p. 233.

17. *Knowledge and Experience*, p. 124.

18. *Selected Essays*, p. 185.

19. Ibid., pp. 187, 185.

20. Ibid., p. 182.

21. *Essays on Truth and Reality*, p. 312.

22. *Selected Essays*, pp. 187–88, 188, 188.

23. "At every moment my state, whatever else it is, is a whole of which I am immediately aware. It is an experienced non-relational unity of many in one" (*Knowledge and Experience*, p. 21).

24. *Selected Essays*, p. 190.

25. Ibid., p. 181.

26. *Essays on Truth and Reality*, p. 303.

27. *The Use of Poetry*, pp. 42, 42, 46, 44.

28. Ibid., p. 45.

29. *Appearance and Reality*, p. 525. See *Principles of Logic* (2d ed. rev., 2 vols.; Oxford: Oxford University Press, 1922), 1: chap. 5; Bernard Bosanquet, *Logic* (2d ed., 2 vols., 1911; New York: Kraus Reprint Co., 1968), 2: chap. 7; idem, *The Essentials of Logic* (1895; London: Macmillan, 1960), lect. 3; H. H. Joachim, *Logical Studies* (Oxford: Clarendon Press, 1948), pp. 21–25, 156–78; R. L. Nettleship, *Philosophical Lectures and Remains*, ed. A. C. Bradley and G. R. Benson (2 vols.; London: Macmillan, 1897), 1: sec. 5.

30. *Appearance and Reality*, p. 528.

31. "Poetry and Propaganda," in *Literary Opinion in America*, 1:107.

32. *On Poetry and Poets*, p. 115.

33. Bradley, *Principles of Logic*, 2:691–94; Joachim, *Logical Studies*, pp. 27–49.

34. *Principles of Logic*, 1:95, 96.

35. *Essays on Truth and Reality*, pp. 304, 307.

36. *Knowledge and Experience*, p. 59.

37. *The Sacred Wood: Essays on Poetry and Criticism* (London: Methuen, 1928), p. 168. Cf. Joachim, *Logical Studies*, p. 32.

38. *Appearance and Reality*, p. 508.

39. See *Knowledge and Experience*, p. 18.

40. *Selected Essays*, p. 245.

41. *Principles of Logic*, p. 475.

42. *Selected Essays*, p. 243.

43. *Appearance and Reality*, p. 124.

44. Joachim, *Logical Studies*, p. 46; see also Nettleship, *Philosophical Lectures and Remains* 1:152.

45. *Appearance and Reality*, pp. 27–28, 502–6, 511.

46. See Joachim, *The Nature of Truth* (Oxford: Clarendon Press, 1906), p. 75; Bradley, *Ethical Studies* (2d ed. rev.; Oxford: Clarendon Press, 1927), pp. 163–64.

47. W. Francis Nelson, *The Structure of American English* (New York: Ronald Press, 1958), p. 28.

48. "Experiment in Criticism," in *Literary Opinion in America*, p. 616.

49. *On Poetry and Poets*, p. 157.

50. Ibid., p. 158; see also *The Sacred Wood*, p. 62.

51. *On Poetry and Poets*, pp. 157–58.

52. *Principles of Logic*, 2:647, 649.

53. *Selected Essays*, p. 185.

54. Ibid., pp. 182, 195.

55. Ibid., p. 124.

56. Ibid., p. 209.

57. *On Poetry and Poets*, pp. 140, 141.

58. Ibid., p. 141.

59. Ibid., p. 140. See also the essay on Byron, ibid., pp. 200–201.

60. *Knowledge and Experience*, p. 75.

61. *Selected Essays*, p. 247.

62. *On Poetry and Poets*, pp. 140–43.

63. *Knowledge and Experience*, p. 66.

64. *Principles of Logic*, 1:60; R. F. A Hoernlé, "Image, Idea, and Meaning," *Mind* 16 (1907): 70–100; Nettleship, *Philosophical Lectures and Remains* 1: 127–29, 169–73; Bosanquet, *Logic*, 1:38–41, 69–73, 2:295–301, and *Three Chapters on the Nature of Mind* (1923; New York: Krause Reprint Co., 1968), pp. 52, 58–63, 75, 82, 95, 112–16, 127–28, 132–37, 155–56.

65. *Knowledge and Experience*, pp. 165, 137, 103, 133, 158.

66. Ibid., pp. 67, 68.

67. *Selected Essays*, p. 204.

68. Ibid., pp. 282–84.

69. Wollheim, "Eliot and F. H. Bradley: An Account," in *Eliot in Perspective: A Symposium*, ed. Graham Martin (London: Macmillan, 1970), p. 189.

70. *Knowledge and Experience*, p. 132.

71. Ibid., p. 130.

72. Ibid., pp. 132, 39.

73. Ibid., pp. 132–34, 129.

74. Ibid., pp. 130–31.

75. See Jean-Paul Sartre, *Imagination*, trans. Forrest Williams (Ann Arbor: University of Michigan Press, 1962), chap. 9, "The Phenomenology of Husserl," esp. pp. 131–36.

76. *Knowledge and Experience*, pp. 15, 137.

77. *Principles of Logic*, 2:517 n. 8.

78. *Knowledge and Experience*, p. 67.

79. *Athenaeum*, no. 4627 (1919), p. 363.

80. "In Memory of Henry James," *The Egoist* 5 (1918): 2.

81. *The Sacred Wood*, p. 23.

82. "In Memory of Henry James," p. 2. By "ideas" Eliot means here "the public, the political, the emotional idea."

83. *Principles of Logic*, 1:69.

84. "Reflections on Contemporary Poetry, 1," *The Egoist* 4 (1917): 118. "It will dissolve into sensations which are not objects" (*Knowledge and Experience*, p. 134).

85. "Reflections on Contemporary Poetry, 1," p. 118.

86. "Tarr," *The Egoist* 8 (1918): 105.

87. "Reflections on Comtemporary Poetry, 2, "*The Egoist* 4 (1917): 133.

88. "Beyle and Balzac," *Athenaeum*, no. 4648 (1919), p. 392.

89. "Observations," *The Egoist* 5 (1918): 69–70, signed T. S. Apteryx.

90. *Knowledge and Experience*, pp. 44, 19.

91. *Selected Essays*, pp. 185, 185, 186, 190, 187.

92. *Knowledge and Experience*, p. 165.

93. *Selected Essays*, p. 195.

94. "London Letter," *The Dial* 71 (1921): 216–17.

7

The Dissociation of Sensibility

1. Tuve, *Elizabethan and Metaphysical Imagery: Renaissance Poetic and Twentieth-Century Critics* (Chicago: University of Chicago Press, 1947), p. 165n.

2. *On Poetry and Poets* (London: Faber & Faber, 1957), pp. 152–53.

3. See H. H. Joachim, *Logical Studies* (Oxford: Clarendon Press, 1948), pp. 184–92.

4. *Knowledge and Experience in the Philosophy of F. H. Bradley* (London: Faber & Faber, 1964), p. 31.

5. "Donne in Our Time," in A *Garland for John Donne, 1631–1931*, ed. Theodore Spencer (Cambridge, Mass.: Harvard University Press, 1931), p. 8.

6. Ibid., pp. 8–9.

7. *Knowledge and Experience*, p. 57; see also p. 157.

8. *Appearance and Reality: A Metaphysical Essay* (2d ed.; Oxford: Clarendon Press, 1897), pp. 460, 140.

9. *Knowledge and Experience*, p. 36.

10. "Donne in Our Time," p. 11. "I easily conceive, I say, that the imagination can work in this fashion, if it is true that there are bodies; and because I cannot find any other way in which this can be explained, I therefore conjecture that bodies probably exist. But this is only a probability; and although I carefully consider all aspects of the question, I

nevertheless do not see that from this distinct idea of corporeal nature which I find in my imagination, I can derive any argument which necessarily proves the existence of any body" (*Discourse on Method and Meditations*, trans. Laurence J. Lafleur [Indianapolis: Bobbs-Merrill, 1960], p. 128).

11. *Knowledge and Experience*, p. 99.

12. Lafleur, *Discourse*, pp. 126, 126, 127, 127–28, 93, 94.

13. "Donne in Our Time," pp. 11–13.

14. *Knowledge and Experience*, p. 23.

15. *The Sacred Wood: Essays on Poetry and Criticism* (London: Methuen, 1928), pp. 162–63.

16. "Donne in Our Time," pp. 15–16.

17. *Knowledge and Experience*, app. 1, p. 177.

18. "Preface to Le Livre des masques," in *Remy de Gourmont: Selected Writings*, trans. and ed. Glenn S. Burne (Ann Arbor: University of Michigan Press, 1966), p. 182.

19. "The Roots of Idealism," in ibid., pp. 155, 166, 167.

20. "The Problem of Style," in ibid., p. 123.

21. Ibid., p. 109.

22. Ibid., p. 125; also pp. 116, 117, 118, 122.

23. Ibid., p. 125.

24. Ibid., p. 121.

25. "Art and Science," in ibid., p. 170.

26. "The Problem of Style," in ibid., p. 122.

27. *Knowledge and Experience*, pp. 153, 165n.

28. Ibid., pp. 85, 154.

29. *Selected Essays* (new ed.; New York: Harcourt, Brace & World, 1950), p. 250.

30. *Knowledge and Experience*, p. 164.

31. *Principles of Logic* (2d ed. rev., 2 vols.; Oxford: Oxford University Press, 1922), 2:504–7.

32. For psychology and physiology see A. E. Taylor, *Elements of Metaphysics* (1903; London: Methuen, 1961), bk. 4, chap. 1. For psychology see also James Edwin Creighton, *Studies in Speculative Philosophy*, ed. Harold R. Smart (New York: Macmillan, 1925), chap. II, "The Standpoint of Psychology." (Other essays in this volume are also worth consulting, "The Standpoint of Experience" and "Two Types of Idealism," to name but these two.)

33. Bateson, "Contributions to a Dictionary of Critical Terms: II. Dissociation of Sensibility," *Essays in Criticism* 1 (1951): 308, 309, 305.

34. Thompson, "The Critical Forum: 'Dissociation of Sensibility,' " *Essays in Criticism* 2 (1952): 207, 208, 213.

35. Ibid., pp. 213, 214.

36. "Contributions to a Dictionary of Critical Terms," pp. 305, 306.

37. "The Critical Forum," p. 214.

38. *Knowledge and Experience*, pp. 165, 137, 67.

39. *Essays on Truth and Reality* (Oxford: Clarendon Press, 1914), p. 190.

40. *The Sacred Wood*, p. 170; *Selected Essays*, p. 248.

41. "The Critical Forum," p. 214.

42. Leone Vivante, *English Poetry and Its Contribution to the Knowledge of a Creative Principle* (London: Faber & Faber, 1950), p. xi. Eliot also draws attention to Vivante's affirmation—the words are Eliot's—that "there is in poetry a genuine creative activity. That something comes into being which is new—in the sense that it cannot be explained by literary or other influences, or by infantile experience that the poet has chosen to forget, or by racial memories and myths of which he is unaware" (ibid.).

43. *Criterion* 4 (1926): 4.

44. "The Noh and the Image," *The Egoist* 4 (1917): 103.

45. *Knowledge and Experience*, p. 55.

46. "Contributions to a Dictionary of Critical Terms," pp. 302–3.

47. "A Sceptical Patrician," *Athenaeum*, no. 4647 (1919), p. 361.

48. "Donne in Our Time," p. 9.

49. Burne, *Remy de Gourmont: His Ideas and Influence in England and America* (Carbondale: Southern Illinois University Press, 1963), p. 166n. 49.

50. Ibid., p. 135.

51. Ibid.

52. *Knowledge and Experience*, p. 25.

53. *Essays on Truth and Reality*, p. 177; *Appearance and Reality*, pp. 76–82.

54. Bernard Bosanquet, *Logic* (2d ed., 2 vols., 1911; New York: Kraus Reprint Co., 1968), 2:297–98.

55. *Knowledge and Experience*, p. 155.

56. *Remy de Gourmont: His Ideas and Influence in England and America*, p. 137.

57. Ibid., pp. 140–41.

58. *Essays on Truth and Reality*, p. 203.

59. *Appearance and Reality*, p. 229.

60. *Selected Essays*, pp. 192–93. "Life is a process of sloughing off. The proper end of man's activities is to scour his personality, to cleanse it of all the stains deposited by education, to free it of all the imprints left by adolescent admirations" (*Remy de Gourmont: Selected Writings*, pp. 123–24). "Flaubert incorporated all his sensibility into his works. . . . Outside his books wherein he transfused himself drop by drop to the dregs, Flaubert was not very interesting" (ibid., p. 125).

61. *Knowledge and Experience*, p. 31.

62. *Appearance and Reality*, p. 207. The "this" or "mine" is "my existence taken as immediate fact," but there is "no inalienable character which belongs to the 'this' or the 'mine,' " for "all tends to refer itself beyond" (*Appearance and Reality*, pp. 209, 206, 211). "Thus, when for instance in despondency I observe my visceral sensations, these feelings are translated into objects, into perceptions and ideas, but none the less, though translated, the original feelings remain" (*Essays on Truth and Reality*, p. 167). "We may confuse the feeling which we study with the feeling which we are"; but "to observe a feeling is, to some extent, always to alter it" (*Appearance and Reality*, p. 205, 205n). "The I who saw the ghost is not the same I who had the attack of indigestion" (*Knowledge and Experience*, p. 121). "You don't really criticize any author to whom you have surrendered yourself." "Even just the bewildering moment counts; you have to give yourself up, and then recover yourself, and the third moment is having something to say, before you have wholly forgotten both surrender and recovery. Of course the self recovered is never the same as the self before it was given" (Eliot to Stephen Spender, in *T. S. Eliot: The Man and His Work*, ed. Allen Tate [New York: Delacorte, 1969], pp. 55–56).

63. *The Sacred Wood*, p. 1.

64. Ibid., pp. 5, 11.

65. *Knowledge and Experience*, app. 1, p. 183.

66. *Posterior Analytics*, 1. 1. 71a, in *The Student's Aristotle*, trans. under editorship of W. D. Ross, vol. 1.

67. See Joachim, *Aristotle: The Nicomachean Ethics*, ed. D. A. Rees (Oxford: Clarendon Press, 1951), p. 34; *Logical Studies*, p. 67.

68. *Principles of Logic*, 2:480.

69. *Knowledge and Experience*, pp. 166–67.

70. *The Sacred Wood*, p. 8. "The writer with an abstract style is almost always a sentimentalist, at least a 'sensitive.' The artist-writer is almost never a sentimentalist and very rarely a sensitive" (*Remy de Gourmont: Selected Writings*, p. 117).

71. *The Sacred Wood*, p. 8.

72. *Principles of Logic*, 2:474. See also Joachim, *Logical Studies*, p. 12.

73. *The Sacred Wood*, pp. 8–9.

74. *Principles of Logic*, 1:76.

75. *Appearance and Reality*, pp. 53, 59, 52.

76. *Principles of Logic*, 2:485.

77. *Appearance and Reality*, p. 425; *Knowledge and Experience*, p. 139.

78. *Remy de Gourmont: His Ideas and Influence in England and America*, p. 138.

79. *The Sacred Wood*, p. 15.

80. *Principles of Logic*, 2:494.

81. *Essays on Truth and Reality*, pp. 209–10.

82. *Logic*, 2:183.

83. *Principles of Logic*, 2:448 n. 27, 486–94, terminal essay 1.

84. *The Sacred Wood*, p. 16.

85. Ibid., p. 5.
86. *Principles of Logic*, 2:486.
87. Bosanquet, *Logic*, 2:182.
88. *Essays on Truth and Reality*, p. 219.
89. *Knowledge and Experience*, app. 2, 203.
90. "A Brief Introduction to the Method of Paul Valéry," *Le Serpent*, by Paul Valéry, trans. Mark Wardle (London: R. Cobden-Sanderson, 1924), p. 9.
91. *The Use of Poetry and the Use of Criticism: Studies in the Relation of Criticism to Poetry in England* (London: Faber & Faber, 1964), p. 44.

8

The Use of Principles

1. "The Three Voices of Poetry," in *On Poetry and Poets* (London: Faber & Faber, 1957), p. 101.
2. "Poetry and Drama," in ibid., p. 85.
3. *Principles of Logic* (2d ed. rev., 2 vols.; Oxford: Oxford University Press, 1922), 2:486, 1:170.
4. "Experiment in Criticism," in *Literary Opinion in America*, ed. Morton D. Zabel (3d ed. rev., 2 vols.; New York: Harper, 1951), 2:616. Cf. Ralph M. Eaton, *General Logic: An Introductory Survey* (New York: Scribner's, 1959), pp. 241–44, 265–72.
5. *Knowledge and Experience in the Philosophy of F. H. Bradley* (London: Faber & Faber, 1964), p. 144.
6. Ibid., p. 132.
7. "The Music of Poetry," in *On Poetry and Poets*, pp. 27, 27, 37–38. See also "Reflections on *Vers Libre*," in *To Criticize the Critic and Other Writings* (London: Faber & Faber, 1965), p. 185.
8. *Principles of Logic*, 2:475.
9. See Bernard Bosanquet, *Logic* (2d ed., 2 vols., 1911; New York: Kraus Reprint Co., 1968), 2:277.
10. "The Music of Poetry," p. 33.
11. See Bosanquet, *Logic*, 2:295, 298; *The Principle of Individuality and Value* (1912; London: Macmillan, 1927), p. 61.
12. "The Music of Poetry," pp. 32–33.
13. See R. L. Nettleship, *Philosophical Lectures and Remains*, ed. A. C. Bradley and G. R. Benson (2 vols.; London: Macmillan, 1897), 1:130–31, 218; Bosanquet, *Logic*, 1:45n, 59; *Individuality and Value*, pp. 31–40; *Science and Philosophy and Other Essays* (1927; Freeport, N.Y.: Books for Libraries Press, 1967), p. 37.
14. "The Aims of Education," in *To Criticize the Critic*, pp. 63–64.
15. Ibid., pp. 64–66.
16. Ibid., pp. 65, 74.

17. Bosanquet, *Individuality and Value*, p. 332; Nettleship, *Philosphical Lectures and Remains*, 1:128.

18. *On Poetry and Poets*, pp. 17, 20, 22.

19. "The Aims of Education," p. 66.

20. Ibid., pp. 66-67.

21. Ibid., pp. 74, 120.

22. *Principles of Logic*, 2:463, 493, 462; *Knowledge and Experience*, pp. 162, 161.

"But the word *pietas* with Virgil has much wider associations of meaning: it implies an attitude towards the individual, towards the family, towards the region, and towards the imperial destiny of Rome. And finally Aeneas is "pious" also in his respect towards the gods, and in his punctilious observance of rites and offerings. It is an attitude towards all these things, and therefore implies a unity and an order among them: it is in fact an attitude towards life.

"Aeneas is therefore not simply a man endowed with a number of virtues, each of which is a kind of piety—so that to call him *pius* in general is merely to use a convenient collective term. Piety is one. There are aspects of piety in different contexts, and they all imply each other" ("Virgil and the Christian World," in *On Poetry and Poets*, p. 127).

23. "What Is Minor Poetry?" in *On Poetry and Poets*, pp. 46, 47, 47.

24. Ibid., p. 50.

25. *Principles of Logic*, 1:191.

26. *Logic*, 1:92-93.

27. *The Essentials of Logic* (1895; London: Macmillan, 1960), p. 58.

28. *Knowledge and Experience*, app. 2, p. 202.

29. Kenner, *The Invisible Poet: T. S. Eliot* (New York: Ivan Obolensky, 1962), p. 48.

30. *Selected Essays*, (new ed.; New York: Harcourt, Brace & World, 1950), pp. 170-71. See also "Rudyard Kipling," in *On Poetry and Poets*, pp. 233-34, 235-36, 237, 241.

31. *Selected Essays*, pp. 171, 172. "We are aware of no inner compulsion." "With no writer of equal eminence to Kipling is this inner compulsion, this unity in variety, more difficult to discern" ("Rudyard Kipling," pp. 236-37). "I am accustomed to search for form: but Kipling never seems to be searching for form, but only for a particular form for each poem. So we find in the poems an extraordinary variety, but no evident pattern" (ibid., p. 237). See the discussion of form by Bosanquet, *Essentials of Logic*, lect. 3, pp. 42-60. "For Kipling the Empire was not merely an idea, a good idea or a bad one; it was something the reality of which he felt. And in his expression of his feeling . . . he was aiming to communicate the awareness of something in existence of which he felt that most people were improperly aware" ("Rudyard Kipling," p. 243). That is a Bradleyan statement.

32. *Knowledge and Experience*, pp. 30, 61.

33. Ibid., p. 138.

34. Ibid., p. 119. See Richard Wollheim, "Eliot and F. H. Bradley", in *On Art and the Mind* (Cambridge, Mass.: Harvard University Press, 1974), p. 237.

35. H. H. Joachim, *The Nature of Truth* (Oxford: Clarendon Press, 1906), pp. 145–46.

36. "The Music of Poetry," p. 32.

37. *Principles of Logic*, 2:628.

38. Ibid., pp. 409–11.

39. Joachim, *The Nature of Truth*, pp. 137–38.

40. *Principles of Logic*, 2:601.

41. *Selected Essays*, pp. 9–10.

42. Joachim, *The Nature of Truth*, pp. 68, 137, 68n.

43. *Knowledge and Experience*, pp. 143, 149; *Appearance and Reality: A Metaphysical Essay* (2d ed.; Oxford: Clarendon Press, 1897), pp. 460, 140.

44. Ibid., pp. 41–42.

45. *Knowledge and Experience*, p. 55.

46. See Bosanquet, *Knowledge and Reality* (1885; New York: Kraus Reprint Co., 1968), pp. 158–62; *Essentials of Logic*, pp. 82–85, 102–3, 106–7; *Logic*, 1:75, 77, 78–83; Bradley, *Essays on Truth and Reality* (Oxford: Clarendon Press, 1914), pp. 389–90, 391, 402–3.

47. *T. S. Eliot: Collected Poems, 1909–1962* (New York: Harcourt, Brace & World, 1963), p. 180.

48. *Appearance and Reality*, pp. 305–6.

49. Ibid., pp. 275, 280–81.

50. Ibid., pp. 306–7.

51. *Knowledge and Experience*, pp. 151, 146, 151.

52. *Selected Essays*, p. 125.

53. *Appearance and Reality*, p. 304.

54. Bosanquet, *Logic*, 1:42–43.

55. "A sign, an unsubstantial and a fugitive mode of expression" (*Appearance and Reality*, p. 338).

56. *Collected Poems*, pp. 61–62

57. *Knowledge and Experience*, p. 120.

58. *Essays on Truth and Reality*, p. 423.

59. Ibid., p. 425.

60. *Collected Poems*, p. 175.

61. *Knowledge and Experience*, p. 55.

62. On Caesar and history see *The Presuppositions of Critical History*, ed. Lionel Rubinoff (Chicago: Quadrangle, 1968), intro., pp. 48–52.

63. *Essays on Truth and Reality*, p. 425; see also p. 426.

64. *Savonarola: A Dramatic Poem*, by Charlotte Eliot (London: R. Cobden-Sanderson, 1926), pp. vii, vii, ix, vii.

65. Ibid., p. viii.

66. *Josiah Royce's Seminar, 1913–1914: As Recorded in the Notebooks* *of Harry T. Costello*, ed. Grover Smith (New Brunswick, N.J.: Rutgers University Press, 1963), pp. 194, 76, 78.

67. Ibid., pp. 193–94.

68. Ibid., pp. 72–87, 118–21, 135–40. See also Eliot's paper on the classification of different types of objects, including the type, if any, which constitutes the subject matter of psychology (pp. 172–77). For "description" and "interpretation" see A. E. Taylor, *Elements of Metaphysics* (1903; London: Methuen, 1961), bk. 3, chap. 6.

69. *Knowledge and Experience*, p. 124.

70. "The Music of Poetry," p. 31.

71. *Knowledge and Experience*, p. 164.

72. "The Music of Poetry," pp. 30–31.

73. Knight, *The Wheel of Fire* (New York: Oxford University Press, 1949), p. xx.

74. *Appearance and Reality*, p. 169.

75. *Knowledge and Experience*, p. 164.

9

Imaginary Objects

1. "On Floating Ideas and the Imaginary," in *Essays on Truth and Reality* (Oxford: Clarendon Press, 1914), p. 34.

2. *Knowledge and Experience in the Philosophy of F. H. Bradley* (London: Faber & Faber, 1964), pp. 89–90; "On My Real World," in *Essays on Truth and Reality*, pp. 460–69.

3. Bradley, *Principles of Logic* (2d ed. rev., 2 vols.; Oxford: Oxford University Press, 1922), 2:662–67; Bosanquet, *Logic* (2d ed., 2 vols., 1911; New York: Kraus Reprint Co., 1968), 1:278–93.

4. *Knowledge and Experience*, pp. 123–24.

5. *Selected Essays* (new ed.; New York: Harcourt, Brace & World, 1950), pp. 284–85.

6. *Knowledge and Experience*, p. 123.

7. Ibid., p. 124.

8. *Selected Essays*, pp. 131–32, 138, 137, 135–36.

9. Ibid., p. 269.

10. Ibid., p. 411.

11. Ibid., p. 130.

12. *Knowledge and Experience*, p. 117.

13. *Selected Essays*, pp. 94, 93, 93, 93, 97, 97, 97, 95.

14. Ibid., p. 133.

15. Ibid., p. 91.

16. "The Three Voices of Poetry," in *On Poetry and Poets* (London: Faber & Faber, 1957), pp. 95–96.

17. *Knowledge and Experience*, pp. 125–26.

18. "The Three Voices of Poetry," p. 94.

19. *Knowledge and Experience*, pp. 121–23.

20. Ibid., p. 118; cf. Bradley, *Principles of Logic*, 2: 631, 702–3; *Appearance and Reality: A Metaphysical Essay* (2d ed.; Oxford: Clarendon Press, 1897), pp. 325–26.

21. *Knowledge and Experience*, p. 82.

22. Ibid., p. 125.

23. "The Three Voices of Poetry," p. 97.

24. Ibid., p. 99.

25. Ibid., p. 97.

26. *Probleme der Lyrik* (Wiesbaden: Limes Verlag, 1951), p. 18.

27. "The Three Voices of Poetry," pp. 101, 100, 101.

28. Ibid., pp. 97–98.

29. Ibid., p. 98.

30. Ibid., pp. 98–99.

31. Wollheim, "Eliot, Bradley and Immediate Experience," *New Statesman* (13 March 1964), p. 401; Allen, *T. S. Eliot's Impersonal Theory of Poetry* (Lewisburg, Pa.: Bucknell University Press, 1974), p. 140.

32. "The Frontiers of Criticism," in *On Poetry and Poets*, p. 110.

33. "Experiment in Criticism," in *Literary Opinion in America*, ed. Morton Z. Zabel (3d ed. rev., 2 vols.; New York: Harper, 1951), 2:610.

34. *Principles of Logic*, 2:547; *Appearance and Reality*, pp. 46, 48–49.

35. *The Use of Poetry and the Use of Criticism: Studies in the Relation of Criticism to Poetry in England* (London: Faber & Faber, 1964), pp. 139, 140.

36. "The Frontiers of Criticism," p. 111.

37. *Knowledge and Experience*, p. 26.

38. H. H. Joachim, "Psychical Process," *Mind*, n.s., 18 (1909): 65–83; *The Nature of Truth* (Oxford: Clarendon Press, 1906), pp. 118–19n.

39. *Knowledge and Experience*, p. 139.

40. Ibid., p. 76.

41. *The Use of Poetry*, pp. 55–56.

42. *Essays on Truth and Reality*, pp. 161–64.

43. *Knowledge and Experience*, p. 26.

44. *Appearance and Reality*, p. 462.

45. *Knowledge and Experience*, pp. 116–17.

46. Ibid., pp. 56, 139, 56, 56, 93.

47. Ibid., pp. 56n, 76.

48. Blanshard, *The Nature of Thought* (2 vols.; London: George Allen & Unwin, 1939), 1:494, 473.

49. "The Three Voices of Poetry," p. 99.

50. *Knowledge and Experience*, p. 56.

51. R. L. Nettleship, *Philosophical Lectures and Remains*, ed. A. C. Bradley and G. R. Benson (2 vols; London: Macmillan, 1897), 1:132–33, 130.

52. Bosanquet, "On the Nature of Aesthetic Emotion," in *Science and Philosophy and Other Essays* (1927; Freeport, N.Y.: Books for Libraries

Press, 1967), p. 398 (reprinted from *Mind*, n.s., 3 (1894): 153–66); *Three Lectures on Aesthetic*, ed. Ralph Ross (1915; Indianapolis: Bobbs-Merrill, 1963), p. 29.

53. "From Poe to Valéry," in *To Criticize the Critic and Other Writings* (London: Faber & Faber, 1965), pp. 39–40.

54. *Three Lectures on Aesthetic*, pp. 58, 57.

55. "From Poe to Valéry," p. 42.

56. "The Three Voices of Poetry," p. 101. In "Ben Jonson": "The plot does not hold the play together; what holds the play together is a unity of inspiration that radiates into plot and characters alike"; the characters have "a kind of power . . . which comes from below the intellect"; they have "an emotional source" (*Selected Essays*, pp. 134, 136, 137).

57. *Knowledge and Experience*, p. 165.

58. Ibid., pp. 23, 99, 23, 75.

59. *Selected Essays*, pp. 240, 241.

60. Ibid., p. 226.

61. *The Sacred Wood: Essays on Poetry and Criticism* (London: Methuen, 1928), pp. 169, 168.

62. Ibid., pp. 161, 162.

63. Ibid., p. 66.

64. *Selected Essays*, p. 115.

65. "From Poe to Valéry," p. 38.

66. Ibid., pp. 34, 38, 39.

67. *Selected Essays*, p. 190.

68. "From Poe to Valéry," p. 35.

69. "On the Nature of Aesthetic Emotion," pp. 396, 402, 396, 396. " 'Objective' knowledge must be a continuation and completion of the 'subjective' knowledge"—"the correlative 'objective' " (Nettleship, *Philosophical Lectures and Remains*, 1:196–97).

70. "On the Nature of Aesthetic Emotion," p. 397.

71. *Three Lectures on Aesthetic*, pp. 32, 29, 30.

72. "On the Nature of Aesthetic Emotion," pp. 398–99.

73. Ibid., p. 405.

74. *Three Lectures on Aesthetic*, pp. 8, 7, 8.

75. "On the Treatment of Sexual Detail in Literature," in *Collected Essays* (2 vols., 1935; Freeport, N.Y.: Books for Libraries Press, 1968), 2:622.

76. Ibid., pp. 623, 623, 620, 623.

77. *Knowledge and Experience*, pp. 124, 125.

78. Cf. Richard Wollheim, "Eliot and F. H. Bradley: An Account," in *Eliot in Perspective: A Symposium*, ed. Graham Martin (London: Macmillan, 1970), pp. 177, 188, and "Eliot and F. H. Bradley," in *On Art and the Mind* (Cambridge, Mass.: Harvard University Press, 1974), pp. 232–33, 246; Brand Blanshard, *The Nature of Thought*, 1:551–54.

79. *Knowledge and Experience*, p. 36.

80. *The Use of Poetry*, pp. 126, 130. "When we define an experience,

we substitute the definition for the experience, and then experience the definition: but the experiencing is quite another thing from the defining" (*Knowledge and Experience*, p. 167).

81. *Knowledge and Experience*, pp. 91, 147.

82. Ibid., p. 159. In poetry of the first voice, "The question of communication . . . is not paramount" ("The Three Voices of Poetry," p. 92). There is in all "experienced activity" an aspect of "theory or contemplation": an idea or judgment, or, what is the same thing, "the self-realization of an idea" (*Principles of Logic*, 2:716; *Knowledge and Experience*, p. 41). Now "we must bear in mind that communication is not the essential of judgment. Therefore we must not go so far as to say that mere desire to inform another, or to influence his action, can produce judgment" (Bosanquet, *Knowledge and Reality* [1885; New York: Kraus Reprint Co., 1968], p. 215). These remarks seem to have a bearing on the question of the first voice; but the matter is obscure, and we cannot pursue it here.

10
A Logic of the Imagination

1. *Selected Essays* (new ed.; New York: Harcourt, Brace & World, 1950), p. 137.

2. Bernard Bosanquet, *Three Lectures on Aesthetic*, ed. Ralph Ross (1915; Indianapolis: Bobbs-Merrill, 1963), pp. 17, 20.

3. The good is satisfaction, the criterion is system, and there are various types of systems or forms of individuality. Cf. Bradley, *Appearance and Reality: A Metaphysical Essay* (2d ed.; Oxford: Clarendon Press, 1897), pp. 364, 365, 366; Bosanquet, *The Principle of Individuality and Value* (London: Macmillan, 1927), pp. 297–99.

4. "Shakespearian Criticism: 1. From Dryden to Coleridge," in *A Companion to Shakespeare Studies*, ed. Harley Granville-Barker and G. B. Harrison (New York: Doubleday, 1960), p. 305.

5. "Contributions to a Dictionary of Critical Terms: II. Dissociation of Sensibility," *Essays in Criticism* 1 (1951): 311.

6. *Romantic Image* (London: Routledge & Kegan Paul, 1957), p. 152.

7. H. H. Joachim, *Logical Studies* (Oxford: Clarendon Press, 1948), pp. 85, 83, 99.

8. *Essays on Truth and Reality* (Oxford: Clarendon Press, 1914), pp. 364, 365.

9. Ibid., pp. 368, 362–63; *Principles of Logic* (2d ed. rev., 2 vols.; Oxford: Oxford University Press, 1922), 2:444–46, 449 n. 34.

10. *Three Lectures on Aesthetic*, pp. 16–17.

11. *Knowledge and Experience in the Philosophy of F. H. Bradley* (London: Faber & Faber, 1964), p. 75. For "the connection of content" see

Richard Wollheim, "Eliot and F. H. Bradley," in *On Art and the Mind* (Cambridge, Mass.: Harvard University Press, 1974), p. 233.

12. *Principles of Logic*, 2: 441–43.

13. *Ethical Studies* (2d ed. rev.; Oxford: Clarendon Press, 1927), pp. 193–94, 194n; *Appearance and Reality*, p. 547; *Essays on Truth and Reality*, pp. 215, 215n, 330, 367; *Principles of Logic*, 2:476–86, 623, 626, 630.

14. *Individuality and Value*, p. 24.

15. "By logic we understand . . . the supreme law or nature of experience, the impulse towards unity and coherence" (ibid., p. 340). This impulse or "striving towards unity and coherence" is exemplified in "art and poetry" (ibid., p. 335).

16. *Elizabethan and Metaphysical Imagery: Renaissance Poetics and Twentieth-Century Critics* (Chicago: University of Chicago Press, 1947), p. 5.

17. Ibid., pp. 44, 14, 166.

18. *John Dryden: The Poet, the Dramatist, the Critic* (New York: Terence and Elsa Holliday, 1932), pp. 63–64.

19. *Principles of Logic*, 1:7.

20. *Essays on Truth and Reality*, p. 309n.

21. *Knowledge and Experience*, p. 43.

22. Joachim, *Aristotle: The Nicomachean Ethics*, ed. D. A. Rees (Oxford: Clarendon Press, 1951), p. 67.

23. Eliot in "Ben Jonson" uses the popular distinction between "the feelings or imagination" and "intellect or invention" in order to make the point that the characters in drama have an emotional source; in "The Perfect Critic" this distinction is a "torpid superstition."

24. *Knowledge and Experience*, app. 1, p. 195. Cf. Joachim, *The Nicomachean Ethics*, pp. 198–200.

25. *Principles of Logic*, 2:481–83; see also 1:28–38, 2:502–14.

26. *John Dryden*, p. 65.

27. *The Use of Poetry and the Use of Criticism: Studies in the Relation of Criticism to Poetry in England* (London: Faber & Faber, 1964), pp. 29, 58.

28. Ibid., pp. 56–58.

29. *The Sacred Wood: Essays on Poetry and Criticism* (London: Methuen, 1928), p. 65.

30. *Selected Essays*, p. 231.

31. *Knowledge and Experience*, p. 168.

32. *The Use of Poetry*, pp. 59–60.

33. *The Spectator*, ed. G. Gregory Smith (4 vols.; London: J. M. Dent, 1933), no. 413, 3:65.

34. *The Use of Poetry*, pp. 61–62.

35. Ibid., pp. 74–75.

36. Ibid., pp. 83–84.

37. "Experiment in Criticism," *Literary Opinion in America*, ed. Morton D. Zabel (3d ed. rev., 2 vols.; New York: Harper, 1951), 2:610.

38. *The Use of Poetry*, p. 58.

39. Ibid., p. 77.

40. Ibid., p. 79.

41. Ibid.

42. For Coleridge's idealism see J. H. Muirhead, *Coleridge as Philosopher* (London: George Allen & Unwin, 1930).

43. *The Use of Poetry*, pp. 146–47.

44. *Essays on Truth and Reality*, p. 365.

45. *The Use of Poetry*, pp. 147–48.

46. *Knowledge and Experience*, pp. 116, 52n.

47. *Selected Essays*, p. 8.

48. Bosanquet, *Logic* (2d ed., 2 vols., 1911; New York: Kraus Reprint Co., 1968), 2:295–301.

49. Perhaps what Eliot says in his discussion of the "idea" is relevant here—that "any expression we can use will remain a metaphor" (*Knowledge and Experience*, p. 43). "And, if all metaphors are to be pressed, then I, and I think all of us, in the end must keep silence. But the question surely is whether such a contradiction is more than formal. And the question is whether on some matters, in order to speak accurately, one has not to use metaphors which conflict with and correct each other" (*Essays on Truth and Reality*, p. 196).

50. *Principles of Logic*, 1:33.

51. "Reflections on Contemporary Poetry [2]," *The Egoist* 4 (1917): 133.

52. *Selected Essays*, p. 208.

53. St.-Jean Perse, *Anabasis*, trans. T. S. Eliot (2d ed.; New York: Harcourt, Brace, 1938), pp. 8, 9.

54. *Implication and Linear Inference* (1920; New York: Kraus Reprint Co., 1968), p. v. See also p. 95n.

55. *Anabasis*, p. 8.

56. *Individuality and Value*, pp. 332–33.

57. Ibid., pp. 329–30.

58. Ibid., p. 329.

59. Ibid., p. 332.

60. Ibid., p. 334.

61. *Ezra Pound: Selected Poems*, ed. T. S. Eliot (London: Faber & Faber, 1928), pp. 9–10.

62. See Bosanquet, *The Essentials of Logic* (1895; London: Macmillan, 1960), pp. 56–57; *Logic*, 1:242–43; *Individuality and Value*, p. 263; *Implication and Linear Inference*.

63. *Knowledge and Experience*, p. 118n; Bradley, *Principles of Logic*, 2:619–20; Bosanquet, *Logic*, 2:179–82, 266–67.

64. "A Note on Ezra Pound," *To-Day* 4 (1918): 3–5.

65. "Ezra Pound," *Poetry* 68 (1946): 331–32.

66. *Ezra Pound: Selected Poems*, pp. 14–15.

67. *Appearance and Reality*, pp. 114–15.

68. *The Presuppositions of Critical History*, ed. Lionel Rubinoff (Chicago: Quadrangle, 1968), p. 134; *Collected Essays* (2 vols., 1935; New York: Books for Libraries Press, 1968), 1:58.

69. *Knowledge and Experience*, pp. 87, 112, 96, 96–97, 97n, 144.

70. Ibid., pp. 156, 143, 100.

71. *After Strange Gods: A Primer of Modern Heresy* (New York: Harcourt, Brace, 1934), pp. 15, 19, 25, 24, 25, 51–52.

72. "American Literature and the American Language," in *To Criticize the Critic and Other Essays* (London: Faber & Faber, 1965), pp. 53, 54, 54, 54, 55, 57, 57, 60, 60.

73. "A Note on Ezra Pound," pp. 4–5.

74. *Principles of Logic*, 2:479, 695–98; *Appearance and Reality*, pp. 512, 517, 521, 522; Bosanquet, *Logic*, 1:90, 2:2–4, 237.

75. "Studies in Contemporary Criticism, 1," *The Egoist* 5 (1918): 113. This is more explicit than the statement in "The Function of Criticism" (*Selected Essays*, p. 21).

76. *Principles of Logic*, 2:459–60, 609–11.

77. *The Sacred Wood*, p. 11.

78. *Knowledge and Experience*, p. 164.

79. "American Literature and the American Language," p. 54.

80. *Selected Essays*, p. 20.

81. *Knowledge and Experience*, p. 125.

82. Ibid., pp. 161–62.

83. Ibid., 117.

84. *Appearance and Reality*, pp. 533–35; *Principles of Logic*, 1:286–88; Bosanquet, *Logic*, 1:135–36, 212–19; *Implication and Linear Inference*, pp. 124–25; Brand Blanshard, *The Nature of Thought* (2 vols.; London: George Allen & Unwin, 1939), 2:152, 155–56, 158–60, 1:609–54.

85. *The Sacred Wood*, p. 13.

86. *Principles of Logic*, 2:627.

87. *After Strange Gods*, p. 60.

88. *Selected Essays*, p. 125.

89. "Life and Philosophy," in *Contemporary British Philosophy*, ed. J. H. Muirhead (1st ser.; London: George Allen & Unwin, 1924), p. 63.

90. *After Strange Gods*, pp. 59–60.

91. *Selected Essays*, p. 242.

92. *Principles of Logic*, 2:431, 437, 463, 471; *Essays on Truth and Reality*, pp. 362–63, 392–93, 402–3; Bosanquet, *Individuality and Value*, p. 335; *Three Chapters on the Nature of Mind* (1923; New York: Kraus Reprint Co., 1968), p. 64.

93. "A Note on Ezra Pound," pp. 6–7.

94. *Ezra Pound: Selected Poems*, p. 14.

95. Bosanquet, *Logic*, 2:233–36; Blanshard, *The Nature of Thought*, 2:99, 143–46.

96. *Knowledge and Experience*, p. 93.

97. Ibid., p. 44.

98. *Principles of Logic*, 2:627, 627n.

99. *Appearance and Reality*, pp. 410–11.

100. *Principles of Logic*, 2:627, 627n.

101. *Logic*, 2:236n. See *Implication and Linear Inference*, pp. 95–96.

102. "Poetry and Propaganda," in *Literary Opinion in America*, pp. 98, 107.

103. *Essays on Truth and Reality*, pp. 37–40; Bosanquet, *Implication and Linear Inference*, chap. 8, "Judgment and Supposition," pp. 166–76.

104. *Selected Essays*, pp. 122, 124.

105. *To Criticize the Critic*, p. 37.

106. *The Use Of Poetry*, pp. 17–18.

107. Ibid., pp. 95–96.

108. *Essays on Truth and Reality*, pp. 312–13.

109. *Appearance and Reality*, pp. 403–4.

110. *Individuality and Value*, pp. 57–58.

111. *Knowledge and Experience*, p. 168.

112. Ibid., p. 46.

Index